August 6, 2001

Dear President Jimmy Carter

with best wishes

Kim Dae-jung

Kim Dae-jung's
"Three-Stage"
Approach to Korean
Reunification

Kim Dae-jung's
"Three-Stage" Approach to Korean Reunification

Focusing on the South-North Confederal Stage

Translated by
Rhee Tong-chin

The Center for Multiethnic and Transnational Studies
University of Southern California
Los Angeles, California
1997

Published in the U.S. in 1997 by
The Center for Multiethnic and Transnational Studies
University of Southern California
University Park Campus
Los Angeles, CA 90089-1694, USA
Phone: (213) 740-1068 Fax: (213) 740-5810

ISBN 1-88-4445-32-2

Library of Congress Catalog Card Number: 97-65449

Published in Korea in 1997 by the
Kim Dae-jung Peace Foundation
for the Asia-Pacific Region Press
Aryung Building, Suite 701
506-20 Chang chun-Dong, Seodaemun-Ku
Seoul, Korea
Kim Dae-jung eui samdangye tongilron:
Nambuk yonhap eul chungsimeuro

IN DEDICATING
THE BOOK TO THE NATION

In offering this publication to the nation on the occasion of the fifty-year anniversary of National Liberation and Division, a million thoughts cross my mind—a mixture of feelings of joy and sorrow. While I feel a relief that I have finally repaid a small fraction of my debt to the nation, that feeling can only be fleeting, for I find myself unable to hide a greater sense of shame and responsibility to the nation and history as the only divided country in the world.

The human mind is a mystery. A soldier facing discharge from service in a month is far more nervous than one who faces it in a year's time. In the same vein, the greater the possibilities of unification become, the sadder and more regretful we feel about the realities of our division, and the greater the burden becomes for our sense of mission to achieve national reunification.

At a time like this, we need composure and patience. Whenever the realities loom large as enormous obstacles and frustrate us, I often look back at history. There are no falsities in history. The truths can be hidden or distorted for a time, but they always surface in the end. History also does not allow pessimism. Justice will always triumph and indefatigable aspiration will always be achieved.

The lessons for us from the fifty-year history of National Liberation and Division can only confirm our belief in the historical truths and great expectations of the future of our peninsula. I still vividly remember the wonderful sensation when the news reached me last October 21 that the North Korean-U.S. negotiations in Geneva were successful. It was a moment of both triumph and humility before the demonstration of historical truth.

The *Three-Stage Approaches to Korean Reunification* is an important culmination of the grand vistas of national unity that I have been working on without any rest or letup for the last quarter century. On this "canvas" which I have drawn, there is the underlying picture of my past pain and agony for being branded as a "pro-Communist" for having the courage and determination to achieve unification. Overlaying it, I have clearly pointed the way towards the future of national unification, promising national reconciliation and prosperity—by overcoming the contradicting realities of aspiration and obstacles to unity.

The road map for our national unification is now in your hands. If we follow the road of self-determination, peace and democracy, and make a gradual and phased journey through a South-North Confederation towards a Federal Stage, we shall eventually reach the height of the unified state. Following the road map, we shall build the roads, cover them with asphalt, install the street lights, plant trees on the roadside, bore tunnels when we encounter mountains, build bridges when we face the rivers, and rest when we are tired; and we shall move on until we reach there. According to a certain poet, The height is over there; how can we chat over here?

I am grateful to the KPF's Secretary General Lim Dong-won and the Foundation's Research Fellows for their long endeavors leading to the publication of this book. Especially, I thank most sincerely Dr. Rhee Tong-chin and Mrs. Robin Rhee for their tireless efforts in translating the book into English with skill and efficiency—not an easy task by any measure. I am hopeful that the English version will inform the public about the desirability and feasibility of Korea's unification for East Asia as well as the world. I also thank many others who have generously shared with us their busy schedules in responding to our requests for their time and advice. Finally, I dare offer the book to the country for study and scrutiny.

August 1996
Kim Dae-jung

PREFACE

This year is the fiftieth anniversary of our National Liberation. And yet, our nation has not had the chance to celebrate it together. We have greeted the anniversary with both the pain of the last half century and a sense of historical mission for national unification.

The Cold War that imposed on us the national division has ended and the internal and external environment, favorable to our unification, is being created. The unification will not be handed to us on a gold platter, nor will it evolve naturally. It is a supreme national task that we will have to accomplish by the sweat and toil of our own people. It must be achieved through reconciliation, mutual exchanges, and cooperation between the South and the North.

At this historic juncture, what we need most urgently are a firm philosophy and clear road map which will point the way and guide our people to national unification. Numerous unification proposals have been made to date. Yet, most of them have disappeared into oblivion without a whimper and without a trace. As time went by, however, Kim Dae-jung's unification formula has made steady progress, broadening its support and consensus. The reason for this has been that his unification ideas contain the wisdom and "his indomitable love for Korea and its people," learned through the tortuous processes of his long struggle in the popular movements for democracy and unification.

Facing the approach of the fifty years of National Division, Dr. Kim Dae-jung felt the need for systemization and specification of his grand blueprints for national unification. As the internal and external circumstances and environments changed for Korea's ultimate unification, there arose a new urgency in concretizing the national will for unity as well as in realizing mechanisms for a peaceful management of the unification processes. Thus, the publication of Dr. Kim Dae-jung's *Three-Stage Approaches to Korean Unification* as a monograph is the culmination of the efforts to add new flesh to his evolving ideas of more than two decades and to revise and/or supplement in parts—all in a response to the emerging new demands of the Zeitgeist of the post-Cold War era.

As is well known to us all, Kim Dae-jung's unification formula has been a target of persecution during the years of the authoritarian rule until the late 1980s. It was then when the government made a Copernican volte face to officially acknowledge and accept his ideas and reflected them in the government's proposal for a "Korean National Community" Unification Formula (made under President Roh Tae-woo's tenure). Even North Korea which had been advocating the "Koryo Democratic Confederation" has admitted the rationality and feasibility of Kim Dae-jung's "South-North Confederal Structure." It is a widely known fact that the leaders of German unification and other foreign experts on Korea have all expressed their agreement with Dr. Kim Dae-jung's unification formula.

Since its establishment in 1994, the Kim Dae-jung Peace Foundation (KPF) has carried on its research activities for Kim Dae-jung's "Three-Stage Unification" Proposal as its pivotal project. Professors Kim Nam-shik, Kim Sung-hoon, Ra Jong-il, Park Jong-hwa, Paik Kyung-nam, and Han Sang-jin—all members of the KPF Consultative Committee—took part in the project. The members of the KPF Research Staff—Drs. Park Kun yong, Park Byeong-seog, Lee Kang-rae, Lee Seok-soo, Lee Sung-bong, Choi

Sung, Ha Sang-sik, Hahm In-hee, and Hwang Ju-hong—bore the central responsibility for the project. Besides, more than a hundred other experts in all areas of specialty assisted in the common effort for research and publication of the project. As a result, the project emerged in its final form by the early part of 1995. Since then the draft version of the manuscript has undergone internal scrutiny; the problems raised in the internal seminars led to revision and improvement; and additional work was done to ensure the consistency of the chapters. The Korean version of the book is the result of all the aforementioned procedures. I am grateful to Dr. Rhee Tong-chin and Mrs. Robin Rhee for their concentration on the masterful translation of this work into English despite other heavy duties in the Foundation—a pioneering venture which will lead hopefully to other foreign language versions in the near future.

Dr. Kim Dae-jung, recognizing that the project was no longer his personal monopoly, assumed the role of providing sharp, focused intellectual guidance in systematizing and concretizing the substance with an inimitable sense of humility. Through word-by-word and line-by-line readings of the entire manuscript with the other project members, Dr. Kim, with his renowned tenacity has exerted focused effort to make the manuscript suitable for the general public.

The well known song—"Our Wish is to Attain Unification" —which so symbolizes our national grievances and aspirations ought to be turned into a memory for our own generation. The achievement of unification depends on what we do from here on.

August 1996
The Project Manager
Lim Dong-won
Secretary General, KPF

CONTENTS

TABLE AND DIAGRAMS

INTRODUCTION

National Unification has been a familiar theme that has been with us for fifty years since Liberation. However, regrettably, unification debates in the past were not for the benefit of the entire nation but for the narrow partisan interest of a specific persona or a specific group of people; or they were excessively idealistic. Those unification formulae which were devoid of seriousness and realism were in fact reflective of the limitations of the general conditions of the times. Notwithstanding the harsh severity of the times of authoritarian dictatorship, there still existed a singular unification proposal which persuasively presented a realistic method and approach to the unification issue—an issue of central import to the Korean national aspiration. Although it has been distorted and misrepresented out of base political partisanship, Kim Dae-jung's unification plan was firmly based on the perceptive understanding of the changes in the international political environment and was properly attuned to the emerging new era. Without question, it was a well thought out unification strategem designed to maximize the interests of the Korean nation.

The Cold War has now disappeared into the dark back alleys of history. Even on our Korean Peninsula, the tides of division and confrontation are ebbing and the tides of unification and peace are upon us. The unification, embracing the national hopes, seems within our reach—entering the realm of realistic possibility. The changing environment for national unification demands from us a clear unification road map. If we are not prepared for unification, the road we shall travel towards our national unity will be tortuous. Since there is an undeniable need for a realistic unification formula, which parallels our national interests, we have here published a monograph on Kim Dae-jung's unification formula that has been consistently advocated with conviction since the early seventies.

"Kim Dae-jung's Three-Stage Unification" Formula, presented in this book, contains all the central elements in his original proposal. Over the years, many different proposals have been floated and jettisoned into oblivion without a trace. Despite intense political oppression and misunderstanding, only the "Three-Stage Unification" formula has maintained its life, smoothly adjusting to changing realities, and made consistent progress in transfiguration.

However, although the proposal has maintained the basic conceptual framework, which is both rational and realistic, until now, it has not assumed the systematized form and substance which is now presented in this book. It is also true that realistic and feasible policy alternatives that can be actually implemented in various areas of society, have not been proposed before this study. That the rapid changes here and abroad provided strong impetus for our project is understandable in that we were convinced of the need for some rethinking and revision in details of the manuscript. Realistically speaking, no unification formula can exactly predict all the possible phases of unification under constantly changing situation. Presenting a formula in neglect of reality and attempting to adjust the evolving phases to the fixed formula would be a sheer folly and act of unjustifiable stubbornness—a Quixotic gesture. In this context, we have started the project for greater systematization and specificity.

In this publication, we shall concentrate on the programs and the guidelines for their implementation in the First Stage of South-North Confederation. The reason for this is obvious: the First Stage is the crucial step leading towards unification. The establishment of a Confederation will be a watershed event that will unleash the tide leading to the indispensable initiative. The Confederal Stage is truly the beginning of the inevitable unification process; and once begun, the rest of the processes will naturally follow. And with the depth and intensity of exchanges and cooperation, the ensuing processes should proceed relatively smoothly.

We expect that the Confederal phase could last for roughly a decade. Accordingly, our elaboration of the unification formula will focus on various facets of programs that can be expected to unfold during the decade after the two Koreas agree to enter the Confederal phase. We shall carefully examine all the possible structural changes that can be expected once the programs, necessary for the ultimate unification, are activated during that crucial phase. We propose to exert our best efforts to portray the expected processes as realistically as possible to avoid superficiality. In so doing, we hope to stress the point that the Confederation is not important merely for peaceful coexistence, peaceful exchanges and cooperation, but as an interim developmental phase it will be a vital step towards the transition to an eventual Federation between the South and the North.

This book is organized as follows:

Chapter 1—An Overview of "Kim Dae-jung's Three-Stage Unification" Formula—systematically introduces the basic principles and implementational guidelines of Kim Dae-jung's unification formula. The examination of the general ideological and philosophical paradigms of the formula will help the readers' basic understanding of the subject and should give them the general outline of the chapters that follow. Chapter 2—The Basic Characteristics of the South-North Confederation and the Principles of Its Operation—will discuss the basic characteristics of the Confederation, its tasks, and the principles of its operation; and offers the policy prospect in the Confederation's ultimate transition to a Federation. Chapter 3—Peaceful Coexistence Under the Confederation—examines critically and comprehensively the issues of arms control and other special measures designed for peaceful coexistence—the two central issues that must be addressed in the Confederal phase. Chapter 4—Economic Exchanges and Cooperation Under the Confederation—discusses the modalities of exchanges and cooperation between the South and the North to create a national economic community. Chapter 5—Social-Cultural Exchanges and Cooperation Under the Confederation—looks at the means for exchanges and cooperation that could be conducive to the creation of the homogeneous national identity as well as the common social-cultural community.

As already been mentioned, Kim Dae-jung's "Three-Stage Unification" Formula has been refined and reinforced progressively in constant adjustment to changing realities despite persistent and pernicious political persecution. To correctly understand, therefore, the particular historical significance of Mr. Kim's unification formula, one has to closely look at its historicity as well as the processes of its systematization. For this purpose, we add the "Supplement" toward the end of the book.

Finally, the important documents, collected to illuminate the unification issues and the relations between the two Koreas, are appended for the readers' benefit.

The book is composed of six chapters. Although we would recommend a thorough reading of the entire book, we have arranged the book in a way that will allow readers to approach the book selectively by their preference of subject matter. Therefore, without reading the preceding chapters, they could easily comprehend the individual chapters which stand independently. For this purpose, we have added introductory segments at the head of each chapter.

The "Three-Stage Unification" Formula will continue to maintain its central policy continuity, based on its three basic principles and ideological/philosophical foundation; and will strive for specificity and feasibility as the formula will undoubtedly undergo further process of verification under the changing circumstances. In our march towards unification, the "Three-Stage Unification" Formula will, we hope, point the direction and provide vision and courage for our nation.

CHAPTER 1

AN OVERVIEW OF "KIM DAE-JUNG'S THREE-STAGE UNIFICATION" FORMULA

Summary

The main purpose of this monograph is to present Kim Dae-jung's "Three-Stage Unification" Formula after giving its basic principles and implementing methods a thorough systematizing logic.

The Formula posits three main principles of unification: self-reliance, peace, and democracy. Under the principle of "self-reliance," we propose that all national issues including unification ought to be solved by ourselves based on the spirit of self-determination and without relying on outside forces. Guided by the principle of "peace," we ought to settle all national issues not through violence but by means of peaceful negotiations. The principle of "Democracy" requires that the unification processes be democratic in that they ought to be based on national consultation and consensus.

Under the "Three-Stage" formula, the first stage is that of a Confederation between the two Koreas; the second stage is a Federation composed of the Southern and the Northern regional autonomous governments; and the third and final stage is either a centralized government or several regional autonomous governments as in the case of the federal systems in the United States and/or Germany. For convenience, we would call the last stage the state of complete unification. Under the "Three-Stage" formula, the first stage of Confederation is considered particularly important as the institutional mechanism for facilitating inter-Korean reconciliation and cooperation. In that context, the establishment of the Confederation would be a watershed event, and an indispensable factor for the ultimate unification. We consider that the Confederal stage can be entered into at anytime, whenever a national consensus is reached and political decisions are made by the two Korean governments, and several other conditions are met.

The primary task for the Confederation is to implement the three basic policy guidelines for peaceful coexistence, exchange, and unification. Peaceful coexistence must begin with the mutual recognition of each other's existence—the co-existence of the two divergent systems. Therefore, it must signify the provision of an institutionalized and practical peace mechanism to avoid any contingency of armed confrontation by building up the structure of political trust between the two Koreas. The peaceful exchange is designed to promote mutual interests and to restore homogeneous national identity by way of extensive exchanges in all areas including the spheres of politics, economy, society, and culture. These are the bridge building efforts between the separated entities to make the unification process easier. Peaceful unification, then, is to prevent the possibilities of either unification through the use of force or absorption through the use of superior economic power at a later date when the conditions for unification will be considered sufficient to warrant a transition from the Confederal stage to a Federation. The transition to a state of unification must be made through the democratic and peaceful process of negotiation.

Under the Confederation, the state of division will have to be managed peacefully and efficiently so as to enable a smooth transition to a Federal Stage. For that purpose, the Confederation is expected to perform other essential tasks. In performing these tasks, several key Confederal organs will have to be established: the "South-North Summit" as the supreme decision making body; the "Council of South-North Confederation" as the representative legislature; and the "South-North Ministerial Council" as the executive body.

Under the Second Stage of Federation, foreign relations/diplomacy, defense, and important internal affairs would come under a Federal government. The remaining internal affairs will still be under the jurisdiction of the two Korean republics functioning as the respective regional authorities.

The reason for setting up the Federal phase under the "Three-Stage" formula was the proper consideration for the heterogeneity in all areas including the spheres of politics, economy, society, and culture between the two Koreas that has developed as the unfortunate consequence of the prolonged national division. The idea is to buffer the expected shock arising from the fusion of the two widely divergent systems; to recognize the autonomous regional government and to respect the idiosyncrasies of North Korea and the self-respect of North Korean residents; and to enable the Federal Government's special assistance to the northern region for a specified period of time.

The "Three-Stage Unification" Formula proposes a progressive transition from Confederation to Federation—a stage of de facto unification—to either a centralized system of government or the existence of several autonomous regional governments similar to the federal system of the United States and Germany. However, given the world trends of regional decentralization or simply regional autonomy, the choice between the two forms of unified government will have to be made by the people themselves.

The "Three-Stage Unification" Formula has the following characteristics. First, it is foremost a strategy of peaceful unification. A unification proposal that inflicts serious damage to the nation through the use of force or imposes unbearable economic burden cannot be seriously considered as a plan. The North Korean policy of unification through Communization or through a bloody revolution is a unification strategy that deserves no debate whatever.

Second, it is a strategy that is eminently feasible, as it offers the optimum modality for rational processes for unification. To immediately enter into a Federal stage with the two divergent systems intact, as proposed by North Korea, is simply unrealistic. Under the prevailing circumstances, when there is an absolutely unbridgeable chasm between the two totally irreconcilable systems, how can we entertain the thought of a sudden and abrupt fusion into a single entity? On the other hand, the direct transition from a Confederation to a complete unification, proposed by our government, is also unpersuasive. If we are truly serious about peaceful unification, we have to account for the time and processes that can overcome the incompatibilities between the two vastly different systems.

Third, the "Three-Stage Unification" formula is, indeed, a very safe proposal for both sides. Most of all, it allows the two sides to take the initial step without fear. As has been already explained, our proposed Confederal stage assumes coexistence between the two states, and provides an adequate institutional mechanism that will tangibly help the two Koreas' reconciliation and cooperation. Thus, even if some unforeseen obstacles occur after the Confederation is effected, no insurmountable threat or burden will have to be borne by either side.

Fourth, our proposal is one of sincere desire for unification. In the past, both Koreas had the habit of making proposals that the other side could not accept. The Confederal stage in our proposal is an innocuous process in which the two sides can promote their mutual cooperation without the burden of giving up their sovereign rights. Hence, neither side is too burdened with obligation that it has no intention of bearing. In that context, the "Three-Stage" formula is cautious and prudent—a truly serious proposal, unprecedented in the last half century of division.

I. Introduction: The Possibility of and Need for Unification

If the division of the Korean Peninsula was the result of the Soviet-American Cold War and the conflict of their interests, the solution to the problem may be found in the fundamental changes in that very Cold War structure. Now the Cold War has ended, and the international environment surrounding the Korean Peninsula is changing in the direction of Korea's unification. The trends of history are pointing to a sea change from confrontation to peace, from conflict and friction to reconciliation and cooperation, and from division to unification. The Republic of Korea has already established normal diplomatic relations with China and Russia, and before long North Korea too will improve its relations with the United States and Japan. If and when the cross recognition of the two Koreas finally occurs, the external factors that obstructed unification will fade into history.

It might be true, however, that Korea's neighboring states may believe that the continuation of the status quo would be in their national interests. Indeed, from the standpoint of "political reality," there could be the possibility that our neighbors would continue to prefer the division of Korea. But if they are somehow convinced that the unified Korea would pose no threat to them and will be a peace-loving state, they may not be able to oppose unification indiscriminately. Because of the vital importance of the Korean peninsula in geopolitical and geo-economic aspects, the stability and peace in Korea could be considered essential for their own respective national interests.

Let us now turn to the changes in unification environment over the Korean Peninsula. First of all, we have to note the fact that the changes in North Korea are inevitable after the collapse of the Communist Bloc. In the Post-Cold War world, the politics and economy are moving towards democracy and market economy. North Korea, too, cannot go against the tides of global historical change. North Korea's changes are detected in its policy considerations for opening its doors to the outside world. In 1991, Pyongyang established Free Economic and Trading Zones in Rajin and Sunbong; enacted a Foreign Investment Law in 1992 and revised the Joint Venture Law in 1994. It is not to gainsay the fact that the policy of economic open doors is becoming a pivot of North Korean policies.

Our own capabilities for unification are also on the rise. As of 1995, in GDP and trade volume, South Korea stands twelfth in the world. Not only in economic power, our international status has grown incomparably greater than in the past. Although there still remain a great many issues to be addressed in terms of genuine democratization, our political development, too, has been remarkable in comparison to our dictatorial past.

The inter-Korean relations are not the same as before either. Under the emerging new conditions of the Post-Cold War era, it seems that North Korea no longer considers its long held policy of communizing the South through revolutionary strategy possible. The result of this change in North Korea's basic policy has been the signing of the "Agreement on Reconciliation, Non-Aggression, and Exchanges and Cooperation between the South and the North" [hereafter cited as the "Basic Agreement"] and the comprehensive package deal on nuclear issues as well as the economic and political issues between North Korea and the United States [the Agreed Framework in Geneva].

In general, the overall conditions, both internal and external, are in the process of change, favorable to Korea's unification. The unification, which was possible only in a dream, is now becoming a distinct possibility. If the unification is becoming a possibility, is it really urgently necessary for our nation? This question being so normal may even sound ridiculous. But beyond the sentimental aspiration of the past, the question now deserves closer scrutiny on the basis of its significance in the context of our realistic need for it under the changing circumstances.

Why do we need the unification? First, there is the historical aspect of continuing with the thirteen centuries of historical tradition of a unified national state since Silla's unification of the peninsula. There have been few states in history which have preserved the political and cultural traditions as unified states like us. The fifty years of our national division is the shameful history of discontinuity of our history and tradition under coercion by outside pressure. The national community of homogeneous people that had been preserved with indestructible persistence was momentarily damaged by outside forces. Accordingly, to break down the wall of division that our nation has found so "unnatural and uncomfortable" is a task that must be accomplished if we are to continue the long historical tradition and to restore the profound national elan.

Second, we must not let the pain and anxiety of the division continue any longer. We have experienced the fratricide of the Korean War. The spiritual agony of the separated families is still with us vividly. The inordinate "fear of war" is still casting a long shadow in the corner of our collective national mind—the fear that gripped us all during the North Korean nuclear crisis. Deprived of freedom and human rights, the spiritual and physical pain of our blood kin in North Korea ought to be immeasurable. We cannot and must not pass on the tragedies of our nation to posterity.

Third, to survive and succeed in the coming era of unlimited international competition, the cost of national division must be transferred to fund increased industrial production and social welfare. Under the WTO structure, only the countries with competitiveness will be able to survive. If we continue the all consuming conflict between the two Koreas, our international competitiveness will be seriously weakened and we shall degenerate into a third class state.

This is not all. There is also a serious political cost due to the national division, namely the control and manipulation of Korea by the neighboring states through the "divide and rule" of the two Koreas. We must make sure that they can no longer use that card to force us to continue to waste our resources on maintaining the separation.

Fourth, if and when we achieve unification, we shall emerge as the central role player in the Asia-Pacific Era of the twenty-first century. South Korea is already a member of the global community of wealthy countries. If we add the quality labor force and natural resources of North Korea, the economic power of the unified Korea will be able to reach the level of the advanced countries in the world, and even the level of the United States, Japan, and Germany. Further, by utilizing our geopolitical condition, we could display outstanding diplomatic ability by playing the role of a "stabilizer" or a "balancer" among our neighboring states. Our national unification must be achieved, if we are to survive successfully in the Post-Cold War competition and to have the fulfillment of national prosperity.

In an age when the possibilities of national unification are higher than ever and when the need for national unity is more urgent, what is the best possible plan for unification? The formula that is needed has to be one that promises both peaceful achievement as well as future national prosperity. Kim Dae-jung's "Three-Stage Unification" Formula satisfies all the optimum requirements.

In this chapter, we shall systematically present its basic principles and methodologies. We shall scrutinize the principles and their ideological bases; and shall examine the significance of each stage and the tasks which must be achieved in each stage. By also comparing the Formula with the proposals of both Korean governments, we shall highlight the differences between them and their respective historical significance.

II. The Principles and Ideological Bases of Kim Dae-jung's Unification Proposal

1. Principles of Unification

Policies that lack principles and philosophies cannot long endure. Ideologies that cannot be verified through history and reality are by nature devoid of specificity and feasibility. In this sub-chapter, we shall examine the principles and philosophies that permeate the "Three-Stage" formula.

The basic principles that Kim Dae-jung has advocated for Korea's unification since the early seventies are self-reliance, peace, and democracy. First, under the principle of "self-reliance," we propose that all national issues including unification ought to be solved by Koreans themselves based on the spirit of national self-determination, without relying on outside forces. Although, under certain circumstances, cooperation and assurances may be needed from our neighboring states, we ought not leave the task of achieving national unification to the decisions of the great powers. The principle of self-reliance has been agreed to as the primary principle by the two Koreas since the adoption of the July 4th Joint Communique (1972)[1] and the same happened at the time of the Basic Agreement in 1991.[2] Being completely surrounded as we are by the four great powers, it is imperative that we firmly observe the "self-reliance" principle that "unification ought to be achieved through our own efforts."

Second, the principle of "peace" requires that all national issues including unification be settled not through violence but through peaceful means. The "peace" principle is especially stressed as the crucial component of the "Three Tenets of Implementation"—namely, "peaceful coexistence" is a fundamental tenet which is to dissolve the inter-Korean hostility and replace it with special inter-relationships to move toward unification. The principle of peace represents the will to "create the condition of peace" through inter-Korean arms control and the estab-

---

[1]Refer to Appendix 1.
[2]Refer to Appendix 1.

lishment of a Northeast Asian multilateral security structure. "Peaceful exchange" is a tenet which is designed to facilitate and expedite the peaceful and free movement of human and material resources between the two Koreas to achieve national prosperity and to restore the common national homogeneity. It is a principle that makes it clear that under no circumstances should there be an attempt to unify the nation through military force or the use of superior power (e.g., economic superiority).

Third, the "democracy" principle posits that the entire process of unification must undergo democratic procedures and national consensus. Unification must occur through the active participation of all Koreans, in both Koreas, and through their free consent. For that purpose, all unification debate must be open and free so Koreans in both Koreas can freely choose the modality of national unity. Only the unification plan which is based on popular consent can possess the necessary legitimacy and authority and will be supported by the international community.

2. The Ideological Bases of the Unification Principles

The three basic principles of self-reliance, peace, and democracy of the "Three-Stage Unification" Formula are deeply rooted in Kim Dae-jung's basic concepts and philosophies of national unification—namely, "Open Nationalism, Positive Pacifism, and Global Democracy."

First, for Kim Dae-jung, democracy is both the ideological foundation and the motive engine of moving toward unification. To him, unification signifies not only the reunion of the Korean nation but the very first establishment of a modern democratic state in Korean history. Kim Dae-jung's "nationalism" referred to here is "Open Nationalism," which opposes the "extensive and aggressive" nationalism that by nature oppresses and exploits other nations for its own narrow selfish national interests. It accepts the "internalized" nationalism that liberates its own nation from foreign colonial oppression to achieve freedom and independence, thus opening the road to its national survival. However, as often seen in Third World nationalism, Kim's concept is against unconditionally anti-foreign and closed minded nationalism. In that context, Kim's "Open Nationalism" is fundamentally different from North Korea's anti-imperialistic notion of "My Country Firstism."

The second ideological basis of the "Three-Stage Unification" Formula is "Positive Pacifism." Peace throughout the Cold War period has been a limited or negative concept of the simple "absence of war." Peace thus defined signified a contradictory phenomenon of angst and tension. Kim Dae-jung's "Positive Pacifism" transcends the negative or minimalist stance of merely opposing war, and is based on the positive concept of peace. It seeks actively the "creation of peace" such as the pursuit of a nuclear-free world or the establishment of a Northeast Asian security cooperation structure, and so forth.

The third ideological basis, Global Democracy, purports to transcend the selfish "single country orientation" of traditional democracy for wider international application of its lofty principles. As the major distinguishing characteristic, it seeks not only the internal application of democratic principles within sovereign states, but also advocates the implementation of those principles to the Third World where the same freedom and prosperity, as enjoyed in advanced countries, could be equally applied for the less developed countries. In addition, its goal is to protect and preserve all living things by beginning a world ecological movement.

The ideas of Global Democracy can be found in Asia's democratic thoughts, institutions, and historical traditions that are not far behind their Western counterparts. We believe the time has come for the broader views of Asian democracy to exert more constructive influence to overcome the limitations of Western democratic practices. There are long-standing democratic traditions and elements deeply rooted in Korea's history such as the concept that "man is heaven' advocated by a native Korean religion, Tonghak; the political and cultural traditions of civilian supremacy; the openness of the civil service examination, assuring extraordinary social mobility; the tradition of the freedom of speech; the tradition of pacifism and non-aggression against other nations; profound educational zeal; and the valuable lessons learned from the democratic struggles against dictatorship. When our democracy is elevated to a new height—a Global Democracy based on Asian traditions and roots—we shall be in a position to achieve our ideals.

We have examined thus far, the three basic principles—self-reliance, peace, and democracy—that form the nucleus of the "Three-Stage Unification" Formula and are rooted in the ideological/philosophical bases of "Open Democracy, Positive Pacifism, and Global Democracy." These principles and the ideological basis play the central role in adding to the universal character of the "Three-Stage Unification" formula and in determining its general direction. We shall now turn to the specific details of the formula.

III. The Processes of "Kim Dae-jung's Unification Formula

The "Three-Stage Unification" Formula rejects unification through war and any other form of violence. It proposes a peaceful unification through democratic procedures and the consensus of all Koreans. Since such a unification cannot be achieved suddenly overnight but only through a gradual process, it advocates "taking the first step as promptly as possible but proceeding with the process as slowly and cautiously as possible."

The first stage of the formula is that of the Confederation of the two Koreas—the South-North Confederation. In this stage, the Confederation is of "One Nation, Two States, and Two Independent Governments." In this phase, the two independent governments form the Confederation, while still maintaining their respective systems. Both Koreas will continue to exercise their existing sovereignty and authority in their respective territories. The Confederation is purported to manage the unification processes efficiently by institutionalizing inter-Korean cooperation. This stage is expected to last roughly a decade. In that period, the South and the North will jointly seek increasing prosperity for themselves and concentrate their efforts to restore the common national homogeneity.

The second stage is a Federation—One Nation, One State, One System, and Two Autonomous Regional Governments. Under the Federation, foreign relations/diplomacy, defense, and other important internal affairs will be handled by the central government, while the remaining internal matters will be administered by the two autonomous regional governments. An elected office of the Federal Presidency and a Federal Parliament will be established under a "Unification (Federal)" Constitution.

As detailed discussion will follow later, in this context, the "Three-Stage Unification" Formula is fundamentally different from North Korea's proposal of "the Koryo Democratic Confederal Republic" [hereafter cited as the "Koryo Democratic Confederation"].[3]

The third and final stage will be the complete unification—a unified state of either a centralized government or several regional autonomous governments as in the case of the federal systems in the United States or in Germany. In fact, by simply entering the second stage of federation, one could argue that de facto unification is achieved. Given the world trends of decentralization or simply regional self-government, the transition from a Federation to centralization or to a system of decentralized federation as in the case of the United States and Germany will have to be decided by the people themselves when the time comes for the final choice. [4]

1. The Stage of South-North Confederation

Within the scheme of the "Three-Stage Unification" Formula, the South-North Confederation is considered particularly impor-

---

[3]The "Koryo Democratic Confederation" proposal was made by Kim Il Sung on October 10, 1980 during the Central Committee session of the 6th Plenum of the Labor Party.

[4]Lee Sang-woo proposes: a ten-year run of a Federal System, composed of the two regional governments of the South and the North to be followed by a unified national federation, composed of four regional governments each in both Koreas. His proposal will be based on the redivision of the South and the North into four regions each. See Lee Sang-woo, "The Unification Scenario: Economic Union in 2000, Political Union in 2010, and the Establishment of a Unified Republic in 2020" in *The Age of Unification Opens in the Year 2000* (Seoul: Dong-A Ilbo, 1993), p. 55.

tant as the institutionalized mechanism for expediting the inter-Korean reconciliation and cooperation. The establishment of a Confederation will be a watershed event to unlock the impasse toward unification, and will be an indispensable prerequisite for eventual national unity. We consider that the Confederal stage can be entered into anytime whenever a national consensus is reached and political decisions are made by the two Korean governments, and several other practical conditions are met.

1) The Significance of the Confederation

While the two Korean governments still maintain their status quo of opposing ideologies and conflicting political and economic systems, the Confederation will mean an institutionalized mechanism that undertakes the tasks of "peacefully managing the division" as well as "efficaciously overseeing the integration process" by the establishment of joint organizations for closer cooperation. As such it will not be merely a fraternal and friendly relationship aimed at the perpetuation of national division, but a deliberate development of a special relationship leading toward unification.

Therefore, unlike the unification plan of the present South Korean government which insists on the prior process of deepening reconciliation and cooperation as the essential precondition to an inter-Korean confederation, the Confederation in our scheme is viewed as essential machinery for inducing the new environment which facilitates the reconciliation and cooperation. We believe that as soon as minimum political confidence is established beginning with the nuclear accord, we could soon begin the deliberate and calibrated process by beginning the Confederal stage as an institutionalized attempt at inter-Korean harmony and cooperation. Needless to say, the South-North Confederation under the "Three-Stage" formula is the end result of inter-Korean exchange and cooperation. Rather it would be the consequence of the Korean people's collective consensus and the political decisions of the two governments as well as the expediter/intensifier of inter-Korean reconciliation and cooperation.

Some will, then, question how it would be possible to enter into a Confederation without first effecting reconciliation and cooperation. Some others will cite the case of Yemen, pointing out that a political integration would be risky without a sufficient level of reconciliation and cooperation. What is clear, however, is that the Confederation in our formula is clearly not a form of political integration. To put it differently, a confederation is not a unification. The Yemeni example is totally irrelevant here for comparison. To elaborate, a South-North Confederation is only a transitional mechanism designed to advance the cause of reconciliation and cooperation. Therefore, even if we are faced with difficulties along the way after the Confederation is established, there will still be no special threat or burden for either side.

The main task of the Confederation is to carry out the three basic guidelines for policy implementation: peaceful coexistence, peaceful exchange, and peaceful unification. Peaceful coexistence begins with mutual recognition of each other's existence and seeks mutual coexistence; and provides an institutional and practical peace mechanism to prevent armed confrontation/conflict under any circumstances through political trust and confidence building.

Peaceful exchange is to promote and expedite inter-Korean exchanges and cooperation in all areas, including political, economic, social, and cultural areas, to increase each other's interests and benefits and to gradually restore the common national homogeneity; and through these steps prepare the bridge for ultimate unification. Especially, the activation of exchanges and cooperation in the economic, social, and cultural areas will increase the level of inter-Korean interdependence, thus laying the firm substructure that will facilitate peaceful and democratic unification through self-reliance.

Peaceful unification posits that all unification processes will proceed peacefully through dialogue and negotiations when the two Koreas discuss the ways to enter into a Federation after all preceding preparation is complete. Unification by military force, as in the case of the Korean War or the Vietnam conflict or by Communist revolutionary tactics, must never be entertained or tolerated. Nor should unification through absorption on the basis of economic superiority be allowed to happen.

2) The Preconditions for the Confederation

The South-North Confederation, the first stage of the "Three-Stage" plan, can be established without much difficulty if the Koreans in both Koreas desire unification and if and when the political authorities in the two Koreas make the necessary political decision based on popular aspiration. On this point, there is a fundamental difference between the views of the present South Korean government and our position. Namely, the South Korean government considers that a Confederation will not be possible until and unless there is mutual confidence between the two Koreas; while we consider the "positive support for unification" by the people sufficient to warrant a Confederal system. Therein lies, in our view, the fundamental difference in perception of the unification issue.

However, because of the serious development of heterogeneous elements between the two Koreas during the last fifty years of division, there must be at least minimal political confidence between the two before a South-North Confederation can be considered. This issue is intimately related to North Korea's nuclear problem. The Agreed Framework between North Korea and the United States in Geneva in 1994 provides a basic framework for its ultimate solution. There could be ups and downs in the negotiations for implementation concerning the supply of the lightwater reactors; however, we believe that the problem will naturally sort itself out through a package deal in a give-and-take of "nuclear issues" and "diplomatic and economic cooperation."

In addition, political confidence building through the implementation of the Basic Agreement, military tension reduction measures, and the completion of the cross recognition of the two Koreas by the four major powers, and others could further facilitate the eventual establishment of the Confederation. But these factors are not necessarily the prerequisites for entering into an agreement on the Confederation, but rather they would contribute to an early entry into a Confederal structure. Hence, the question of whether or not to agree on a Confederation or when that agreement can best be made, is entirely up to the Koreans themselves and their respective authorities in both Koreas.

3) The Confederal Organs and Their Operation

Under the Confederation, six major tasks will be implemented based on the three guidelines for peaceful management of the national division and for efficient entry later into a Federal phase. The six major tasks will be discussed later in detail.

The following Confederal organs will be inaugurated to carry out the six tasks: the "South-North Summit" [hereafter cited as the "Summit Conference"]—the supreme decision-making body; the "Council of South-North Confederation" [hereafter cited as "Confederal Council"]—representative legislature; and the "South-North Confederal Council Secretariat" [hereafter cited as the "Secretariat"]; the "South-North Ministerial Council" [hereafter cited as the "Ministerial Council"]—the executive body; and the "South-North Confederal Committees" [hereafter cited as the "Confederal Committees"] for designated areas.

The "South-North Confederal Charter" [hereafter cited as the "Confederal Charter"] is the basic law that will regulate the inter-Korean relations under the Confederation, and will be effective until a "Unification (Federal) Constitution" is established. It will be adopted by the decision of the Summit Conference and will go into effect through the ratification of the Confederal Council.

As the supreme decision-making body, the Summit Conference will meet regularly, rotating between the two Koreas. It will make the political decisions on the problems of the nation, unification, and inter-Korean relations with its eyes firmly set on unification. It will decide whether to accept or reject the matters passed by the Confederal Council; ratify the decisions of the Ministerial Council; and oversee the implementation of the agreed items.

As a permanent legislative body, the Confederal Council will hold sessions in different parts of both Koreas in rotation. In implementing the three policy guidelines of peaceful coexistence, exchange, and unification, it will listen to the views and opinions of the people, discuss, and vote on the matters, and refer the decisions to the Summit Conference.

As a Confederal body that represents the two states, linked in a state to state fusion, its mode of decision-making will be based on unanimity so that both sides can maintain their respective independent positions. The Confederal Council will be composed of representatives elected by the parliaments of both sides; and the decisions made in the Confederal Council will be adopted or rejected by the Summit Conference. The Summit Conference has the veto power over the matters referred to it by the Confederal Council.

The Secretariat's task is to support the operation of the Confederal Council, and is organized by the officials designated by each side.

The decisions made by the Summit Conference will be turned over to the Ministerial Council for implementation. The Ministerial Council will decide how to implement the referred matters from the Summit Conference. The Ministerial Council will set up South-North Confederal Committees [the Confederal Committees] to deal with different areas; the Committees' function is to respond to the consultations with the Ministerial Council on the details of the referred matters and devise means to implement them for the Ministerial Council. For example, the "South-North Confederal Military Committee" will discuss and devise measures to implement the following matters: the contingencies of military accidents, military confidence-building measures, arms control negotiations, supervision and verification systems, and other related matters.

2. The Stage of Federation

1) The Characteristics of Federation and Its Significance

The stage of Federation would mean unification. Under the Federation, foreign relations/diplomacy, defense, and important internal matters will be handled by the Federal Government. But other less important and routine internal matters will continued to be dealt with by the two republics, functioning as autonomous regional authorities. More specific decisions on the roles of the regional governments cannot be specified at this time as the matter will be considered more than a decade away. We shall, however, present general outlines here.

Why is the Federal system necessary? What is the reason for a Federation as a transitional stage prior to complete unification? The reasons are as follows:

First, in order to push for an integration, one must consider the overall situation of the two Koreas such as the significant differences in economic and social development; the structural and systemic differences in political, social, and cultural areas after a half century of deepening and intensifying heterogeneity. In fact, the Federal stage would be essential to ameliorate the tremendous shock and confusion of the people in both Koreas— from daily life to values—that is expected from integration. Second, there is a distinct need for regional self-government for North Korea, considering the unique idiosyncrasy of the North Korean system and the self-esteem of Northern residents. Third, the need will arise for the Federal Government to offer "special assistance" to the northern region for a considerable period of time. Particularly, it would be unavoidable and indispensable to allow the northern region special consideration such as the concentrated indirect social capital investment in infrastructure to minimize the confusion in the integrated labor market[5] and to rationally allocate social welfare funds.

For these reasons, a transition from Confederation straight to complete unification, as proposed by the South Korean government, without going through a transitional phase like the Federation would be foolhardy. At the same time, the North Korean proposal that the two Koreas ought to enter the Federal stage without further preparation while maintaining the two divergent systems also lacks realistic feasibility because it completely ignores the existing reality. Accordingly, the South-North Federation is possible only after a considerable period of Confederal phase as a preparatory unification stage—a unification stage that will mitigate the expected shocks and confusion from integration, and a stage in which special assistance will have to be offered the north Korean region by the Federal Government. In this context, the Federal phase must precede what follows next.

2) The Preconditions for Entering the Federal Stage

The transition to a Federation from Confederation requires the fulfillment of the following conditions:

---

[5]A sudden and extra rapid integration of the labor market through the massive internal migration of the northern labor force to southern Korea would create an industrial vacuum in the northern region, a serious housing problem in the south, and either a sharp reduction of southern workers' incomes or massive layoffs. On the other hand, if the large-scale southerly migration of the northern labor force is physically controlled, while an increasing number of the unemployed in northern Korea, due to large scale industrial bankruptcies, are not meaningfully assisted, the northern residents' nostalgia for the old Kim Il Sung era might be unavoided.

First, North Korea must democratize by accepting a multi-party system and free elections. A political integration between the two Koreas will become possible only when both Koreas have a democratic political system.

Second, an inter-Korean economic community must be established through the North Korean acceptance of a market economy; and further integration must take place in the areas of currency, the monetary system, and finance.

Third, there must be a "new military balance at a reduced force level" through an arms control agreement, leading eventually to an integrated military forces between the two Koreas. A diplomatic integration to represent a single sovereign state in the international community must take place simultaneously.

Fourth, the socio-cultural heterogeneity between the two Koreas must be considerably reduced so that a common national homogeneity can be restored. All this would be essential if we are to effect socio-cultural integration.

As mentioned earlier, we believe that, under the "Three-Stage Unification" formula, the changes in all areas of society will occur not from external pressure but by the voluntary will of the two Korean authorities and by increasing popular demand.

To briefly introduce the organization and the operation of the Federal System, foreign relations/diplomacy, defense, and important internal matters will be handled by the Federal Government, but general internal affairs will continue to be dealt with by the two autonomous regional governments in the two Koreas.

Under the Federal System, the two regional governments will be autonomous, while the Federal Government, representing the two regional authorities, will concentrate its "pan-national" efforts for national prosperity and development, based on the universal values of a market economy, democracy, and social welfare. Based on the Federal Constitution, agreed on by the two Korean governments, a Federal President and Legislature will be established during the period. The latter will be bicameral, based on regional as well as functional representation.

Under the Federal System, the two Koreas will be represented at the United Nations as a single entity, and the relationship with foreign powers will also be unified. So will be the membership in all international bodies, all seeking to promote the national interest of Korea as a single state.

3. The Stage of Complete Unification

The process of South-North integration under the "Three-Stage" formula is from Confederation to Federation— composed of two autonomous regional governments—to either a centralized government or several autonomous regional governments as in the case of the federal systems in the United States or in Germany. In fact, by entering the stage of Federation with two regional authorities, Korea will have achieved a de facto unification. The decision between the centralized form of government or several regional authorities will have to be made by the people themselves at that time.

The exact timing of the complete unification in the form of either system is not very important. What is really important will be to restore complete mutual confidence and trust and to thoroughly embark on the task of establishing a unified national community—such as the balanced development of all Korea and the restoration of a homogeneous common national identity.

IV. The Future Vision of the Unified State

There is one thing we should always keep in mind during the long processes of national unification: that is to be clear about the vision of the future unified state. First, the political system of the unified state shall be founded on democracy that guarantees people's liberty, freedom, and rights, especially human rights. Korea's division has been the major obstacle to democratization in both Koreas. Fortunately, however, democracy is gradually taking root in South Korea, mainly because of the high political consciousness of its citizenry. On the other hand, as a totalitarian state North Korea is far from being a democratic society. However, as general exchanges and cooperation begin and increase in depth and intensity between the two Koreas after a Federal system is agreed upon, it is expected that North Korea will inevitably accept a gradual democratization. Before the entry into a Federal phase and complete unification, concentrated efforts will have to be made during the Confederal stage to maximize the spread of democratic values in both Koreas, especially North Korea.

The achievement of democracy in the unified Korean states will not be confined to Korea alone. It is highly desirable that unified Korea, in cooperation with the other advanced democratic states around the world, offers its material and moral assistance to other states which have not yet begun to democratize as well as to other developing democratic states. The unified Korean state that will unfold before us will not stop at efforts for Korean democracy alone, but will make efforts to spread the benefits of democracy not only to the rest of Asia but throughout the entire world for the ultimate concept of Global Democracy, wherein "all will live together" and "all humans will have dignified lives."

Second, the unified state's economic system will be a market economy. In the late eighties, we learned through the experiences of various states in the world that between the planned and market economic systems, the latter should be the inevitable choice for us. Based on the principle of equal opportunity and on unlimited creativity, the market economy should be able to bring forth national prosperity and development. However, the market economy, advocated by the "Three-Stage" formula, does not mean unlimited free competition and unlimited maximization of profit. The economic principles endorsed by it will be founded on Kim Dae-jung's concept of "growth and stability, and fair distribution of wealth."[6]

Three, the unified state will create a society that honors and respects human dignity through social justice and welfare. Through Korean unification, we do not merely aim for territorial reunion or economic prosperity alone. Rather through it, we aspire to the heightened state of equality in the quality of life for all Koreans. The focus of the fundamental social policies of the unified state will be to provide meaningful opportunities for job training and employment for low income employees and economically and socially alienated groups within the larger framework of "equal opportunities," designed to pursue a genuine welfare state.

Fourth, as an advanced moral state, unified Korea shall contribute to world peace and coprosperity for all members of the human community. In the past, a great many advanced states had committed the errors of imperialism, routinely impinging

---

[6]Kim Dae-jung, *My Way and My Ideas: The Grand Transition of World History and Strategies for National Unification* (Seoul: Hangil-sa, 1993), p. 236.

on others' sovereignties and exploiting their resources and labor. As a unified state, we shall oppose all aspects of imperialism, and in close cooperation with the under-developed states, assist in their development and prosperity.

Fifth, reunited Korea will decisively deal with any act of insult against it and shall contribute to world peace on the foundation of adequate national defense. However, we shall threaten no one. And by the wise utilization of Korea's vital geopolitical position, we will do our part in securing regional stability and security in Northeast Asia, thereby making a valuable contribution to permanent world peace.

Thus the five major pillars for the future of the unified Korea will be: democracy in politics; just and fair market economy; social welfare; and pacifism and moralism for world peace.

V. The Characteristics and Significance of "Kim Dae-jung's Three-Stage Unification" Formula

What is the best among all the unification proposals that have been presented to us thus far? Considering the uniqueness of the two Koreas' situations and international political dynamics, the answer to this question depends on the following:

The most ideal unification proposal is the one that: (1) strictly observes the principle of peace; (2) has the highest possibility for success; (3) is safe for both sides due to its non-threatening quality; and (4) demonstrates the highest possible sincerity and firmness of will for unification. Now we shall compare and contrast the proposals of the two Korean governments and our "Three-Stage Unification" Formula based on the above criteria, and discuss the unique nature and significance of our proposal.

As is shown in [Chart 1-1], the proposals of the two Korean governments posit the first stage of reconciliation, cooperation under the three principles of self-reliance, peace, and democracy; the second stage of Confederation of states; and the third and the final stage of the unified state. In South Korea's government plan, it recognizes the existence of two different political entities during the phase of reconciliation and cooperation; and does not consider the other side as the object of overthrow and emphasizes that the other side is a partner for coexistence and coprosperity. In the next stage of Confederation, the South Korean proposal calls for the maturing of conditions for political integration by way of a firm establishment of peace structure, and the establishment and development of economic and social community; and the institutionalization of South-North Summit meetings and a Ministerial Council through an inter-Korean agreement. In the final phase, a political integration will be completed, thus forming a single nation and state. The ultimate purpose is a national community that guarantees peace, welfare, and human dignity.

Based on the grand principles of self-reliance, peace, and national unity, North Korea's Koryo Confederation calls for the immediate entry into a Federation (with the existing two systems intact) without going through any preparatory stages. Under the unified state in the form of a Federation, a "Supreme National Federal Congress" would be established, composed of an equal number of delegates from the two Koreas and an agreed number of delegates from overseas Koreans; and under it, "Standing Federal Committees," authorized to supervise the Southern and Northern regional governments. The Supreme National Federal Congress shall deal with national defense, external affairs, and the matters of general national issues touch-

*[Chart 1-1] Comparison between the Unification Proposals of
the Two Koreas and the "Three-Stage Unification" Formula*

	South Korean Government	North Korean Government	Kim Dae-jung
Names	The "Three-Stage Unification Plan for the Establishment of the Korean National Community"	Plan for the Establishment of the Koryo Democratic Confederal Republic	The "Three-Stage Unification" Formula
Stages	3 stages Reconciliation/Cooperation/South-North Confederation—Unified State	1 stage Unified State in the form of a Federation	3 stages South-North Confederation/Federation/complete Unification
3 Principles	self-reliance; peace; democracy	self-reliance; peace; grand national unity	self-reliance; peace; democracy
First Stage	The Stage of Reconciliation/Cooperation (1 Nation, 2 States, 2 Systems, 2 Independent Gov'ts.) Recognition of Two Political Entities; Expansion of Exchanges/Cooperation; Political Confidence Building; Settlement of Peace Structure	Unified State in the form of a Federation (1 Nation, 1 State, 2 Systems, 2 Autonomous Regional Governments The Supreme National Federal Congress and the Standing Federal Committees decide on national defense, external relations, and unification issues.	The Stage of inter-Korean Confederation (1 Confederation, 1 Nation, 2 States, 2 Systems, 2 Independent Gov'ts.) Implementation of Policy Guidelines: Peaceful Coexistence, Exchange, and Unification; the establishment of the inter-Korean Summit and the Council of South-North Confederation for the peaceful management of national division and the unification processes; the firm establishment of a peace structure through an arms control agreement and others; the enhancement of mutual interests through all around exchanges / cooperation and restoration of common national homogeneity.

[Chart 1-1] Continued

	South Korean Government	North Korean Government	Kim Dae-jung
Second Stage	The Stage of South-North Confederation (1 Confederation, 1 Nation, 2 States, 2 Systems, and 2 Independent Gov'ts.)	**Possibility of allowing a greater degree of power to two regional gov'ts. on external affairs, defense, and international matters—as a transitional arrangement.	The Stage of Federation (1 Nation, 1 State, 1 System, and 2 Autonomous Regional Gov'ts.)
Third Stage	Buildup of conditions for political integration by establishing and developing a Economic-Social Community; the institutionalization of an inter-Korean Summit Conference and a Ministerial Council, and others through agreement.		A Federal Government in charge of external, defense, and major internal matters; and two autonomous regional gov'ts.
	Unified State (1 Nation, 1 State, 1 System, and 1 Govt.)		The Stage of Complete Unification. (1 Nation, 1 State, 1 System, and 1 Central Gov't (or Several Federal Regional Gov'ts)
	National Community with guaranteed freedom, welfare, and human dignity.		Democracy, market economy, social welfare, advanced moral state, pacifism.

ing on the general interests of common concern.[7]

Compared with the two Korean governments' proposals, the "Three-Stage Unification" Formula has the following special features. First, it is a plan for peaceful unification. A unification proposal that inflicts serious damage to the nation through the use of military force or imposes unbearable economic cost cannot be considered a genuinely serious plan. The approaches to unification ought to begin with the objective and correct understanding of the realities faced by the two Koreas. Radical and emotional notions about unification must be guarded against at all cost and rejected. Unification through absorption, advocated by some people, is neither possible nor desirable under the existing circumstances. Unification through Communication of the Peninsula by violence, advocated by North Korea, is not even

---

[7]Of late, however, there are signs of changes even in North Korea's proposal. In his New Year's Address in 1991, Kim Il Sung stated that he intended "to allow tentatively greater authority and power to the regional governments under the Confederation and was willing to discuss the problem of gradually achieving the unification through phased increase of the future Central Government in order to make the national consensus easier to reach on the problem of establishing the Koryo Confederation." This statement seems to indicate his acceptance of the transitional nature of the Confederation between the two Koreas as a means toward unification. What is particularly noteworthy was the fact that Yoon Ki-bok, Chairman of the Unification Policy Evaluation Committee, the Supreme People's Council, told the South Korean parliamentary delegation to the 85th meeting of the IPU General Conference in Pyongyang in April 1991 that "Let's create a Confederal Unified State with the two Koreas' political systems intact. But we could allow tentatively a greater degree of power, especially in the area of external, military, and internal affairs, to the two regional governments." This statement should be re-analyzed and re-interpreted. Meeting with former U.S. President Jimmy Carter, Kim Il Sung said that if there were problems with North Korea's Confederation proposal, he would be willing to discuss Kim Dae-jung's "Three-Stage" proposal as well as the South Korean government's unification proposal."

worthy of debate. To re-emphasize, the "Three-Stage" formula is a peaceful and gradualist concept which supposes a consensual entry into a Confederation. After a proper and decent interval, it will move forward to a transitional Federation and thence to a complete unification.

Second, the formula is highly feasible, mainly because the unification processes can be managed smoothly only through this plan. The North Korean idea to move immediately toward unification through its Confederation proposal while there are still two wholly irreconcilable and divergent systems is extremely unrealistic. How can we be one overnight when there still exists such a chasm between the two systems? For example, the means of production such as plants and machinery are private properties in the South, while North Korea does not allow private property. The price is set by the market principle of supply and demand in the South, while it is decided by central planning the North. Especially, an abrupt and sudden integration of the two Koreas' military will be particularly impossible under the circumstances.

On the other hand, the South Korean plan of a direct transition from a loose Confederal stage to complete unification is equally unpersuasive. For a peaceful unification, time and procedures are crucial elements for bridging the irreconcilable differences between the two wholly different systems. As advocated in our proposal, it is vitally important to mitigate as much as possible the expected shocks and confusion from the integration of the two systems and their multifaceted differences. In view of North Korea's unique conditions and the sensitive nature of North Korean residents' self-esteem, it would be indispensable to recognize the North Korean regional authorities for a certain length of time, while allowing the Federal Government (as an evolving central authority) to provide special assistance to the North to smooth the critically important transition.

Third, the "Three-Stage Unification" Formula is a safe plan for all. It allows all parties to take the step toward unification with ease and without worries. As mentioned earlier, the South-North Confederation has great significance as an institutional mechanism for building mutual harmony and cooperation, based on state-to-state coexistence. For this reason, even if difficulties arise after the Confederation is established, there cannot be any special danger or burden to either side.

Fourth, our formula is one that demonstrates a strong determination for unification. Never before has there been such a favorable set of conditions for achieving unification. Perhaps there will never come a better opportunity. Therefore, a plan which lacks a firm will and determination cannot but be an empty gesture no matter how it seems on the surface. We have to bear in mind the bitter lessons of the past—in which the dictatorial regimes of both Koreas exploited the unification issue as the means of political self-preservation. The Confederation, advocated under the "Three-Stage" formula, as a mechanism for facilitating harmony and cooperation under the existing status quo, has to be judged a reasonable and equitable format because it does not cause difficulties or psychological or actual burdens for either side in starting the actual process of national unity.

VI. Conclusion

Thus far, we have examined and analyzed the "Three-Stage Unification" Formula and we hope we have verified its specificity, rationality, and feasibility, and confirmed that it offers direction and vision for the nation.

The international climate for Korea's unification has become more favorable than ever because of the end of the Cold War, and is expected to improve as time goes by. On greeting the fifty year anniversary of National Liberation, Korea must clear its ignominy as the only divided nation in the world. As a nation, we ought to seriously reflect on the nation's future; the necessary decisions for unification must be made decisively and promptly, while the actual process for its achievement must be prudent and cautious through carefully calibrated phases.

For this, we must try our best to change North Korea's reluctant stance toward dialogue and negotiation. While actively engaged in efforts to improve its relations with the United States, North Korea refuses to talk to its own people in the South. In so doing, it violates its own touted principles of Juche ideas and national self-determination. Thus, to achieve national unification based on the principles of self-reliance, peace, and democracy—common to both Koreas—North Korea ought to take a more forward looking posture to facilitate the inter-Korean contacts. Moreover, to achieve the atmosphere of minimum confidence between the two sides, we urge North Korea to observe and implement scrupulously all the agreements reached thus far between itself and the United States.

The Southern government, too, must exert greater efforts to improve the inter-Korean relations. It ought to refrain from unnecessarily provocative statements or attitudes which could offend North Korean sensibility. Along with it, we must positively look at the issue of either an amendment to or the abolition of our controversial National Security Law. At the same time, North Korea ought to re-examine the preamble of its own Workers' Party covenant and the provisions of the Penal Code.

For greater effectiveness in our approaches to North Korea, it must be pointed out that although the policy decisions and implementation rightly belong to government, the work for the national consensus must come from all Koreans. Therefore, the dictum must be: unify the ultimate decision-making authority, but multiply the points of contact and dialogue with North Korea.

We urge our government to redouble the efforts to persuade and induce North Korea to accept some of the humanitarian projects that we have been pushing for, such as the postal exchange between the separated families, the establishment of a place for their reunion at Panmunjom, the re-joining of these families on a voluntary basis, and mutual visits. However, we must reiterate as many times as necessary that we do not intend to impose unification on North Korea against its will through any form of absorption. Since North Korea is particularly sensitive about this issue, perhaps we ought to consider a parliamentary resolution to reconfirm our opposition to absorption.

The "Three-Stage Unification" Formula will continue to maintain its central policy continuity, based on its three basic principles and ideological/philosophical foundation; and will strive for specificity and feasibility as the formula will undoubtedly undergo a further process of verification through changing history and circumstances. In our march towards unification, the "Three-Stage Unification" Formula will, we hope, point the direction and provide vision and courage for our nation.

CHAPTER 2

THE BASIC CHARACTERISTICS OF THE SOUTH-NORTH CONFEDERATION AND THE PRINCIPLES OF ITS OPERATION

Summary

The purpose of this chapter is to discuss and clarify the Confederation's basic characteristics and tasks, the principles of its operation, and to present the general policy perspectives in the context of the eventual transition to a Federation.

The South-North Confederation, once established, is a preparatory and transitional stage rather than unification per se. Before unification becomes possible, it is a stage in which the two Koreas through increasing exchanges and cooperation—"through coming and going, and sharing with each other"—create "a climate for actual unification"—so that they can jointly experience approximated "life under the unification."

The biggest task for the Confederation will actually be to practice the three basic policy guidelines—peaceful coexistence, exchange, and eventual unification. To accomplish this, the Confederation is charged with the following six major responsibilities:

The first is political confidence building through inter-Korean reconciliation and cooperation: by recognition of and respect for each other's systems, through restraint of recrimination and defamation, and desisting from all acts of destruction and sabotage, and through non-interference in each other's internal affairs.

Second, there is the task of establishing a peace structure through military confidence building between the two sides and attaining a "new military balance at a reduced force level." This can be done *inter alia* through the redeployment and reorganization of the forward deployed offensive weapons and forces on both sides in close proximity to the Demilitarized Zone (DMZ); secure the balance of military forces through an arms control agreement; and institutionalize the system of mutual inspection and verification.

Third, another task is to develop a balanced national economy in preparation for unification and to improve the national welfare by establishing a Korean economic community; and broaden and intensify the inter-Korean economic exchanges and cooperation to assist North Korea's opening and reform efforts.

Fourth, maximum efforts will be made to restore the common national homogeneity between the two Koreas by broadening and intensifying all forms of social and cultural exchanges. These exchanges are highly significant not only in terms of carrying on with the legacies and traditions of Korean history but also to alleviate the social and cultural heterogeneity, created by the division, which will be conducive to seeking the *modus operandi* of future social integration between the two sides.

Fifth, the two Koreas shall dispose of the existing laws and regulations that hinder unification and together enact new laws, common to both Koreas, and implement them. Each side must on its own undertake efforts to correct, improve, and supplement their existing legal and systemic factors so that they could contribute significantly to the task of peacefully and democratically achieving national unity.

Sixth, greater efforts must be mounted to create an international environment favorable to Korea's unification. Unification must be achieved by the Koreans themselves. However, to expedite the process, it is highly desirable to improve the international conditions by heightening the level of cooperation from the world community.

The common endeavors in the six areas described above will benefit both sides and through them their relations will become closer and broader. As North Korea moves towards a market economy and democracy while South Korea, too, further improves its own social justice and social welfare structure, the transition to the Federal phase of the unification process will be increasingly less burdensome. The smooth transition to a Federation will be the most central task of the South-North Confederation.

To carry out the six tasks mentioned above, we shall need appropriate legislative and executive bodies. As the supreme decision-making body, the Summit Conference shall meet regularly in both Koreas in rotation. The Summit will deal with all national problems related to unification and others, and will make political decisions on all pending issues. It will also discuss the decisions made by the Confederal Council, and accept or reject them. A veto can be cast by either side at this time.

The Confederal Council [the Council of South-North Confederation] will be composed of an equal number of members and each delegation to the Council will have the veto power; and hold its meetings by travelling to different locations throughout the peninsula. The Council's main task is to listen to the views and opinions of the residents of both Koreas, and discuss and vote on the problem of implementing the three major policy guidelines—Peaceful Coexistence, Peaceful Exchange, and Peaceful Unification; and refer its final decisions to the Summit Conference.

The structural and institutional problems that will have to be solved before the transition to a Federal Stage would be: the writing of the Federal Constitution; the transition from the Confederal Council to a Federal legislature; the decision on the method of choosing a president under the Federation; the revision and/or abolition of all laws of the two Koreas which conflict with each other, and other necessary overhauling of the legal systems; and the membership status change in the United Nations as a single state.

Along with the writing of a Federal Constitution, the Federal legislature will decide on the method of selecting a Federal president. When the transition is complete to a Federal phase, the Confederal Council will be replaced by a Federal Parliament. The amendment or repeal of all legal codes that had existed in both Koreas during the Cold War confrontation will have been completed prior to the Confederation to Federation switch over. In the case of the South, the territorial provisions in its present Constitution and the National Security Law, and in North Korea, its Penal Code and the Preamble of the Workers' Party Covenant will have to be changed or repealed. In the latter stage of the Confederation, there has to be a general overhaul of the legal system on both sides which could either be an obstacle to unification or that which would have no usefulness. And to more effectively manage the institutional problems which may arise unexpectedly in the process of transition to a Federation, there may have to be a series of legislation common to both sides. The United Nations membership, the dual representation by the two Koreas, will have to be changed to a single representation as a unified state. Simultaneously, the two sides must coordinate and cooperate with each other to induce an international environment favorable to Korean unification. Although the Koreans are the the main role players in the task of forming a single national community, it would still be necessary to secure the understanding and cooperation of the neighboring powers to make the unification process go forward more smoothly.

I. Introduction

The ideological rivalry and conflict between the superpowers that has for so long imposed on us the inter-Korean distrust and confrontation have not been put to rest with the collapse of the Soviet Socialist Bloc. The inertial power of the end of the Cold War is now showing its impact even in Northeast Asia and the Korean Peninsula. After a long and difficult period, a beginning was made for the solution of North Korea's nuclear issue, and as the implementation of the agreement begins, cautious optimism is being prognosticated for the prospect of Korea's unification.

The Cold War's end has drastically reduced the importance and significance of intra-bloc cooperation in political and military matters, and heavily impacted on the change of nations' strategies toward narrow national economic interests as the supreme priority. Particularly, as the United States has been making special efforts to enhance its economic competitiveness based solely on a nationalistic perspective, the world economy is headed toward a mixed structure of free trade—as its foundation— and "Neo-Mercantilistic" limited case-by-case competition. The "Age of Political Cold War" has ended and the "Age of Economic War" has arrived. To survive in an age of global economic war, we must transcend the paralyzing and consuming confrontation and conflict between the two Koreas and unite national power. This is, indeed, the historical reason for us to go forward more expeditiously with the task of national unification.

Korean unification is now not only "feasible," but "absolutely indispensable." Then, what is the optimal approach to unification? The answer has to be found in peaceful approaches that also promise national prosperity. Kim Dae-jung's "Three-Stage Unification" Formula offers just such a solution.

The "Three-Stage" Formula states that Korea's unification must be achieved through three consecutive and mutually interrelated stages based on the three basic principles of self-reliance, peace, and democracy—slowly, gradually, and prudently. The South-North Confederation, as the opening stage of the processes, is designed to peacefully manage the national division and to achieve the "conditions of *de facto* unification" by rendering assistance to North Korea's self-motivated changes; and can be formed at any time with the political decisions of the leaders of both sides.

The purpose of this chapter is to discuss and elaborate the Confederation's basic characteristics and tasks, its operational principles, and to present the policy perspectives for an eventual transition to the Federal phase of the unification process. By providing the possible details of these procedural issues based on the best case of projectable reality, this chapter will hopefully demonstrate how the actual task of unification is expected to proceed.

II. The Characteristics of the Confederation and the Conditions for Its Establishment

1. The Characteristics of the Confederation

It is realistically impossible to expect a unification taking place overnight between the two Koreas which have maintained wholly different ideologies and systems for the last half century. It is much more realistic and wiser, therefore, to proceed with the unification processes gradually, slowly, and cautiously.

Prior to unification, the two Koreas must exert efforts to recognize and respect each other's systems, prevent a recurrence of war, achieve balanced economic development of both sides with their eyes on ultimate national unity, and solve "brick-by-brick" all the problems concerned with the restoration of the common national homogeneity. These tasks can be achieved only when the two Koreas manage to have close cooperation and coordination. The Confederation is a mechanism devised to promote cooperation and coordination between the two sides to take care of these very issues.

Accordingly, the Confederation does not pertain to unification itself but rather is a step taken jointly to prepare for ultimate unification—through cooperation. Before political unification becomes possible, this stage is for each side to exchange visits, to help and share with each other so that they can jointly experience approximated "life under the unification."

The establishment of the Confederation will be beneficial to all Koreans for the following reasons. First, as a process of peaceful coexistence and a step, taken consensually, for the ultimate unification, the people of both Koreas will become free from the fear of another war. Second, since, under the present circumstances, the Confederation is not devised to rush toward unification, neither side has to worry about the worrisome after-effects, unacceptable to both sides. Third, not being an organ of a unified state, the Confederation is merely a structure for cooperation between two independent states. Thus, there will be no economic burden on our side for North Korea's economy. However, the realization of a Confederal structure should pave the way for a giant leap toward coexistence and coprosperity of the two Koreas by institutionalizing the inter-Korean cooperative system.

The South-North Confederation, established as the first stage of the three-stage unification process under our format, is different in several areas from the Confederation under the present South Korean government proposal. First, under the South Korean government proposal, the South-North Confederal Stage (which is the Second Stage in the government plan) is entered into after a prior phase of reconciliation and cooperation. In our case, however, we do not consider the increasing reconciliation and cooperation as necessary preconditions for the establishment of the Confederation. In fact, the Confederal Stage itself is one of reconciliation and cooperation, thus requiring no special preparatory period, and can be commenced forthwith. To enable our proposal to be activated, we would obviously require at least minimum confidence-building between the two Koreas and the expressed will for ultimate unification. Once a minimum political confidence-building is underway through, for instance, a satisfactory settlement of North Korea's nuclear issue, then we could begin the task of institutionalizing the cooperative phase in the form of a Confederation through and by which we could deliberately increase and upgrade inter-Korean harmony and cooperation. Hence, the Confederation in our formula is not the consequence of inter-Korean exchange and cooperation, but of "political will, determination, and agreement" as well as the facilitator/expediter of reconciliation and cooperation between the two sides.

Second, the government expects a direct transition from Confederation to complete unification, while in our plan, we expect another transitional period after the Confederal Stage—the Federal Stage—before we move finally towards complete unification. The obvious reason for our difference is to alleviate the shock and confusion of integration, to make room for accommodating North Korea's unique situation and the sensibilities of North Korean residents, to recognize the autonomous nature of the Northern government, and to allow for a reasonable period of special assistance to northern Korea by the Federal Government.

On the other hand, the South-North Confederation in our formula is even more different from the Federation proposed by North Korea under the so-called "Koryo Democratic Confederal Republic [hereafter cited as 'Koryo Democratic Confederation']." The "Koryo Democratic Confederation" proposes a unification based on the "One State, Two Systems" concept. The North Korean proposal calls for an immediate fusion in which the Confederal Government is to control all defense and foreign relations. Considering the realities of the division, it is simply unrealistic. The difference between our proposal and that of North Korea is that in our case a Federation is judged possible only if North Korea makes a considerable transition towards a market economy and a democratic system of government.

2. The Conditions of Its Establishment

In light of the innocuous nature and necessity of the Confederation, the "Three-Stage Unification" Formula urges as prompt an entry as possible into the Confederal phase by eliciting the support of the people of the two Koreas and through the political decisions by both governments. It also illustrates several factors that could facilitate such political decision-making: *inter alia*, the political confidence-building between the two sides, the implementation of measures for military tension reduction, and the cross recognition of the two Koreas by the Four Major Powers. However, the fact is that there already exists a basic inter-Korean agreement on "Reconciliation, Non-Aggression, and Exchanges and Cooperation," additional protocol agreements which detailed its implementation, and specialized joint committees, tasked to implement the agreed items. Furthermore, the two Koreas have agreed on de-nuclearization of the Korean Peninsula, and have been operating a joint committee for nuclear control. Between North Korea and the United States, there has been a comprehensive package agreement covering the nuclear issues and the improvement of political and economic relations with the result that there now exists a possibility for reducing the North Korean-U.S. hostility as well as reducing the tension on the peninsula. Following the normalized relations between South Korea and China, and South Korea and Russia in recent years, the process for normalization is underway between North Korea on the one hand and the United States and Japan.

But these developments are not absolutely necessary preconditions for the two Koreas to enter the Confederal stage. Rather, it would be more correct to see them as factors that could contribute to the earlier achievement of the Confederal stage.

Therefore, the questions of whether or not to enter into a Confederation or, if so, when would be the proper time to do so, would entirely depend on the judgment and decision of the two Korean governments.

III. The Tasks for the Confederation

The biggest responsibility of the South-North Confederation is to make sure that the three basic policy guidelines—Peaceful Coexistence, Peaceful Exchange, and Peaceful Unification—are implemented. "Peaceful Coexistence" signifies the peaceful management of the division. For this, all necessary measures ought to be taken to prevent any and all military confrontation/conflict under all circumstances: namely, serious and sincere military confidence-building, arms reduction, and verification. It would be imperative to induce and create an improved international environment, favorable and friendly to Korea's unification through the establishment of a system of multilateral security and cooperation in Northeast Asia that would involve not only the two Koreas but the United States, China, Japan and Russia— all designed for the firm establishment of a peace structure in the Korean Peninsula.

"Peaceful Exchanges" signifies concerted efforts to restore the common national homogeneity and to expand mutual interest by way of expanding all phases of exchanges, including political, economic, and cultural areas, within the structure of the Confederation.

"Peaceful Unification" signifies the peaceful management of unification processes. Peaceful unification, then, would prevent any possibility of unification through the Southern absorption of the North or the Northern Communization of the South through conspiratorial scheming, coercion, or by military force. Rather, the unification must be achieved cooperatively between the two Koreas based on agreement via mutual reconciliation and cooperation; and the processes for achieving it must be by gradual inter-related phases, with carefully and prudently calibrated incremental development.

Under the Confederation, the two Koreas will assume the task of implementing the following six specific operations.

First is to build political confidence between the two sides. Maximum efforts must be made and all necessary steps ought to be taken for it through mutual respect, prohibition of mutual recrimination, slander, subversive activities such as sabotage or any destructive act, and interference with each other's internal affairs.

Second, the Confederation must strive for a stable foundation for peaceful coexistence by military confidence-building and balancing military forces through meaningful reduction of force levels. The concentration of offensive weapons and units, forward-deployed in proximity to the truce line ought to reorganized and redeployed for defensive positions; and an arms control agreement must be reached and implemented with a reliable system of mutual inspection and verification. In addition, a system of multilateral security cooperation must be aimed for in Northeast Asia as political insurance for the peace structure in Korea.

Third, common efforts must be made for a genuinely national economic community "to promote an integrated and balanced development of the national economy and the welfare of the entire people" of Korea. Extensive and variegated forms of economic exchange and cooperation must be vitalized in support of

North Korea's open door policy and economic reforms. Such inter-relations must be based on the principles of equality and mutual respect.

Fourth, vigorous social and cultural exchanges must be promoted in order to restore our common national identity. Except for the half century of division, we as a nation have been able to preserve and maintain homogeneous national identity for more than one thousand years. To continue with the national historical bonds and tradition and to alleviate and ultimately eradicate the differences that have emerged during the last fifty years, it would be vitally important to carry on with vigorous programs of socio-cultural exchanges between the two sides.

Fifth, all existing laws and regulations on both sides that hinder and obstruct the cause of national unity must be abolished, and legal codes common to both sides must be enacted and implemented. A systematic study must be made to identify anti-unification legal and systemic factors so that they can be largely disposed of; and common and incremental efforts must be made to enact laws common to both sides. For genuine progress towards unification, each side must on its own undertake efforts to correct, improve, and supplement their existing legal and systemic factors so that they could contribute to the task of achieving national unity.

Sixth, greater efforts must be mounted to create an international environment favorable to Korea's unification. Unification must be achieved by the Koreans themselves. However, to expedite the process, it is highly desirable to improve the international conditions by heightening the level of cooperation by the world community. Geographically, since Korea is surrounded by the world's four great powers, it is imperative for us to pursue more active diplomatic endeavors to create and improve an international environment conducive to our cause.

The common endeavors in the six areas described above will benefit both sides and through them their relations will become closer. As North Korea moves towards a market economy and democracy while South Korea further improves its own social justice and social welfare structure, the transition to the Federal phase of the unification process will be increasingly less burdensome. The smooth and painless progression to a Federal System will be the central task of the South-North Confederation.

To efficiently carry out the above tasks, rational executive and legislative bodies will be needed. In the following section, we shall examine and explain the establishment and operation of such Federal organizations.

IV. The Establishment of Confederal Organs and Their Operation

In accordance with the "South-North Confederation Charter" agreed to by the two Koreas, the cooperative structure of Confederation will have under it the following organs: (1) the "South-North Summit Conference [hereafter cited as the "Summit Conference"]—the supreme decision-making body; (2) the "Council of South-North Confederation" [hereafter cited as the "Confederal Council"]—representative legislature—and the "South-North Confederal Council Secretariat [hereafter cited as the "Secretariat"]; (3) the "South-North Ministerial Council" [hereafter cited as the "Ministerial Council"]—the executive body; and (4) the "South-North Confederal Committees" [hereafter cited as the "Confederal Committees"] for designated areas.

The Confederal Charter will be the basic law which regulates the inter-Korean relations and will remain in effect until the adoption of a "Unification [Federal] Constitution." It will be adopted by the Summit Conference between the supreme leaders of the two Koreas, and will be referred to the Confederal Council for ratification and implementation.

The Confederal Charter shall reflect the basic spirit that constitutes the foundation of the Confederation itself and the three major policy guidelines that will be implemented during the period of its duration, namely, Peaceful Coexistence, Exchange, and Unification. The Charter should also reiterate and reflect the spirit of national cooperation and unity, contained in both the "July 4th Joint Communique" (1972) by the two Koreas and the "Basic Agreement" (1991). It needs, however, to be pointed out that there is a vast difference between the Charter and these two documents in the area of whether or not to have any actual cooperative mechanism and how that mechanism should be empowered to actuate the inter-Korean cooperation. Hence, the Charter may reflect the fundamental intent and spirit of both documents but does not have to be confined by them. The substantive parts of the aforementioned documents should all be reflected in the anticipated Charter, however, the new basic law will spell out the specific tasks the Confederation will be responsible for—including the function, organization, and operation of the Confederal organs as well as their legal bases and effects.

More specific functions and roles of the various Confederal organs will be spelled out by an additional number of sub-Charter level agreements dealing with different specialized areas. The authority of the Confederal bodies will be limited to matters that will be delegated to them by the agreements of the two Korean governments, and such important matters will also be specified in the Charter. The tasks that the Confederal bodies will deal with, will naturally be designated as "joint projects"; and these joint projects will be carried out in the territory of one side or on both sides, or in "third areas," or in all areas of both Koreas.

[Diagram 2-1] profiles various organs of the Confederation. As the supreme decision-making body, the Confederal Summit Conference will be truly the central organ of the Confederation, especially in the context of its very existence and in light of the fact that the Confederation can be a reality at any time through the political decisions by the supreme leaders of the two Koreas. Regular meetings of the Summit Conference will be held in both Koreas in rotation. As mentioned earlier, the main task of the Summit Conference will be to discuss and make decisions on all relevant national issues, including unification and other pending issues related to that ultimate goal; and to discuss the decisions voted by the Confederal Council. In deciding on the matters thus referred to it by the Confederal Council, the Summit Conference can exercise a veto, or confirm/ratify the agreed matters by the Ministerial Council and oversee their implementation.

As a legislative body, the Confederal Council will be composed of an equal number of members, selected by the parliaments of each side; and will meet in rotation at sites in both Koreas. The equal membership signifies that as a unicameral system, the Council is designed to allow higher priority to regional representation than to "resident representation" for the obvious reason of the basic spirit and intent of the Confederation itself. The intended equality in power and status between the two components of the Council is based on the recognition that the seat allocation between the two Koreas on the basis of population would be contrary to the central purpose of a "state-

[Diagram 2-1] Confederal Organs

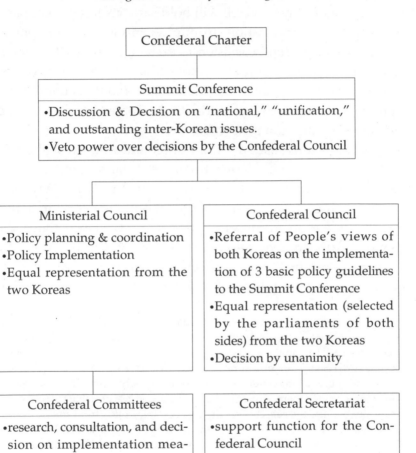

Confederal Charter

Summit Conference
- Discussion & Decision on "national," "unification," and outstanding inter-Korean issues.
- Veto power over decisions by the Confederal Council

Ministerial Council
- Policy planning & coordination
- Policy Implementation
- Equal representation from the two Koreas

Confederal Council
- Referral of People's views of both Koreas on the implementation of 3 basic policy guidelines to the Summit Conference
- Equal representation (selected by the parliaments of both sides) from the two Koreas
- Decision by unanimity

Confederal Committees
- research, consultation, and decision on implementation measures on detailed items

Confederal Secretariat
- support function for the Confederal Council

to-state" integration into a Confederal structure.

The Confederal Council will hold sessions in different parts of both Koreas in rotation. In implementing the three policy guidelines of peaceful coexistence, exchange, and unification, it will listen to the views and opinions of the people, discuss, and vote on the matters, and refer the decisions to the Summit Conference; and the decisions made in the Confederal Council can be vetoed by the Summit Conference.

All decisions made by the Confederal Council will be by "unanimity," meaning either Korean delegation can exercise a veto over any matter that it cannot accept. The "unanimity" formula is a useful decision-making method to arrive at an agreement between divergent social groups.[1] As explained above, the South-North Confederation is to be established based on the minimum reconciliation between the two Koreas which have undergone a long period of deepening heterogeneity. In that

---

[1]The typical decision-making method in democracy is majority rule. However, the principle of majority rule can only operate well in relatively homogeneous society. The obvious reason is that only in such a society can there be common denominators of a similar world view (*Weltanschauung*), value systems, and life style among the members of the society, thus ruling out serious differences among them. Accordingly, majority rule is acceptable without much difficulty because the rule chooses the best possible option from among the sets of similar views of the members of the society. Needless to say, however, in societies with serious disparities among their members, the application of majority rule would be difficult to apply since the decisions thus derived would not likely be accepted or obeyed easily. Therefore, in some democratic European states, burdened by persistent heterogeneity and internal conflict due to religious, ethnic, linguistic, cultural differences, efforts are being made to search for a political method of political integration and social consensus in the "Consociational Model" based on the principle of the majority rule so as to prevent intense friction/conflict from those differences. *Per* Arend Lijphart, *Democracies: Patterns of Majoritarian & Consensus Government in Twenty One Countries* (New Haven: Yale University Press, 1984), *passim*.

context, the decision-making method for the Confederal Council is to be based on the principle of unanimity whereby the two sides can sufficiently preserve and maintain their respective independence. The adoption of the unanimity rule signifies not only the symbolic nature of the Confederal Council as representing the common national destiny of Korea, but also demonstrates that its decisions are founded upon genuine pan-national support.

The President of the Confederal Council assumes a very important role because he/she will be in charge of managing and expediting the unification process from a grand national perspective. As it is expected that the Confederal Council, to be established under the condition of national division, will be faced with numerous unexpected obstacles and operational trials and errors during its infancy, the political savvy and leadership of its president will be of paramount importance. The Confederal Council will have two presidents [Co-Presidents]—one from each side. The Co-Presidents will have to be persons with moral qualities as well as political leadership qualities who can accommodate the positions of both Koreas.

The power of selecting the Council members will be in the hands of the parliaments of the respective Koreas. The primary criteria for selection of the members should be their representativeness as well as their professionalism/expertise. The "representativeness," for instance, should reflect the pluralism of each Republic such as groups representing age, region, social class, and political associations; while the "Professionalism/expertise" should reflect the level of professional expertise on issues that would be discussed in the Confederal Council such as political, military, economic, social, cultural, women's affairs.

The Secretariat is a supporting body to the functions of the

Council, and will be composed of members detached to it by both Koreas. If necessary, the Secretariat will send the resident liaison offers to Seoul and Pyongyang and empower them to liaise and conduct business with the Co-Presidents of the Council.

The decisions reached by the Confederal Council will be referred to the Summit Conference. The matters that are finalized by the Summit Conference will then be turned over to the Ministerial Council for specific policy decisions and implementation. For research, consultation, and deciding on the implementation measures, the Ministerial Council shall establish Joint Committees to deal with various areas of specialization. To wit, the "South-North Economic Committee" will discuss policies on the exchange of goods and materials, investment, the currency exchange rates, the issue of loans and credits, mediation of conflicts, and financial and monetary policies, etc. The "Joint Military Committee" shall deal with the problems of devising implementation measures on: prevention of accidental military confrontation/conflicts, military confidence building, arms control/reduction negotiations, and the establishment of inspection and verification structure.

V. The Transition to a Federation

In view of the fact that the Confederation is a system of coexistence between the two independent states, too ambitious a rush for unification and/or integration could either completely nullify its significance or even threaten its very existence. In order to achieve a smooth transition from a Confederation to Federation, it would be highly important to undergo a carefully calibrated phase of incremental maturation and development of the Confederation itself. Needless to say, therefore, a considerable period of time will be needed for the Confederation to accomplish its assigned tasks. Our "Three-Stage Unification" formula considers the optimum period to be about a decade.

The formation of the national political community for Korea will be the end result of the process of intimate interaction between the two Koreas through the deepening social, cultural, and economic exchanges and cooperation on the one hand, and the strong determination and unshakable will for unification and the expansion of inter-governmental policy cooperation/coordination between the two Korean governments.[2] There are several important tasks in institution building prior to the transition to a Federal stage—a period of political integration: the writing of a Federal Constitution; the transition from the Confederal Council to a Federal Legislature; the decision on the method for choosing the Federal President; the general overhaul—either revision or outright abolition—of all laws and regulations on both sides that would be contrary to the cause of inter-Korean harmony/cooperation and unification; and the transition from dual to single representation at the United Nations. These are just a few examples of such tasks.

The Federal Constitution will be necessary to accommodate the changes in the inter-Korean relations. Quite different from the Confederal Charter under which two independent governments interacted minimally, the new basic law, the Federal Constitution, defines a wholly different political set-up, representing a *de facto* integration. And this new Constitution will be applied

---

[2]Inter alia, refer to Park Young-ho and Park Jong-chul, *On the Method of Establishing a South-North Korean Political Community* (Nambuk-han Jungchi Gongdongchae Hyungsung Bang-an Yungu) (Seoul: The Research Institute for National Unification, 1993), pp. 10-12.

equally to all of Korea and to all areas, including political, military, economic, social, and other areas. The Federal Constitution will be drafted by the Confederal Council and becomes effective after the ratification by the parliaments of the two Koreas.

The Confederal Council, along with the drafting of the Federal Constitution, will decide on the method of choosing a Federal President. The Summit Conference can exercise a veto over the Confederal Council recommendation on the Federal presidential selection method. When, finally, the Federation is created, the Confederal Council will be replaced by a Federal Legislature.

The revision or repeal of all anti-unification laws and regulations, maintained through the period of Cold War hostility, would be undertaken throughout the Confederal phase. In the South Korean case, the territorial provisions in the Constitution and the National Security Law, and in the North, its Penal Code and the Preamble of the Workers' Party Covenant will have to be overhauled. In the latter stage of the Confederation, laws and regulations that could be an impediment to unification and others that are outdated will have to be dealt with in a similar fashion. At the same time, new common legislatiion will have to be undertaken to institutionally manage and control the newly emerging situation at the time of the transition to a Federal stage.

Under the Federation, the dual independent representation in the United Nations will have to be changed to a single representation. The two Koreas will have to cooperate and coordinate their efforts to create an international environment favorable to' Korea's unification. Unification must be achieved by our own efforts. But, to expedite the process, it will be highly desirable to improve the international conditions by heightening the level of cooperation by the world community. Although we shall play the key role in forming a single national political community, to smooth the way for its processes, we will need closer cooperation and assistance from our neighboring states.

As we approach the end of the Confederal period, we should go a step beyond the institutional integration to a more systematic and positive stage of political and cultural integration, thus paving the foundation for establishing a Federation. The twin tasks of gradually reducing the heterogeneity between the Koreans in the South and the North and the firm implanting of democratic ideas among the North Koreans must be successfully accomplished to eliminate the stark differences in political ideology/philosophy, thinking processes, value systems, and beliefs.

VI. Conclusion

As shown above, we believe that the Confederation is, indeed, the best and the most plausible transitory phase for unification—as it is based on the uniquely flexible management and operation of the twin structures of the "reality of division" and the "rational approach to unification." The true significance of the Confederation, therefore, lies not in the completeness of the Confederal stage itself, but in its role as the facilitator or inducer of conditions that will make the smooth transition to a Federation possible. However, imagining a Confederation as the very first step toward unification at this juncture is to merely plan for the future, and planning for a Federation is even more so. Because we feel the need for more thorough and systematic reflection of the changed political perceptions and national sentiment in the future, we have deliberately avoided detailed discussion of the Federation and refrained from unreasonable assertions.

Without the kind of noble self-abnegation, expressed by our esteemed Kim Koo, that he would gladly be a door keeper or even a janitor, if he could somehow achieve the national unification; and without the genuine courage of the two Korean governments and the people on both sides to yield a little, our national unification will never become possible. We must seek a unification in which "both sides can win" rather than one in which "only one side triumphs." To earn unification, we will have to pay the price in some form or other. We shall never succeed if we try to impose sacrifice on the other side without ourselves assuming the just and fair burden. There will be no unification without cost. If there is a genuine will for national unity, both Koreas ought to begin the task by solving the pending problems one by one based on the wisdom of concession and the principles of coexistence.

Our national journey to a Confederation and from there eventually to a Federation will be protracted and difficult. There will be an array of unexpected exigencies and crises or we could be headed in a wholly unimagined direction. To be ready for such contingencies and to prevent their occurrence, we should prepare long and short-term contingency plans, based on the "collective national rationality," to be ready for all possible developments. The "Rationality Critical of Division" that cannot be swayed by the inertia of division and the excuses of reality is the fundamental and indispensable basis of the "Will and Reason" for national unification. Thus, we must overcome the division with cold-blooded reflection and incisive observation, and go forward toward our national goal with realism and flexibility.

As in all human endeavors, the first step is always the most difficult in great projects. But a great many conditions around us point toward national unity. Under the evolving situation, the will, determination, and support of the people of the two Koreas are greater than ever, and we can sense their historic pulse. Now is the time for us to take that historic first step.

CHAPTER 3

PEACEFUL COEXISTENCE UNDER THE CONFEDERATION

Summary

The purpose of this chapter is to present the plans for peaceful coexistence under the Confederal Stage.

The plans for realizing peaceful coexistence can be discussed in three major areas: a peace agreement, arms control, and the international guarantee of peaceful coexistence between the two Koreas. On the issue of negotiating a peace agreement, there is the question of its possible signatories, its substance, and the timing of its fulfillment. North Korea's position to exclude South Korea from a peace agreement cannot be a subject for discussion as the matter in question has already been settled by the inter-Korean concord through the "Basic Agreement"; and in view of that fact the two Koreas will have to be the most directly concerned parties in the implementation of the peace agreement, if and when it materializes, there cannot be any argument that the two Koreas will have to be the signatories to that future compact.

The substance of the agreement will have to be more than a mere end to the state of war; it should include realistic measures to guarantee peace on the peninsula—such as plans to deal with the Demilitarized Zone, to prevent hostile military acts, to achieve a new military balance at a reduced level, and to replace the Armistice Commission and the Neutral Nations Supervisory Commission which have thus far managed the armistice system. We should also provide measures to achieve an international guarantee of peace in Korea.

An early conclusion of a peace agreement is desirable, in fact the sooner the better. However, the necessary conditions for it must precede, although its conclusion is not the necessary condition for entry into a Confederal stage.

As for arms control, the important thing is to assure each other's existence and completely eliminate the threat of war by way of an arms control agreement that creates a peace-oriented military equilibrium based on the meaningful reduction of force levels on both sides. Military confidence-building and arms control must take place in tandem. Particular priority should be placed on controlling weapons of mass destruction such as nuclear and chemical weapons and other offensive weapons. Lastly, the arms control agreements must be accompanied by a clearcut agreements on inspection and verification regime.

For military confidence-building, there has to be, first, a phased exchange of military information and a stable communications link between the two sides. Second, all military activities must be made public and disclosed to the other side. Third, an agreement must be reached against surprise attacks and accidental military incidents. The Demilitarized Zone must be turned into a "zone of peace" by withdrawing the forces, weapons, and other hardware from it. A new "Limited Deployment Zone" (LDZ) must be created beyond the existing DMZ, in which the emplacement of offensive forces should be specifically prohibited to eliminate the possibility of armed confrontation/conflict and to enhance the early warning capabilities.

The purpose of arms control is to achieve a mutually acceptable balanced forces on each side on the basic principle of a "one-to-one" ratio. After the arms control agreement, the force levels will have to be reviewed and re-determined taking into account the status of unified Korea and the estimation of the force requirement at the time. Although at this time, a force level of 300,000 each can be considered, the exact determination of the total size of the forces should be postponed to the latter stage of Confederation.

Concerning the arms control agreement, there are two major questions: "how to reduce?" and "what to reduce?" Arms reduction must be phased in gradually, but the correction of the present military imbalance must be tackled as a priority item. Although the capabilities for surprise attack and offensive capabilities must be removed, the reduction and elimination of offensive weapons must begin with those that can be verified, as in Europe. Once the reduction of weapons is achieved, then a proportional cut must be made on troop levels to dovetail with the weapons reduction.

While ensuring the strict observance of arms control agreements, the problem of verification can often hinder an agreement itself. Because of this dual character of verification, it is the most important aspect of any arms control agreement. The authority and responsibility of verification must be based on strict reciprocity. Also the selection of verification targets must be symmetrical. It must be pointed out that demand for too stringent a verification could actually lead to failures in making progress in military confidence-building and an arms control agreement. We must guard against such a possibility.

The two Koreas must agree on a plan to phase in an incrementally higher level of verification. First of all, military observer teams must be invited and sent to all war games; on-site inspection must be allowed to verify the implementation of agreements and resident verification teams must be exchanged for the sustained inspection and verification of the implementation process; and the air space must be open and special and instant inspections must also be permitted.

The question of achieving an international guarantee of peaceful coexistence on the Korean Peninsula entails of necessity the discussion of the United States military presence in Korea and the formation of a multilateral security cooperation structure in Northeast Asia. On the former, there must precede the political and military confidence-building between North Korea and the United States. Once the North Korean-U.S. agreement on the nuclear issue is faithfully implemented, a degree of political confidence-building between the two will be possible through the establishment of an appropriate level of diplomatic and economic relations. If such a development is followed by military confidence-building over the U.S. forces in Korea with simultaneous confidence-building between the two Koreas, the continued U.S. military presence in Korea does not have to be an obstacle to achieving a stable and secure peace structure on the peninsula.

A multilateral security cooperation regime in Northeast Asia ought to be established based on the following principles. First, the multilateral security cooperation structure can coexist with the existing bilateral alliances. Second, the multilateral security framework must be established as soon as possible based on the existing discussions on security cooperation. Third, the role and function of the security cooperation structure should be strengthened by gradual stages. Specifically, cooperation must begin with non-military areas and be expanded later to military areas as well. Fourth, the system of security cooperation in small areas (such as in Northeast Asia) will not conflict with one covering a large area (such as ASEAN Region Forum).

When the very last phase of the Confederation is reached, the mutual threat between the two Koreas will largely dissipate as the result of the common efforts made thus far for arms control measures and an international guarantee of peace in Korea. At that point in time when the two Koreas face the task of entering a Federation, a stage of de facto integration, the most important policy task will be the fusion of the two military establishments into a unified Federal armed force. The fundamental measure for the transition to a Federal armed force will be to freeze the force levels at an appropriate point and expand the common inter-Korean military cooperation, and to seek ways to increase security cooperation with the Northeast Asian states.

I. Introduction

The Cold War which has been characterized by the ideological and military conflict between the United States and the Soviet Union since the end of the Second World War has now ended. Having been the symbols of the Cold War, the two Germanys are unified and Eastern European Socialism has collapsed, while the old Soviet Union has been dissolved. These unprecedented political changes in the international arena have made a considerable impact even on the regional order of Northeast Asia. Although there still exists a degree of uncertainty in regional security, at least the security environment, created by the strategic conflict between the United States and the Soviet Union during the Cold War, is being transformed into a new regional order of peace and cooperation.

The impact of the Post-Cold War has now reached even the Korean Peninsula. The move toward cross recognition of the two

Koreas by the Four Major Powers is underway, and the first stage withdrawal of the American forces in Korea and the withdrawal of the tactical nuclear weapons have now been completed. Besides, there have been other important developments: the simultaneous entry of the two Koreas into the United Nations, the inter-Korean agreements on reconciliation, non-aggression, exchanges and cooperation, and the de-nuclearization of Korea, and others.

To be sure, there are still other obstacles to overcome. As we are well aware, there was a time only recently when the dark cloud of war hovered over Korea because of the complications related to North Korea's development of nuclear weapons. However, even this crisis was brief as the powerful tide of history—the end of the Cold War—demonstrated its strength even in Korea. The North Korean nuclear issue which brought crisis and tension for some time, without any signs of resolution, was finally resolved by an agreement in Geneva between North Korea and the United States in October 1994. The Cold War is about to end in Korea as well, and Korea's unification, hitherto the subject of mere debate, is about to enter the realm of real possibility.

Although the dissolution of the Cold War world order has brought a new environment of peace and cooperation, it has also caused the rise of a non-ideological universal competition based on naked national economic interest. The United States whose economy has been exhausted through the excessive cost of the Containment Policy against the Soviet Bloc, has decided to rebound its economy as its foremost national priority. Such a distinct change of policy has plunged the world into an era of unconditional and unlimited economic competition and rivalry.

In an age where economic power is the sole measure of

national strength, Korea's unification is not only a mere possibility but a necessity. If we are ever to enter the ranks of the advanced nations in the world, the extraordinary cost of national division must be converted to finance increased economic growth and production, and to promote adequate social welfare. This is the real reason why unification is so vital for the survival of both the South and the North, and for all Koreans.

Then, under the circumstances, what is the best possible means for Korea's unification? What is needed is a formula that promises peaceful unification as well as national prosperity. We believe firmly that Kim Dae-jung's "Three-Stage Unification" formula is a plan which promises to deliver on both counts. It spells out a comprehensive plan and offers the most realistic blueprint for the nation's future.

The purpose of this monograph is to present and elaborate on the scheme for achieving peaceful coexistence during the period of Confederation, designed as the first stage of national unification. This chapter is divided into five sections. Following the general description and discussion of the changed international and regional environment for unification, the evolution and reality of the inter-Korean military confrontation will be discussed. Next we shall discuss the basic principles of peaceful coexistence under the Confederation, and offer specific and detailed ideas and concepts on a peace agreement, arms control, and the international guarantee of peace on the peninsula. The last section will raise such issues as the integration of the armed forces of the two sides during and after the transition from Confederation to Federation.

II. The Evolution of the Military Confrontation/ Conflict between the Two Koreas

Soon after Korea was liberated from Japanese colonial rule, our people suffered the tragedy of national division, brought on by external forces. The United States and the Soviet Union, victors of the Second World War, moved their forces into Korea and established military governments under the pretext of disarming the Japanese forces in Korea; consequently, Korea was divided and became a victim of the U.S.-Soviet Cold War.

When two separate governments were established in South and North Korea under different ideologies and systems, supported by the United States and the Soviet Union, North Korea had already formed its People's Army as its official military establishment.[1] In June 1950, North Korea made a surprise attack against the South with ten divisions, equipped with 240 T-34 tanks and 3,000 heavy guns, for the purpose of communizing the Korean Peninsula. The attack was made with the support of the Soviet Union in pursuit of Joseph Stalin's "post-war offensive" strategy.

South Korea, too, established its own national military forces with the birth of the Republic of Korea. As North Korea was provided military assistance by the Soviet Union, so too was South Korea by the United States. But before the war began, South

---

[1]North Korea's People's Army was begun in early 1946 as Internal Security Forces (Bo-an-dae) and became an official military establishment in February 1948. At the time, the North Korean forces already had two infantry divisions and one combined arms brigade. To this, three Korean divisions from the Chinese People's Liberation Army were added. Equipped and trained by the Soviet Union, the North Korean forces were far superior to South Korean forces when the Korean War began in June 1950.

Korean military assets were limited to eight lightly armed divisions with approximately 1,000 field guns of all varieties and not a single tank. This stark military imbalance between the two sides and the American Secretary of State Dean Acheson's statement of the Pacific Defense Perimeter on January 12, 1950 that excluded South Korea from American responsibility and guarantee played the major role in inducing the North Korean attack.[2]

It must be pointed out, however, that the military confrontation was not begun with the war in 1950. It was begun well before the start of the war itself. By assisting the Southern Workers' Party, North Korea was responsible for the internal violence—major guerrilla activities—throughout South Korea beginning in earnest in 1948. For example, the Communist agents who had penetrated the National Constabulary (the predecessor to the Republic of Korean Army, ROKA) were responsible for a military mutiny of a South Korean army regiment in Yosu and Sunchon (in Cholla Province) in 1948. Subsequently, a force of roughly a thousand Communist mutineers moved into the mountain region and began a guerrilla movement against South Korea. In concert with the development in the South, North Korea had sent guerrilla warfare cadres to South Korea in large numbers, and activated the strategy of a general offensive by September 1949. To frustrate and impede South Korean counter-insurgency activi-

---

[2]The controversial Acheson statement was made on January 12, 1950 before the National Press Club, in which the U.S. Secretary of State declared the American policies on Asian security by drawing an Asia-Pacific defense line for the United States. Acheson's statement was meant to deter the territorial ambitions of the Soviet Union and China, and the Defense Perimeter that he defined ran from the Aleutians through Japan, Okinawa, the Philippines, to Australia, and New Zealand, excluding from it South Korea, Taiwan, Indochina, and Indonesia. These excluded territories, Acheson stated, would be under the protection of the United Nations.

ties in the South, the North Koreans made large scale probes all along the thirty-eighth parallel line to tie down the Southern forces. However, the general counter-insurgency efforts by the South in the winter months proved to be successful.[3]

The Korean War, thus begun by the North, eventually turned into a major East-West military conflict with the intervention of the United States as the principal force of resistance and sixteen other United Nations member states along with the eventual entry into the war by the Chinese Communist forces. The tragic war, lasting three long years, took a monumental toll in terms of human casualties and material loss and left a deep and irreparable psychological scar on the Koreans. Finally, in July 1953, the war was "stopped" by an Armistice Agreement between the United Nations forces on the one side and the North Korean and Chinese representatives on the other. A Demilitarized Zone was drawn along the Truce Line, the existing battle line, and the Military Armistice Commission and the Neutral Nations Supervisory Commission were established to manage the Armistice System.

After the Armistice Agreement and the end of the hostilities, South Korea and the United States had agreed to take joint measures to guard against the Northern threat by signing the "R.O.K.-U.S. Mutual Defense Treaty" on October 1, 1953.[4] In accordance with the treaty, the United States decided to station

---

[3]Lim Dong-won, *The Communist Revolutionary War and Counterinsurgency* (Seoul: Tamgudang, 1967), pp. 222-242.

[4]Although at first the United States was lukewarm to the idea of an alliance with South Korea, it would eventually change its position and signed the treaty in a hurry, mainly due to President Syngman Rhee's attempt to jeopardize the truce negotiations by unilaterally releasing the Chinese and North Korean "anti-Communist" Prisoners-of-War.

some 60,000 troops in Korea—two army divisions and their support units, and one air force division. Because of the fact that the United States assumed the responsibility for South Korea's defense, the two nations agreed further that the operational control of the South Korean forces be exercised by the Commanding General of the United Nations Forces in Korea (an American general) and that the United States would continue to render military assistance to South Korea.[5] South Korea, having firmly established a joint defense structure with the presence of the American forces in Korea, began its ground force-oriented military buildup by increasing its ground component to twenty divisions, a total strength of 720,000 troops by 1955.

On the other hand, North Korea signed a treaty of "Friendship, Cooperation, and Mutual Assistance" with the Soviet Union and China in 1961, and with their assistance, built up an air force-oriented military power. The troop strength was increased to 410,000 by 1955 from 260,000 at the end of the war. In general, it is estimated that the South maintained generally superior forces vis-a-vis the North from the Armistice Agreement to the early 1960s.

However, a noticeable change was detected in North Korea's position in the 1960s. A new set of circumstances—the intensification of Soviet-American arms competition and the Sino-Soviet ideological conflict, the Vietnam War, the April 19th Revolution (1960) in South Korea that toppled the Syngman Rhee regime, the May 16th Military Coup (1961) against the constitutional government of Prime Minister John Chang, and others—were the turbulent background to Pyongyang's decision in September

---

[5]Ministry of Foreign Affairs, Republic of Korea, *Thirty Years of Korea's Diplomacy, 1948-1979* (Seoul: Ministry of Foreign Affairs, 1979), pp. 107-111.

1961 to aim for a revolution in the South ["The National Liberation and Democratic Revolution in South Korea"],[6] followed by
the strategy of "Four Major Military Policy Lines" (1962) and the
"Policy of Consolidation of Three Revolutionary Capabilities"
(1963).[7] Clearly, it was an attempt to achieve an independent
security posture and was an unmistakable reflection of North
Korea's new determination to unify the country by communizing the South. To upgrade its military strength, Pyongyang felt it
had to further incite anti-Southern sentiment among its population, and as part of its strategy of increasing tension between the
two Koreas, it carried out several highly provocative and dangerous acts against the South: the commando attack against the
presidential residence, the Blue House, on January 21, 1968, the
commando attacks against the East Coast cities of Samchuk and
Ulchin, and the capture of the USS *Pueblo*.

As the result of North Korean military buildup, the two
sides reached a balance of forces in the mid-1960s. Under the
umbrella of the alliance with the United States, South Korea was
committed to economic development since the early sixties, and

---

[6]This strategy was to duplicate a Vietnam-style revolutionary war in
South Korea.

[7]As part of stepped-up preparations for war in 1962, Kim Il Sung decided
on four major policy lines: the arming of the whole population, fortification of
all regions, transformation of the entire military into an organization of cadres,
modernization of all forces. Again in 1963, Kim enunciated a policy of "Three
Revolutionary Capabilities": "First, the firm and successful establishment of
Socialism in the Northern half of the nation, and the political, economic, and
military consolidation of its revolutionary base; second, the consolidation of
revolutionary capabilities of South Korea through raising the political consciousness of South Koreans; and third, the consolidation of unity between the
revolutionary capabilities of Koreans and the international community." The
Research Institute for North Korea, *Bukhan Chong-ram [North Korean Handbook]*
(Seoul: Research Institute for North Korea, 1983), p. 1605.

because of the vastly decreased American aid between the early sixties to the mid-seventies, was not able to upgrade its military power to any significant degree. Through persistent efforts, however, North Korean military power began to surpass that of the South by the late sixties. By the early seventies, it enjoyed a considerable superiority.

Toward the late sixties, the Soviet-American strategic equilibrium was being established, and the two powers began to show signs of detente, if only to reduce their excessive military outlays over the nuclear rivalry. Reflecting the emerging trends in the security environment and the Nixon Doctrine in 1969,[8] the United States decided to withdraw one army division from Korea. Needless to say, American military assistance to South Korea also showed an increasingly downward trend. Along with this development, the entry of the People's Republic of China into the United Nations in 1971, the collapse of South Vietnam in 1975, and the rapid growth of North Korean forces began to take their toll on South Korean confidence in its national security. The new security environment, caused by these threats made the South turn to a new posture of independent defense capabilities.

Thus, since the mid-seventies, South Korea began its policy of self-reliant defense—the "Yulgok Project"[9]—by general mili-

---

[8]The central message of the Doctrine as far as South Korea was concerned was that "the primary responsibility of defense in Asia rests with the countries directly concerned."

[9]Named after one of the two greatest philosophers during the Yi Dynasty and an official, Li Yi [or Li Yulgok] (1536-1584), who among other things, proposed a buildup of 100,000 elite forces for national defense before his death in 1584, eight years before Toyotomi Hideyoshi's Japanese invasion of Korea in 1592. His recommendation was never accepted or acted upon.

tary buildup and setting up its own national defense industries. North Korea, too, continued its defense buildup with special emphasis on the strategy of "blitzkrieg"—emphasizing its mobility and fire power. The inter-Korean rivalry in military buildup picked up its momentum through the eighties and continues to date.

What is the present status of the South-North military confrontation? Broadly speaking, it can be summarized in two ways. First, although the Armistice has been maintained by the two sides thus far, the two Koreas both face a high degree of security dilemma and continue to maintain the state of hostility under great tension. The visible index ratio of 70 (South) to 100 (north), demonstrating the quantitative imbalance between the two opposing forces, can be seen in the disparities in troop strengths—650,000 vs. one million—and in the number of tanks —1,800 vs. 3,800—on both sides. But the seriousness of the question is rather in the composition of forces and the mode of their deployment. Contrary to South Korea's "defensive force structure," the North Korean forces are organized in an "offensive mode."

In addition to infantry divisions, comparable to those of the South, North Korea possesses forces designated for a blitzkrieg. Forming its "Central Mobile Fighting Forces" are 38 tank and mechanized infantry brigades, 30 artillery brigades, and 24 special forces brigades. Most of these offensively organized forces are forward deployed close to the Truce Line for an easy surprise attack against the South.[10]

During the Cold War in Europe, the early warning time

---

[10]Ministry of Defense, Republic of Korea, *National Defense White Paper, 1993-1994* (Seoul: Ministry of Defense, 1993-1994), p. 50.

available for the NATO forces against the Soviet invasion was 30-45 days. However, in the case of South Korea, it is merely 12-24 hours—an extremely dangerous situation which gives no lead time to prepare for a surprise attack. The highly mobile North Korean forces have such a powerful offensive capability that it constitutes a serious threat to South Korea and is its single biggest source of uncertainty.

On the other hand, North Korea considers the presence of the American forces in the South and the combined deterrence strategy of the South Korean-U.S. forces, including the potential use of the nuclear weapons against it as the single most serious external threat to its security. Especially, North Korea has viewed and reacted violently against the joint annual South Korean-U.S. military exercise—Team Spirit—as the war game for nuclear war against it.

Second, as the result of intense competition in military buildup, the two sides now possess military forces of great destructive power. For instance, at the beginning of the Korean War, North Korea had 240 tanks, and South Korea had none. Today, the total number on both sides is almost 6,000. There were only 4,000 artillery pieces (including 1,000 on the South) in the Korean War, however, both sides now total more than 30,000.[11] Should war break out again in Korea, the losses in human casualties and in property would be monumental in comparison to the last war. The competition in arms buildup continues not only quantitatively but also qualitatively, and forces on both sides tremendously excessive military outlays.

---

[11]*Military Balance, 1994*, IISS.

III. The Principles of Peaceful Coexistence
Under the Confederation

Through the vicious cycle of action-and-reaction in arms buildup, both sides possess truly excessive military power today, and to maintain it, both sides continue to waste enormous national resources. The solution to this unending dilemma can only be found in peaceful coexistence and political confidence-building based on mutual recognition and respect. The Confederal phase is a mechanism designed for that very role.

In this section, we shall offer specific political and military measures with which both Koreas can achieve and consolidate peaceful coexistence. But before that, we will explain and evaluate the institutional background of the purpose of peaceful coexistence in relation to the "Three-Stage Unification" Formula.

1. Peaceful Coexistence and the Significance of the Confederation

Under the Cold War confrontation, the two Koreas maintained uncompromising hostility toward each other by adamant refusal to recognize each other's existence and rejection of all official contacts and negotiations. Since the temporary cessation of hostilities, the two sides have been planning to absorb each other by looking at the other side merely as an object of "liberation" or "restoration." The South insisted on crushing Communism before it could achieve unification while the North dreamed of "liberating the South"—prolonging the ever intensifying political and military confrontation, and arms buildup competition.

In the early 1970s, against the background of a changing international situation caused by the reduction of tension and reconciliation between the Superpowers, Kim Dae-jung proposed for the first time in Korea plans for the improvement of relations between the two Koreas and for a gradualized process for national unification based on international guarantees of peace on the peninsula by the Four Major Powers and the inter-Korean exchanges. His proposal called for the realization of peaceful coexistence first through the mutual recognition, reconciliation and exchanges, and argued for the peaceful management of the division as the foundation for a gradual process of unification.

Pressured by the new strategic environment, even the Park Chung-hee regime which had insisted on the inflexible position of anti-Communism as the primary national policy tacitly acknowledged the political entity of North Korea; and stated that it would not oppose the simultaneous membership of the two Korean states in the United Nations and that it would accept the policy peaceful "competition in good faith" with the Northern regime.

Before long, however, inter-Korean relations relapsed to a deep freeze as the two sides demonstrated continued intent to destroy and/or overthrow the other side, resulting in an unending cycle of intense competition for military buildup.

Reaching the nineties, however, the Cold War finally ended after forty years of intense conflict. This historic shift precipitated epochal changes: the collapse of the central economic planning in the Soviet Union and Eastern Europe and its replacement by a market economy and the transition of the one-party Communist dictatorship to a pluralistic democracy with a multi-party structure; and most importantly, the disappearance of the East-West conflict between the Free World and Communism. The winds of change through the demise of the Cold War were felt even in Asia. For one, China has achieved a spectacular economic growth through the policy of economic open doors and reforms. Vietnam is also travelling a similar path of economic restructuring. Unlike Eastern Europe, however, in some parts of Asia the change is confined to the economy, still under the continuing leadership of the Communist party. Nevertheless, it is inevitable that the economic reforms toward the policy of open doors and market economy will eventually change the political consciousness of the people themselves, inducing the conservative-progressive conflict and ultimately will compel the Chinese government to move towards the next phase of democratic political reforms.

What will happen in North Korea? On the whole, there are two contrasting views on that prospect. One view predicts the imminent collapse of the North Korean system—at least sooner or later; and the other predicts a gradual systemic transformation roughly along the Chinese line. Be that as it may, it is an accepted truism that the already difficult North Korean economy has taken a turn for the worse since the historic global changes and the collapse of the Communist Bloc. But even more undeniable is the fact that the increasing tempo of deterioration in North Korea has not visibly affected the North Korean population. Having already endured hardship for the last half century under a completely closed system, poverty has become North Koreans' second nature and shielded them from a sense of relative aggravation of their deprived life style. Accordingly, life under the draconian Orwellian system of surveillance and control makes it totally impossible for the emergence and sustenance of any viable opposition to the existing political structure. What this means is that contrary to the general prognostication in the West, the present system in North Korea could have far greater endurance than generally conjectured. And as long as

Socialist China is able to maintain its power and supports North Korea's existence, and exerts its power and influence to block the sudden demise of North Korea, it would be impossible to forsee a collapse of North Korea. Rather, the likely development would be that the North Korean leadership, sensing its critical situation would begin on their own cautious program of reforms to prevent the collapse of the system itself. We would rather support the notion that North Korea will opt for a course of reforms to ensure a very conservative and gradual systemic transformation. It is reasonable to foresee that North Korea will follow the Chinese pattern of change—a gradual economic opening and cautious economic reforms—and attempt an economic recovery by way of importing foreign capital and technology rather than through the failed system of the mobilization of its people.

Even from the South Korean perspective, the sudden collapse of North Korea is not desirable. The crossing into South Korea by an army of several million unemployed North Koreans, caused by the sudden and rapid collapse of North Korea would inevitably create massive chaos and dislocation of the labor market, not to mention unacceptably enormous budget outlays for unification expenses, including gigantic social welfare expenditures. Of greater concern is the high probability of unpredictable after-shocks of socio-psychological conflict between the peoples from the two Koreas, similar but vastly more serious than anything experienced by the Germans since their unification. For these reasons, instead of a sudden collapse of North Korea, we would rather prefer a cautious and gradualistic process in which the sides can increase their exchanges to help and share with each other in the confirmed environment of peaceful coexistence—approximating common national life under the unification. Therefore, we have no doubt whatever that peaceful coexistence is the only viable shortcut to national unity.

The "Three-Stage Unification" Formula which aspires to peaceful national unification is a credible mechanism that will facilitate inter-Korean reconciliation/cooperation and points the way toward a South-North Confederation. If and when a very minimum of political confidence is achieved through agreement on nuclear issues and others, we could go forward to a path of reconciliation and cooperation with deliberation and speed through the establishment of a mechanism—a Confederation. Hence, the South-North Confederation under the "Three-Stage" plan cannot be the consequence of inter-Korean reconciliation and cooperation but rather the "result of the national consensus and the political decisions of the two Korean governments" as well as the catalyst for broadening and deepening the structure of mutual harmony and cooperation between the two sides.

The Confederation as the first unification stage, presented in the "Three-Stage" plan, is a Confederation of states. First, under the Confederation, the two existing Korean governments will be operating various cooperative organs in close cooperation while continuing to retain their respective authorities and power over their own diplomacy/foreign relations, defense, and innately internal matters.

Second, the Summit Conference, composed of the supreme leaders of the two Koreas, shall discuss and decide on the direction of all major policies, based on the three major policy implementation guidelines: Peaceful Coexistence, Exchange, and Unification. Its decisions will be referred to the Ministerial Council for specific policy decisions, and turned over to the relevant Confederal Committees for discussion, agreement, coordination, and detailed measures for their final implementation. One of the most important tasks for the Confederal stage is to work for arms control agreements and the establishment of a firm structure for ensuring peace between the two Koreas.

The Confederal Council, as the legislature, and composed of an equal number of representatives from the two sides, will consult the views and opinions of the people, discuss, and vote on the implementation of the three policy guidelines of peaceful coexistence, exchange, and unification, and refer the decisions to the Summit Conference. The latter shall have a veto power on the referred matters.

Third, towards the end of the expected ten years for the Confederation, we expect the following will have been accomplished: (1) the firm establishment of the structure for peaceful coexistence; (2) the broadening and deepening of exchanges in all areas; (3) the fusion of the two military forces and foreign relations/diplomatic activities through the achievement of a military balance and through arms control agreements. Generally speaking, the foundation will have been laid for an eventual unification.

Thus far, we have looked at the Confederation in the larger framework of the "Three-Stage Unification" Formula. We shall now turn to the principles of peaceful coexistence and the specific plans for it under the system of Confederation.

2. The Principles of Peaceful Coexistence Under the Confederation

The significance of peaceful coexistence under the Confederation is not just peaceful coexistence between the two systems merely for the purpose of "maintaining the status quo"—it has quite a different goal. As a special relationship, established as a partial process for unification for a tentative purpose, the Confederation is not quite a "state-to-state" linkage, but a phase of peaceful coexistence aiming for the dissolution of the national division.

We shall present the following as the principles for peaceful coexistence under the Confederation. First, the two sides ought to recognize and respect each other's system. Neither the exchanges and cooperation nor peaceful coexistence will be possible without these important conditions. Second, neither side shall encroach on the other through the use of military force, nor shall attempt to destroy, subvert or overthrow the other. Third, they shall not interfere with each other's internal affairs. Fourth, the two sides shall promote their common interests and prosperity through exchanges and cooperation.

The political and military tasks that the two sides must pursue under these principles are as follows. First, inter-Korean relations of distrust and confrontation must be transformed to that of reconciliation and cooperation through recognition and respect for each other's entity. This can be achieved only through expanded dialogue and contact, and broader exchanges and cooperation. Therefore, the very basic responsibility of the Confederation is to build up its institutional ability to manage the unification processes under the cover of peaceful coexistence by constantly raising the level of political confidence between the two sides.

Second, the state of armistice must be converted to a state of peace. Since the end of the Korean War, the two Koreas have maintained a precarious truce based on the Armistice Agreement. The two sides now must take legal steps to replace the Armistice Agreement and achieve the means for the peaceful management of the national division.

Third, arms control measures must be taken through agreement between the two. Since the armistice, the two Koreas have experienced intense military competition and have expended an enormous amount of national resources for it, resulting in tremendous potential of power for destruction aimed at each other. Despite these efforts, however, there is a serious military imbalance between the two; and even today, South Korea depends on foreign forces for deterrence. For genuine and stable peaceful coexistence, military confidence must be built up through viable arms control measures; and a new military equilibrium must be achieved through a balanced reduction of forces on both sides. Under the Confederation, genuine arms control will be the most important task to be accomplished.

Fourth, there is the question of an international guarantee of peaceful coexistence. The measures taken for peaceful coexistence may be the necessary conditions for it, but are not by themselves sufficient. Namely, firm peace is not possible without them, but they are not completely adequate for reliable peace. The reason is simply that peace in the Korean Peninsula is integrally linked to other regional states. As we are aware, the fundamental cause of Korea's division was the intervention by the United States and the Soviet Union. Even today, the United States, Russia, China, Japan, and others are affecting the interrelationship between the two Koreas. The United States and South Korea are allied through a Mutual Defense Treaty. Russia and China are in a state of treaty relations with North Korea under the "Friendship, Cooperation and Mutual Assistance" treaty. Japan, too, for strategic reasons and its own national interest, maintains a high concern for the peninsula. From this perspective, although all the important questions concerning the future of the Korean Peninsula (such as the realization of the Confederation, the transition from truce to peace, and arms control) must be solved by the Koreans themselves, it is still vitally important to get support, cooperation, and assurance from all the neighboring countries as well.

IV. The Modality of Peaceful Coexistence Under the Confederation

We shall now present our views on the negotiation of a peace agreement, arms control, and international guarantees for peaceful coexistence in the peninsula as means toward peaceful coexistence under the Confederal phase.

1. A Peace Agreement

For the present, under the Armistice Agreement, the two Koreas maintain the state in which war was temporarily stopped. Section 62 of Article 5 (Miscellaneous) of the Armistice Agreement provides that the Agreement will remain in effect until it is replaced by a proper political agreement for a peaceful settlement of the Korean question. Accordingly, for peaceful coexistence, it would be necessary at some point in time to negotiate a "proper agreement" for the conversion from the state of cease fire to a state of peace.

The "proper agreement" means a peace agreement in the normal definition of that term, namely to replace the Armistice Agreement to end the state of war and to ensure peace. The agreement in question can either be named a "peace agreement," the "South-North Confederal Charter," or it can called by a different name and take a different shape. For convenience, it is called a "peace agreement" here.

As for the peace agreement, there are three problems: the parties to the agreement, the contents, and the timing of the agreement. The root cause of the debate over who the parties should be is the fact that the Armistice Agreement was signed between the Commander of the United Nations Forces, led by the United States on the one side, and the Commanders of North Korean forces and the Chinese Volunteers on the other. As for the possible signatories of the new peace agreement, there could be two alternative plans. One plan would be based on an approach in which a procedural linkage could be made between the negotiation of a peace agreement and the international guarantee of the Korean peace—for instance, the formulae of "two plus two," "two plus four," or even "two plus two plus the UN." In other words, the two Koreas would first agree on a peace pact, followed by a guarantee by other concerned states. The other approach could be to pursue both avenues simultaneously—such as a meeting among the four powers concerned. That is to carry on simultaneously the negotiations among all the concerned parties to convert the existing agreement to a peace agreement for the Korean Peninsula, and the task to achieve an international guarantee for it.

The "Three-Stage Unification" Formula proposes that the most desirable way is to: first, "convert the present cease-fire to a stable peace status" through the efforts of the two Koreas as provided under Article 5 of the Basic Agreement, followed by post-facto support and recognition by the United States and China, and to have the UN Security Council approve and guarantee it later.

To date, North Korea has insisted on an unsupportable and unjustifiable argument that South Korea can not be a party to a new peace agreement because it was not a party to the Armistice

Agreement. However, because of the Basic Agreement between the two Koreas, such an argument can no longer be a subject for discussion. Not only is South Korea a proper party to the Armistice Agreement because along with other UN member states which took part in the War, it was represented in the armistice negotiations through the Commander of the UN Forces, but since the agreement, it has been the most important custodian for the maintenance of the armistice system since cease-fire went into effect. South and North Korea will continue to be the main parties in maintaining the new peace structure in Korea. It is sheer nonsense and an empty argument that the rules of the game for the negotiation and the maintenance of peace in Korea can and should be made without the presence and/or agreement of the main player in the whole drama.

The next best alternative would be to agree on a peace pact through the participation of the two Koreas, the United States, and China. In this case, the format would be to negotiate and sign a four-party peace agreement. If and when the United States becomes involved in the four-party negotiations, the issue of the future American military presence in Korea would be inevitably raised officially among the four countries. However, it ought to be pointed out that this issue is entirely between South Korea and the United States.

Second, the peace agreement will have to confirm the will and determination for peace and national unification, and deal with all necessary measures for the preservation and mainte-nance of peace on the peninsula rather than a mere termination of the state of war. Initially, it will have to formulate specific plans to replace the armistice system, operated under the Armistice Agreement such as ways to deal with the de-milita-rized zone, measures to prevent military hostilities, plans to create a new military balance at a much reduced force level, and plans to replace the Military Armistice Commission and the Neutral Nations Supervisory Commission which have so far managed the existing armistice system. The peace agreement will also have to include the basic principles for unification as well as international guarantees for peace.

Through the Basic Agreement, the two Koreas have already committed themselves to the non-use of military force against each other, non-aggression, the "peaceful settlement of disputes, and the "inviolability" of the military demarcation line as provided under the Armistice Agreement. They also agreed in principle to the peaceful use of the DMZ and the phased reduction of the forces on both sides. Accordingly, the Basic Agreement must be considered to contain most of the items that should be included in the future peace agreement. But the remaining task will have to deal with the specific formulae for the abrogation of the Armistice Agreement and its replacement.

However, in the final analysis, peace cannot be ensured by a documentary agreement alone; there must also be an equilibrium of power. For this self-evident reason, it will be imperative to agree on and implement specific measures for peace through the balancing of forces on each side. Hence, the peace will have to include much more than a mere declaration of intent.

Third, the sooner a peace agreement is reached, the better it would be for all parties. One way to do this would be to consider the inclusion in the Confederal Charter of a specific and definite inter-Korean commitment for the peace agreement at the time of the transition to Confederation. But as has been referred to earlier, although the problem of replacing the Armistice Agreement with a peace agreement must be settled by the two Koreas themselves, the reality makes it impossible for the Koreans to solve the problem alone. The stable balance of power and the international guarantee must be achieved for the peace agreement to be truly effective. Therefore, although it would be advantageous to have an early peace agreement, it cannot be done without the advance maturation of proper pre-conditions. Nevertheless, we still feel that simultaneous entry into the Confederation and the conclusion of a peace agreement is best. But, in our view, the absence of a peace agreement does not necessarily make the transition to Confederation impossible. A gradual process for peace settlement can go forward under the Basic Agreement already in place between the two Koreas. The position on the peace agreement is summarized in [Chart 3-1].

[Chart 3-1] The "Three-Stage Unification"
formula for a Peace Agreement

- Parties: The Optimum Plan — A peace agreement between the two Koreas, Support by the U.S. & China, UN Recognition & Guarantee.

   The Second Option — A 4-Power participation by the two Koreas, U.S. & China

- Contents: Specific Provisions for Insuring Peace
   – ways to deal with the de-militarized zone, measures to prevent military hostilities, plans to create a new military balance at a much reduced force level, and plans to replace the existing Armistice management machinery, and decisions on the basic unification principles and international guarantees for peace.

- Timing: Although it would be advantageous to have an early peace agreement, it cannot be done without the advance maturation of proper pre-conditions such as the genuine balance of forces and measures for international guarantee.

---

2. Arms Control

By pursuing the goal of arms control, the two Koreas will be able to go forward to reduced military tension and peaceful coexistence. The basic concept of the "Three-Stage Unification" formula for arms control is as follows: first is the removal of the danger of renewed war by guaranteeing each other's existence and achieving a balance of power at a much reduced force level. Second, the military confidence-building and arms control should proceed together simultaneously. Mass destruction such as nuclear and chemical weapons and particularly offensive forces must be reduced as the prime priority. Third, a verification and inspection system for arms control measures must also be taken in tandem to ensure the faithful implementation of the agreements.

There are two ways to prevent war and to insure national security. One is the usual and realistic method of maintaining superior military forces to those of the enemy—through buildup of forces, alliance relations with foreign powers, and the possession of mass destruction weapons like nuclear weapons. However, these measures will be matched by the other side, resulting in spiraling competition in military buildup, increasing defense costs, and ultimately weakening the national economic power. The other more idealistic approach is to agree on arms control by consensus and maintain the state of peaceful coexistence. To help understand this issue, refer to [Diagram 3-1].

Arms control has two competing concepts: one involves an aspect of how to prevent the temptation and/or miscalculation and misjudgment in starting a war, or war provocation; and the other is how to reduce or eliminate altogether the military capabilities to provoke a war.[12] The former is the concept of opera-

---

[12]Lim Dong-won, *op cit.*, pp. 28-29.

tional arms control. To wit, the idea is to notify and publicize to the other side the status of one's own military forces, their movement, field exercises/war games and other military activities, thus raising the level of predictability so as to create an atmosphere of mutual trust and confidence. Obviously, the whole process can be called an important part of military confidence-building. The latter concept is to control the composition, structure, and size of the military power, including limitations on military buildup, freeze, and reduction of force levels. A stable military and/or political situation can thus be achieved through a new military balance by agreeing on the reduced force levels. An arms control, therefore, is both the process and the method for strengthening national defense and security by way of inducing a proper balance of power based on mutual military confidence.

Through arms control, the two Koreas should be able to transform the structure of confrontation to one of cooperation. They will do this by: 1) converting unilateral security to one of common security; 2) moving from mutual distrust to mutual confidence; 3) progressing from military imbalance to equilibrium; and 4) by transforming an offensive force structure to one of defense. Needless to say, however, since the arms control process, will be very difficult and tricky, it will be possible only when the two sides are firmly convinced that peaceful coexistence will benefit their respective interests.

Verification is a process by which the signatories of arms control can make a judgment as to whether all the military measures taken to implement the arms control agreement are in strict accordance with its provisions. It will also serve the increasing military confidence and assure the observance of the agreement itself through mutual consultations on the proper interpretations of the provisions of the agreement and the evidence collected by the verification process. The verification itself performs various tasks for the integrity of the agreement and its implementation: 1) to build mutual confidence and trust by verifying the implementation of the respective sides; 2) as a safety valve to detect and identify early the violations of the arms control agreement by the other side so as to deter the possibility of further violations and to reinsure strict observance of the agreement; 3) to build a new structure of security by increasing the

[Diagram 3-1] The Conceptual Structure of Arms Control

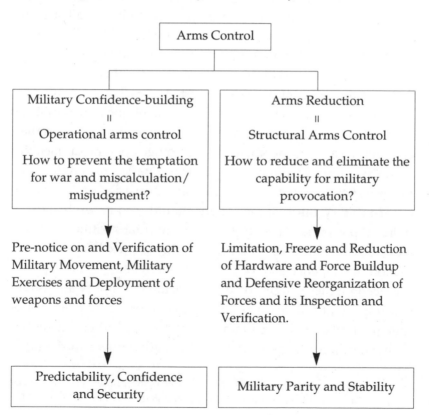

transparency and predictability.[13]

In the next section, we will look into the ways and means for military confidence-building, arms control, and verification methods on the basis of the arms control concepts discussed above.

1) Military Confidence-Building

As for the measures to be taken for inter-Korean military confidence-building, there will be three categories: the exchange of military information and the maintenance of communications links, the public notification of military activities, and the prevention of surprise attacks and/or accidental military face-offs.

First, the two Koreas ought to exchange military information by phases and maintain communications links between them to build up mutual confidence and trust. The exchange of information should cover such areas as the status of one's own military power, the composition of military units above certain designated level, weaponry, deployment, and other operational facilities including underground tunnels, the details and contents of defense spending, the status of military industries, and other relevant military information. There should also be exchanges of military personnel in order to reduce mutual hostility and distrust; and the direct communications links for exchange of information/intelligence and for crisis management.

Second, there ought to be an agreement to notify and publicize important military activities to the other side. Movement of military units above a certain size and level, military activities such as military maneuvers must be made known to the other

---

[13]Chun Sung-hoon, *On Verification of Arms Control: Based on Theories and Historical Cases* (Seoul: Research Institute for National Unification, 1992), p. 21.

side, and for the purpose of ensuring mutual confidence, it should be obligatory for the other side's military observers to be present in those activities and/or exercises so that they can confirm or verify that these are not for surprise attacks The invitations sent to the North Korean military observers to the South Korean-U.S. joint military exercises—Team Spirit Exercises—in the past were just such cases in point. Such steps must become a reality as soon as possible.

Third, regulatory steps must be taken to prevent either surprise attacks or accidental military flare-ups. Troops, weapons, and military facilities must be withdrawn from the de-militarized zone so that the DMZ can be truly de-militarized and eventually converted to a genuine peace zone. It would be highly desirable to establish in that peace zone cultural and sports facilities, facilities for the reunion of the separated families, and marketing facilities for the exchange of goods and services between the two Koreas. A superhighway can also be built along the DMZ cutting across the peninsula east to west to be used for both the purposes of mutual inspection and as an indirect capital investment for national infrastructure.

In addition, territorial belts of a certain distance on both sides of the DMZ should be designated as "Limited Deployment Zones" (LDZs), and no offensively structured forces should be allowed to be deployed in them. Such an arrangement would be highly useful to deter undesirable accidental military conflicts as well as to increase the early warning capabilities on both sides.[14] Along with it, the problem of the de-nuclearization of Korea is truly an important task.

---

[14]Lim Dong-won, "Arms Control on the Korean Peninsula is the Historic Demand of Our Times," *Hankuk Nondan* (A monthly journal in Seoul), July, 1990, p. 35.

[Chart 3-2] The "Three-Stage Unification" Formula's Plans for Military Confidence-Building

- •The Exchange of Military Information/Intelligence & Maintenance of the Communications Links
  - – the exchange of information on the status of each side's military power, the deployment of military units above a certain designated level, weaponry, and other operational facilities including underground tunnels, the details and contents of defense spending, the status of military industries, and other relevant military information.
  - – the exchange of military personnel.
  - – the direct communications links between the two military authorities.
- •public notice of important military activities.
  - – Movement of military units and military maneuvers, and the obligatory invitation of the other side's military observers.
- •prevention of surprise attacks and accidental military flare-ups.
  - – the withdrawal of troops, weapons, and military facilities from the DMZ, replaced by a genuine peace zone.
  - – establishment in the peace zone of cultural and sports facilities, facilities for the reunion of the separated families, and marketing facilities for the exchange of goods and services.
  - – the building of an east-west superhighway along the DMZ to be used for mutual inspection and as an indirect capital investment for national infrastructure.
  - – the designation of "Limited Deployment Zones" (LDZs) on both sides of the DMZ and prohibition of offensively structured forces in them to deter accidental military conflicts and to increase the early warning capabilities.
- •the de-nuclearization of Korea.

Under the Basic Agreement, already in place between the two Koreas, the following measures can be taken at any time depending on the political will of the two sides: the military confidence-building measures such as the establishment and operation of a direct military telephone link, the peaceful use of the DMZ, the exchange of military personnel, and others. Some of the measures, central to the military confidence-building, which must be taken are the movement of troops which involves certain procedural difficulties, the notification and control of military maneuvers, and the exchange of information.

The position taken by our "Three-Stage Unification" formula on inter-Korean military confidence-building is shown in [Chart 3-2] below.

2) Arms Reduction

As for the principles of arms reduction, the "Three-Stage Unification" Formula offers the following: the purpose of arms reduction is to achieve the proper level of military power based on the principles of a "one-to-one" ratio in military power and mutual balance. The level of forces allowed after the reduction should be determined in consideration of not only South-North confrontation, but also in terms of Korea's geopolitical position, national status and dignity, and the projected military needs for national interest. At this point, however, we could consider a force level of some 300,000 for each side.

The question of "how to achieve arms reduction?" must be dealt with through reduction in phases, aiming for the correction of the existing imbalance between the two opposing forces in Korea. The new balance must be achieved at a slightly lower level than that of the inferior side at this point in time, and proceed from there to phased reductions.

What is to be reduced? The focus of reduction should be the elimination of surprise attack and offensive capabilities; and as in Europe in the past, the prime objective ought to be the reduction of offensive weapon systems that can be verified. Mass destruction weapons such as chemical weapons must be abolished as the first priority following the pattern of international trends. An attempt to reduce all weapons will not be practical or feasible under the existing circumstances. Once the agreement for reduction is reached on such clearly offensive weapons as battle tanks, armored vehicles, self-propelled field guns, attack helicopters, and fighters and fighter-bombers, all other weapon systems could easily be reduced later.

Once the reduction of weapons is achieved, it must be followed by reductions in troop units and military manpower. The ready forces as well as reserves must be also cut.

Arms reduction can occur either through a unilateral decision or by negotiation. The inter-Korean arms reduction is to be carried out by the inter-Korean Confederal Military Committee,

[Chart 3-3] The "Three-Stage Unification" Formula's Plans for Arms Reduction.

- the achievement of proper level of military power based on the principles of a "one-to-one" ratio in military power and mutual balance.
- the level of forces to be determined based on internal & external factors and on national status and the projected military needs of the unified state.
- the prime objective must be the elimination of the mass destruction weapons and the reduction of battle tanks, armored vehicles, self-propelled field guns, attack helicopters, and fighters and fighter-bombers to prevent surprise attacks and/or offensive operations.

which will oversee the entire process.

The position of the "Three-Stage Unification" Formula on arms reduction is summarized in [Chart 3-3] below.

3) Verification

One cannot overestimate the importance of the verification process to see to the faithful implementation of the arms reduction accords for the ultimate purpose of military confidence-building. The verification, however, can be a double-edged sword in that on the one hand, it can insure the faithful observance of the arms control agreements, but on the other hand can impede in some cases the agreements themselves. For this reason, it must be dealt with with prudently and carefully. To put it differently, undue insistence on watertight verification to insure the binding effect of agreement could even abort the arms control negotiations themselves. The verification, therefore, must be one of balanced wisdom which can satisfy both the agreement itself and the implementation as well.

The verification must be based on the following principles: first, the power and obligations of verification must follow the principle of reciprocity, and the selection of the object of verification must be based on symmetry. Too meticulous or cumbersome a verification process must not be allowed to sabotage the arms control agreements themselves.

Since the two Koreas are without the means to verify the implementation of the arms control accords through intelligence satellites or by intelligence aircraft, the verification must utilize the method of on-site inspection.

In light of the low technology status of both Koreas, such an agreement will have to use on-site inspections and verification,

particularly remote controlled television cameras, and/or resident on-site inspection teams, and open-sky arrangements.
Multi-national verification or by the United Nations should be
avoided as much as possible based on the principle of national
self-reliance and to avoid the possibility of revealing too much
defense information to the outside.

The objects of verification should be: the exchanged military
material (on ready forces, logistics and support facilities, military facilities, and military industries, etc.), pre-notified military
activities, the actual implementation of de-militarization in the
DMZ, the level of combat readiness, the observance of the limitation of deployment, and the mass destruction weapons and
the offensive weapons.[15] The two Koreas should agree to elevate

*[Chart 3-4] The "Three-Stage Unification" Formula's Plans for
Arms Control Verification.*

•The verification objects: the exchanged military material, pre-noti-fied military activities, the actual imple-mentation of de-militarization in the DMZ, the limitation of military deployment, the observation of combat readiness, and the mass destruction weapons and the offen-sive weapons.
•The level of verification: The gradual elevation of the levels of inspection through the invitation and dis-patch of the military observers → the on-site inspection → the exchange of resident inspection teams → the open sky program and inspections on challenge.

[15]Nam Man-kwon, "On Inspection and Verification of the Inter-Korean
Arms Control," *Kukbang Nonjib (Defense Studies)*, 14, Summer 1991. pp. 193-209.

the level of verification by stages. Military observers must be invited and sent first to the military maneuvers, and in the next stage, the preparations for and the implementation of the arms control agreements ought to be verified. These should be followed by the exchange of the resident on-site inspection teams for the uninterrupted implementation, and finally by the open sky program and inspections on challenge.

The position of the "Three-Stage Unification" Formula on arms control is summarized in [Chart 3-4].

3. International Guarantee for South-North Peaceful Coexistence

As mentioned earlier, the efforts by the two Koreas for peaceful coexistence can either be helped or hindered by the external factors. For this reason, it is vitally important to get international support and cooperation. Most of all, the question of the U.S. military presence in Korea must be addressed with wisdom. And this must be followed by the firm establishment of peace in the Korean Peninsula and international cooperation for Korean unification through the organization of a Northeast Asian security cooperation structure.

1) The United States Forces in Korea

The American and Soviet forces that occupied South and North Korea from August 1945 were withdrawn in 1949. However, with the North Korean invasion of the South in June 1950, the United States entered the war as part of the United Nations' efforts for collective security, and have remained in the South since then under the Mutual Defense Treaty signed in 1953. As South Korea has felt seriously threatened by the powerful North

Korean forces, so, too, North Korea has feared the presence of American forces in the South. Indeed, the presence of United States forces in South Korea has been a subject of intense conflict between the two Koreas whenever the two were involved in talks to relax tension and has in fact been a great obstacle to the realization of arms control. The position of the "Three-Stage Unification" formula on the settlement of the American forces in Korea is based on the following principles: first, it is imperative to realize both political and military confidence-building between North Korea and the United States. Although the seriousness of the inter-Korean hostility and distrust have been noted thus far, the mutual distrust between North Korea and the United States has not been sufficiently highlighted. The degree and intensity of the Northern sense of fear of the United States originates from its intense distrust of the United States. Hence, to solve the problem of the American forces in Korea with wisdom and prudence in the process of building up the peace structure in Korea, it requires the dissipation of hostility and the buildup of political and military confidence between North Korea and the United States. If and when North Korea's nuclear issue is resolved through faithful implementation of the agreement between the two, they would be able to create a degree of political trust between them through the establishment of an appropriate level of diplomatic and economic relations. Along the way, if the pursuit of North Korean-U.S. political and military confidence-building measures parallel those between the two Koreas, it can be expected that the North would not continue to view the U.S. forces as an inhibiting factor to the peace structure on the peninsula. We would still face ups and downs in the future, but there is no doubt that the Agreed Framework between North Korea and the United States, signed in Geneva, was a giant step forward for the ultimate establishment of trust and confidence between the two countries.

Second, the reduction of American forces in Korea and the readjustment of their role must be pursued in tandem with the arrangement of the inter-Korean arms control. North Korea has been insisting on the withdrawal of American forces as the precondition for an arms control agreement. However, at least since 1987, Pyongyang has shown signs of change in its attitude on this issue. In the "Proposal for Phased Reduction of Forces," announced on July 23, 1987, North Korea called for the phased withdrawal of American forces from Korea, and repeated its clear change of policy through the "Arms Control Plan for Korean Peace" in 1990 in which North Korea linked the phased American withdrawal to the progress made in the inter-Korean arms control negotiations. This obviously signifies that the problem of the withdrawal of American forces from South Korea is no longer a pre-condition for arms control but an integral issue linked to the larger process of arms control.[16]

Under the circumstances, we believe the following are reasonable procedures for settling the problem of American forces in South Korea. First, the size and role of the American forces must be readjusted. For this, the South Korean-U.S. military alliance

---

[16]During the period of North Korean-U.S. confrontation over the issue of Pyongyang's nuclear weapons program, Kim Il Sung stated in an interview that "[I] have never insisted on the immediate withdrawal of American forces from Korea. What I said was that the American forces could withdraw in stages when and if the phased reduction of forces is achieved and when self-defense becomes feasible for the Korean Peninsula." Also in his meetings with former U.S. President Carter, Kim proposed the "proportional reduction of American forces to the reduction of force levels between the two Koreas." These specific cases seem to show that the hitherto stubborn posture of North Korea toward the issue of the American forces has considerably mellowed.

structure must be overhauled. As of December 1, 1994, South Korea regained operational control of its forces in peacetime from the United States. South Korea ought to move toward independent authority in operational control and independent national defense capabilities by regaining war-time operational control of its forces as well.[17] A major adjustment must be made in which the central role for defense must now be borne by South Korea while the American forces in Korea must assume a complementary role, and the American forces ought to be reduced in stages.

Second, the question of the continued presence of the United States forces in Korea even after the establishment of the peace structure in Korea will have to be addressed at that time based on careful scrutiny of the security conditions in Northeast Asia and the role of the American forces. However, in consideration of all these issues, we must pay attention to the fact that the American forces continue to remain in Europe and in Japan even after the end of the Cold War. Although the proper size of American forces in Korea can and should be readjusted toward the latter half of the Confederal stage based on the careful examination of the security conditions surrounding the Korean Peninsula at the time, it is our view that their continued presence at a proper force level is desirable as the "Balancer of Regional Security and Peace in Northeast Asia."

The position of the "Three-Stage Unification" Formula on the U.S. Forces in Korea is summarized in [Chart 3-5] below.

---

[17]Cha Young-koo, "[We will] Enter an Era of Common Defense between the Two Koreas from Year 2000," *The Unification Era That Will Open in Year 2000* (Seoul: The Presidential Commission on the 21st Century, 1993). pp. 156-176.

*[Chart 3-5] The "Three-Stage Unification" Formula's Plans for
the Settlement of the Problem of American Forces in Korea.*

•the central defense role must be borne by South Korea while the American forces in Korea must assume a complementary role, and the American forces ought to be reduced in stages.
•the desirability of the continued American military presence in Korea as the "Balancer of Regional Security and Peace in Northeast Asia."

2) Multilateral Cooperative Security Regime in Northeast Asia

Military stability in Northeast Asia will play a major role in the successful management of peaceful coexistence between the two Koreas for the following two reasons: first, if the regional states are involved in an arms race due to the instability of security in Northeast Asia, it would have a negative impact on Korea's own security as well as on the efforts for inter-Korean arms control.

Second, regional insecurity even after the peaceful coexistence is achieved in Korea, will still make it difficult for the Koreans to benefit from the peace dividends because the conversion of military expenses to peaceful use would not be entirely possible. One must note that this problem is caused by the duality of threats to the Korean Peninsula. An arms control agreement between South and North Korea will reduce the military threats between them and could firmly establish their peaceful coexistence. However, as peaceful coexistence becomes firm towards the latter half of the Confederation, the two Koreas could face a new security situation that did not exist before, as hitherto dormant potential external threats might surface. Such a possibility becomes real when one considers the strategic implications of the quiet yet on-going military rivalry between China and Japan, and the possibilities of regional feuds/conflicts among nations over economic and environmental issues and others which could easily spill over to other unexpected areas. Since the strategic conditions surrounding the peninsula could seriously affect the conditions of peace in Korea, arms control should not be confined merely to the two Koreas, but should be pursued in the larger context of Northeast Asia as a whole.

The "Three-Stage Unification" Formula shall seek an institutionalization of a Multilateral Northeast Asian Security Cooperation not only for peace and stability in Korea but for the peace and prosperity of the entire region. A system of multilateral security cooperation is obviously a regional peace structure, designed to prevent errant behavior of the member states as well as to increase the trust and confidence among them. Its purposes are: first, to enhance among the member states, mutual understanding, confidence building, and security transparency through consultations on comprehensive security issues; and on that basis, either reduce or eliminate altogether regional instability and uncertainties. Second, to accumulate the collective habits or traditions through routinized discussions on matters of common concern among the member states, and to pursue the commonality of rules, applicable to all so as to heighten the level of predictability in the mode of actions among the signatories. Third, to lay the foundation for serious arms control measures. And finally, the structure is designed to settle all problems and disputes through peaceful means only.[18]

---

[18]Kim Kook-jin, "An Approach to a Multilateral Security Regime in North-

The multilateral security cooperation that we seek through the "Three-Stage" plan is similar to Europe's Conference on Security and Cooperation in Europe (CSCE)[19] that produced the

---

east Asia," *Journal of Area Studies*, 6, 1994 (The Korean Consultative Research Council for Area Studies/*Hankuk Jeeyuk Yunku Hyup-eui-hoe*), pp. 65-67.

[19]It is highly interesting to note that originally the idea of a European Security Conference was floated by the Soviet Union in 1954, and was consistently pursued by the Warsaw Pact through the 1960s. But NATO states rejected the Soviet proposal because of the suspicion that it was a political ruse designed to "decouple" the United States from Europe and effectively neutralize the NATO alliance. However, after the Berlin crisis in the early 1960s, Europe was calmer without direct confrontation between NATO and the Soviet Bloc, while France under Charles de Gaulle and later West Germany under Willy Brandt began serious approaches to Moscow for detente; and by 1971, for reasons including the Vietnam War, the United States too became interested in detente in the East-West relations. After Henry Kissinger's secret trip to Beijing and the entry of China into the United Nations, the Atlantic Council finally accepted the Warsaw Pact proposal for a Security Conference in December 1971, although NATO continued to insist on negotiations for conventional forces reduction. Following the development, preparatory talks began in November 1972, followed by a conference in Helsinki, Finland in July 1973, attended by thirty-three states, including NATO, Warsaw Pact, non-aligned and neutral nations. Albania was the only country which did not attend the conference. The Conference included two non-European countries—Canada and the United States. From July 30 to August 1, 1975, President Gerald Ford, General Secretary Leonid Brezhnev and other leaders met in Helsinki and signed the "Final Act" of the talks, which included the so-called "Three Baskets": (a) On security issues, the basic principles were for the respect of sovereignty, non-interference in internal affairs, and the "inviolability" of the post-World War II borders in Europe; (b) cooperation in trade, technology and cultural exchanges; and (c) the respect for fundamental human rights and the free exchange of ideas and people across Europe, [It was hoped that this agreement would one day help undermine the Communist system in Eastern Europe.] And most importantly, it was decided that the process of detente should continue through the meetings of a "Conference on Security and Cooperation in Europe" [CSCE]. The Helsinki Accords represented the height of European detente in the 1970s, and strengthened the policies of *Ostpolitik*, committing

Helsinki Accords in 1975. The Northeast Asian structure of multilateral security cooperation will not only be a community for military and economic issues, but a community of humanity for cultural exchanges as well as for common security.

Although it is evident that the Northeast Asian structure of multilateral security cooperation will have a positive effect on the establishment of a peace structure on the Korean Peninsula, the timing of its establishment will still be a problem. If its establishment coincides with the decision for the inter-Korean Confederation, many of the difficult issues such as the agreement for the Confederation and its eventual implementation could be solved within the framework of a multilateral security system.[20]

But because of the extremely complex interests of the concerned states, institutionalization of a multilateral security cooperation would require a very long time. What is important, therefore, is to have Korea's neighboring powers first endorse and guarantee the structure of peace in Korea and induce them later to cooperate with each other in increasing tempo. To wit, Northeast Asian multilateral security cooperation could eventually emerge via this vicarious route.

---

both sides to the cause of maintaining peace in Europe. The significance of the "Final Act," however, was greatly diluted by the fact that there still existed two irreconcilable military blocs and that there was no real respect for human rights in the East Bloc, symbolized by the intense suppression of the "Charter 77" human rights group in Czechoslovakia. At the CSCE meeting in Belgrade in 1978, NATO and the Warsaw Pact states collided over the touchy issue of human rights and the CSCE talks would not resume again until the late 1980s. By then, the Gorbachev regime in Moscow and the Soviet reforms (*Glasnost and Perestroika*) created an entirely new international environment for the successful continuation of the CSCE.

[20]For example, the reduction of bio-chemical weapons and other mass destruction weapons would be such problems.

Concerning the task of institutionalizing regional multilateral security cooperation, the "Three-Stage Unification" Formula will pursue the following principles: first, the regional multilateral security cooperation can coexist with the existing bilateral alliances and security commitments. Second, an early establishment of the multilateral security cooperation through the initiatives of the involved governments based on the security consultations thus far. Third, the role and function of the multilateral security cooperation will be strengthened gradually in phases. Cooperation should begin in non-military areas and be expanded gradually to the military arena. The degree and level of institutionalization could begin first in a basic format of the structure itself and gradually extend towards organizing a specified organ for security cooperation. Fourth, multilateral security cooperation in smaller territorial scope (e.g., in Northeast Asia) does not necessarily conflict with one covering a larger territorial area (e.g., the Asia-Pacific Region).

Under these principles, the following six member states would be desirable—the two Koreas, the United States, Japan, China, and Russia.[21]

Like the CSCE, the agenda for the Northeast Asian security structure should include a broad spectrum of issues in both the military and non-military areas such as the economy, science and technology, environment, human rights, culture, refugees, addictive drugs, etc. In the military area, an attempt must be made to establish the tradition/habit of dialogue and consultation and to create common rules for all members—first through an extensive discussion of the regional situation. Also a common commitment must be made to the non-use of military force, non-

---

[21]Due to the economic potential, Mongolia could also be included.

aggression, and the non-use of nuclear weapons within the region for political confidence-building. These initial measures ought to be followed by the active participation in and strict observance by the member states of the global confidence-building system[22] so as to enable the minimum military confidence-building in the region—such as the publication of the defense budget, the exchange of military personnel, pre-notification of military exercises, the exchange of military data and information, the invitation to and dispatch of military observers to military exercises, and the publication of military strategies and doctrines. As the security cooperation matures into a firm pattern of institutionalization, the reduction and/or freeze ought to occur with respect to the weapons of mass destruction and other important conventional weapons. In the process of cooperation in military and non-military areas, sovereignty must be respected as a matter of principle. The problem of human rights guarantee, as was shown to be the issue of prolonged controversy and conflict in the CSCE between the West and the East, must be approached prudently and flexibly based on the European experiences and lessons.

The two Koreas will have to maintain close cooperation with the member states of the multilateral security structure in Northeast Asia for the peaceful management and solution of the Korean problems. Special efforts would have to be made in this regard to elicit particularly strong support from them for Confederation, arms control measures, and the conversion of the Armistice System to a new peace structure

---

[22]The United Nations' systems of conventional weapons registration, military expenses registration, Nuclear Non-Proliferation Treaty, treaties banning chemical weapons, the missile technology control regime, etc,

The position of the "Three-Stage Unification" Formula on a Multilateral Security Cooperation in Northeast Asia is summarized in [Chart 3-6] below.

[Chart 3-6] The "Three-Stage Unification" Formula's Plans for Multilateral Security Cooperation in Northeast Asia

•the regional multilateral security cooperation can coexist with the existing bilateral alliances and security commitments.

•an early establishment of the multilateral security cooperation through the initiatives of the involved governments.

•cooperation should begin in non-military areas and be expanded gradually to the military arena.

•multilateral security cooperation in smaller territorial scope (e.g., in Northeast Asia) does not necessarily conflict with one covering a larger territorial area (e.g., the Asia-Pacific Region).

•member states: the two Koreas, the United States, Japan, China, and Russia.

•agenda:

– declaration of the principles of non-use of military force, non-aggression, and the non-use of nuclear weapons.

– active participation in the global confidence-building system

– military confidence-building at the minimum level.

– reduction and/or freeze of the weapons of mass destruction and other important conventional weapons.

– economic, science/technology, environmental, human rights, cultural, refugees, addictive drugs, and other issues.

4. The Comprehensive Program for Peaceful Coexistence

We have examined thus far our plans for peaceful coexistence under the Confederation basically through the three main areas of peace agreement, arms control, and the international guarantee of peaceful coexistence between the two Koreas. We shall now look at the modalities of their implementation by chronological periods.

The most pressing priority in the early period of the Confederation would be to lay the firm foundation for peaceful coexistence between the two Koreas by achieving political confidence. All the necessary steps ought to be taken for political confidence-building through mutual respect of each other's systems, prohibition of mutual recrimination, slander, subversive activities such as sabotage or overthrow of each other's government, and interference into each other's internal affairs—and through all around exchanges and cooperation.

What is important is the very firm will and vision of not only all the Koreans in South and North Korea but especially of the leaders of both governments for the cause of peaceful coexistence between the two Koreas. Accordingly, in the long and painful process of political confidence building, we ought to be extra patient and careful not to let misunderstandings and differences mar the entire process.

Another central task during the period of Confederation would be to prevent temptations for war and/or misjudgment and miscalculation so as to enable the strict observance of non-aggression for peaceful coexistence. To this end, a slow but gradual process of military confidence-building must not slacken; both Koreas ought to notify each other about their respective military power and deployment, and major military movements. The exchange of military personnel and military intelligence/information, the maintenance of the communications links, pre-notification of the movement of major units, war maneuvers, the invitation and dispatch of military observers to military maneuvers, measures to prevent surprise attacks and other accidental clashes, the conversion of DMZ to a peace zone—these are the steps that ought to be taken and carried out by both sides to build up the necessary trust and confidence between the two Koreas. The task of de-nuclearizing the Korean Peninsula will be of particular significance. The North Korean nuclear program must be made completely transparent so as to make all of Korea nuclear free.

Along with the confidence-building, there ought to be parallel negotiations for arms control; and weapons of mass destruction must be abolished as a matter of supreme priority. Implementable arms control measures ought to be taken either through negotiation or by unilateral decision.

The two Koreas must commit themselves to gaining international support, guarantee, and cooperation for the firm establishment of the structure for peaceful coexistence during the period of the Confederation. The tasks of converting the Armistice to a peace agreement within the framework of peaceful coexistence and eliciting international cooperation for inter-Korean arms control would be highly significant. The institutionalization of multilateral security cooperation for Northeast Asia will be an effort that will greatly contribute to the cause of peaceful coexistence in Korea.

Towards the latter half of the Confederation, a more systematic consolidation and more efficient management of the peace structure will become possible based on the foundation of political and military trust and confidence built during the early phase. The DMZ will have been converted to a peace zone, then to an LDZ, from which all offensive forces and weapons will be pulled further back to the rear or entirely be de-activated. The most important task during this phase would be to achieve a more systematic arms control in order to reduce the forces on both sides to much lower levels, to be followed by additional steps to completely convert the offensively structured forces to a purely defensive posture. A single caveat to all this will be the necessary adjustment fine tuned to the nature and level of future external security threats and due consideration of the structure, composition, and size of the military forces for the unified state vis-a-vis the expected/predictable national security situation in the future.

The size of the American forces in Korea will also be adjusted in accord with the progress made toward a balanced adjustment of the two Korean forces through arms control decisions; and the continued presence of a proper level of American forces in Korea as the balancer for regional equilibrium may still be possible at that time.

In addition, in the later period of the Confederation there should be a multilateral security cooperation in some shape or form in Northeast Asia to enable enhanced intra-regional cooperation and arms control. Intra-Korean arms control should be assisted tremendously by region-wide arms control, which in turn will have a salutary effect on peace and stability on the peninsula.

Under a market economy, the North Korean economy shall experience robust growth, gradual opening to the outside world and improvement of living standards for its residents should change the general consciousness of the North Korean population, ultimately resulting in the budding of political democracy even under the North Korean political system. These changes in

North Korea will be accelerated under the weight of the arms control achievement which will, in our estimation, become significant factors for the peaceful unification of Korea.

V. The Transition to a Federation

Near the end of the Confederal stage, it is expected that the mutual threats between the two Koreas will have been dissipated largely because of the cumulative efforts made up to that point by the two sides for arms control and the international guarantee of peace on the peninsula. By this time, the two Koreas will be at the threshold of crossing into the Federal stage of the unification process, and the most important policy issues that will face the two sides will be to merge the two military establishments into Federal armed forces. Although the two Koreas under the Confederation were autonomous in defense and foreign relations, when the Federal stage is entered, the Federal Government will exercise unitary authority over the unified armed forces. The basic steps towards the transition to Federal forces would be to attain and maintain appropriate force levels for both sides through the arms control measures, the gradual expansion of cooperative efforts for common military activities, and the consolidation of security cooperation among the regional states in Northeast Asia.

First, in the area of arms control, the two Koreas will have achieved during the Confederal phase the reduction of ready forces and equipment to an appropriate degree. The decision for further reduction will have to be made logically at the time based on the careful consideration of the likely external threats against unified Korea.

Second, the problem of merging the two military forces, hitherto controlled exclusively by each side, into Federal armed forces will be extremely complicated and difficult. To offer a very rough outline of this project, we would propose the formation of a "Planning Group for Military Integration" under the "Combined South-North Military Committee" to generally design the strategy for military integration, to hold consultations on the related issues, and to devise specific and detailed blueprints for the difficult task.

This body will be charged with the systematizing of comprehensive reports and plans for the combined Federal Forces: its composition, structure, and operation. The central subject for the Planning Group's purview will be: military strategy, war fighting structure, control and command structure, determination of proper force level, deployment, and other major related issues.

In coordination with the activities of the Planning Group, the two existing forces of the Koreas will have to reinforce and upgrade their cooperation and coordination for the smooth transition to a Federal military establishment. For this, there ought to be an increased exchange of military officials and upgraded combined training and education of military personnel by areas/fields, holding of joint exercises whose accumulated experiences could be useful for the efficient operation and management of the combined Federal Forces when they are formed. As mentioned earlier, when the final stage of the Confederation is reached, there could be heightened regional threats which have lain dormant during the period of the inter-Korean division. It is, therefore, incumbent on the two Koreas to exercise their utmost efforts to overcome such potential regional threats by way of increasing and ensuring international cooperation and guarantee.

In this context, the problem of how to handle the issue of the American forces in Korea will arise once more. Our view, under the "Three-Stage Unification" Formula, is we do not consider their withdrawal urgent or necessary. If the regional security situation in Northeast Asia remains unstable even after the Federation is formed, we would consider it desirable for the American forces to remain in the region as the balancer of regional equilibrium. Today, the United States forces continue to remain in Europe and Japan: their continued presence in Korea is judged to be conducive not only to our national interest but to those of other nations in Northeast Asia.

The vital importance of a Northeast Asian multilateral security cooperation has already been discussed above: it will help us to overcome the regional security threats and to achieve an international guarantee of peace on the peninsula. The two Koreas will have to strive consistently for the institutionalization of a multilateral regional security cooperation through governmental efforts and channels.

VI. Conclusion

The "Three-Stage Unification" Formula sets its sights on three major goals for peaceful coexistence between the two Koreas during the Confederal Stage: the dissolution of hostility, arms control, and the realization of Northeast Asian multilateral security cooperation. In this chapter, we have tried to discuss the ways and means of realizing these goals with specificity. We shall close the chapter by discussing several idiosyncrasies of the proposals for peaceful coexistence under our unification formula.

First, the "Three-Stage Unification" Formula presents specific ideas for peaceful coexistence which can be implemented through an inter-Korean agreement. We believe our proposals in their substance are eminently acceptable to either side as well as feasible and implementable—because they are balanced towards the vital interests of both sides.

Second, our formula offers a comprehensive schedule for implementation based on the proper timing of each step and issue, and takes into account the processes of the Confederal phase and the speed with which these processes are to be put into effect. We proposed, in the early phase of the Confederation, an emphasis be placed on military confidence-building with the caveat that arms control measures be taken on plans which can be easily agreed to and implemented by the two sides. For the later phase of the Confederation, our proposal calls for the dual track approach of achieving the actual agreements and the strict implementation of substantial arms control measures, and those other undertakings hitherto unattempted during the early stage for the ultimate purpose of military confidence-building.

Third, going beyond the issue of peaceful coexistence under the Confederation, we presented important policy matters that have to be addressed jointly by the two Koreas before they can enter the Federal stage. Especially to ease the transition to Federal Forces, we have stressed the importance of inter-Korean military cooperation and the importance of regional security cooperation.

CHAPTER 4

ECONOMIC EXCHANGES AND COOPERATION UNDER THE CONFEDERATION

Summary

The purpose of this chapter is to present the plans for economic exchange and cooperation under the Confederation.

Economic exchange and cooperation during the Confederation, as part of the grand strategy for the upgraded inter-Korean cooperation, will be pursued under the following principles: the two Koreas shall proceed with economic exchange and cooperation in the spirit of achieving a "National Economic Community" while simultaneously pursuing their respective interests. In so doing, they should faithfully abide by the principles of the separation of politics and economics, the rational division of labor between government and business, focused assistance to medium and small businesses, political consideration for North Korea's open doors, economic rationality, environment friendly development, and others.

To expand and intensify economic exchange, direct trade and the internalization of national trade are two indispensable steps. Economic cooperation must be pursued in tandem with economic exchanges, while the two governments ought to concentrate their efforts indirectly on such things as agreeing on the rules/regulations, systems, loans and credits on the needed capital, leaving the rest to civilian initiatives. Because of the possibility of loss, large scale investment in infrastructure and exploration and development of natural resources in North Korea for revitalizing its economy could be done through a consortium or other such means to lessen the risks. And as an active means to attract foreign loans and credits for North Korea, one can consider South Korean guarantees for them. For greater efficiency and feasibility of inter-Korean economic exchanges and cooperation, the two Koreas should set overall short-and long-term goals and specific programs, suitable for their systematic and phased implementation.

Although the independent efforts of the two Koreas are the primary factors in the dynamic process of their economic exchanges and cooperation, it would be equally important to induce a friendlier international atmosphere for the common project. Regional organizations for economic cooperation such as the "Asia-Pacific Economic Cooperation" (APEC) and "Northeast Asia Economic Bloc" will add to inter-Korean trade and to the general stability of the investment environment, and will help expand North Korea's external economic contacts and relations, thus immeasurably contributing to the opening of North Korea to the outside world. For this reason, it would be highly important for the two Koreas to exert common efforts to vitalize APEC and the Northeast Asian Economic Bloc.

On the other hand, the two Koreas ought also to prepare themselves for the undesirable side effects that are likely to occur from the intensification of the economic exchanges and cooperation. Because of the possibility of environmental damage from economic development, an institutionalized multilateral cooperation must be advanced to ensure harmony between environmental protection and development. The two sides, therefore, ought to make concerted efforts for the common utilization of environment-friendly industrial technology and common economic planning.

With deepening economic exchanges and cooperation under the Confederation, we can expect the following changes in the North Korean economy: to begin with, the North Korean economy will overcome to a considerable degree its capital shortage and technological backwardness through its policy of open doors to the outside; and will show greater vitality in its economic relations with the outside world. As the planned economic system gradually turns toward a market economy, the North Korean economy is expected to experience rapid growth, and the economic disparity with South Korea will begin to narrow. When and if such developments occur, along with improved living standards for its citizens and the inevitable change as well in their world view and/or perception of the outside world, we would project that there would inevitably be demands for changes even in their political system. As these trends take root, it would be unavoidable for the North Koreans to tolerate or even accept the multi-party system and the principle of free elections. But most of all, through the process of economic exchanges and cooperation, the two Koreas will expand the scope of mutual understanding, and realize the natural bond of close interdependence.

The maturing of these developments, not easy but steady and unstoppable, will have paved the foundation for the eventual transition to the Second Stage of the Unification process— the Stage of Federation. When such a point is reached, the two Koreas will have to undertake seriously the task of polishing up the overall economic policies for inter-Korean economic integration—such as the establishment of a rational exchange rate system and a common currency policy for the efficient management of the integrational process. As cooperation in the currency policy will not be possible without cooperation in fiscal policy and coordination, such problems must be left to the Joint South-North Economic Committee for resolution. The work for economic integration at this stage will be unlike the previous periods, and is designed to lay the foundation for systemic integration in expectation of the transition to the Federal Stage of Unification. The historic significance of the economic integration of the two Koreas can be appreciated in light of its being: 1) the first giant step for the unified national economy; 2) the first brick in laying the economic foundation for a single modern nation-state; 3) the quantum expansion of the domestic market for the expanding national economy.

Although, in principle, the change in the North Korean system must precede the inter-Korean economic integration, we must bear in mind that changes must also come in South Korea as well. The inter-Korean economic integration must become the turning point in which the South Korean economy, as an advanced system, must also be elevated to an even higher level. Well in advance of the national economic integration between the two Koreas, it would also be important for the South Korean economy to overcome and rectify its own contradictions and shortcomings prior to taking initial steps toward an economic link with North Korea. Only such preparations on our part will provide the process with the necessary drive and dynamism, and help make the ultimate economic integration a truly significant national economic event.

The great tides of world history are already pointing toward the trends of unification and peace from division and conflict. Even in Korea, a powerful silent tide is moving forward to unification and peace. We believe that the principles and plans for inter-Korean economic exchanges and cooperation, presented in this chapter, are the essential conditions necessary for the gradual and peaceful unification of Korea and for the future prosperity of the national community.

I. Introduction

We are witnessing changes on a global level. The waning days of the twentieth century have brought an end of the Cold War conflict built on the clashes of opposing ideologies. Along with it has come the decline of the "Hegemony of the Dollars."

The dissolution of the Cold War world order has severely diluted the sense of common destiny and common responses against the Communist Bloc among Capitalist states and dramatically and precipitously reduced the political and military component of the previous pattern of economic cooperation. Newly emerging international relations are surely reverting to the traditional pattern of a self-centered quest for narrow national interests devoid of ideological distinctions. Consequently, the world economy that once sought stability based on American economic power has veered to a new direction of economic rivalry and competition resting on "selective Free Trade Policies"[1] and economic regionalism. To a large extent, this new trend owes its origin to declining global hegemon, which using the pretext of the end of the Cold War, has now returned to the traditional form of hegemony based on economic domination. As a result, the world is leaving the age of "politico-military" Cold War, and is about to enter an era of "Economic Hot War."

In an era of global economic "war" wherein ideology plays no role and economic power itself is the foundation of national power, Korea's unification is not only "feasible" but "absolutely necessary."[2]

---

[1] The "Selective Free Trade Policies" describe the situation in which the principles of Free Trade are not applied evenly in all situations but applied differently depending on the cases and/or the categories of objects.

[2] Kim Dae-jung, *My Roadmap and My Ideology: The Grand Transition in World*

The answer to the question of "whether we would lag behind to the fringes of the world action or enter into its center" will surely depend, without exaggeration, on whether or not we can utilize the tangible or intangible[3] costs of national division as fresh new resources for production and improved national welfare. Herein lie the "reasons of absolute necessity" of national unification for the very survival and prosperity of the two Koreas.

The "buds" of Korea's unification are about to blossom. North Korea's strategies for communizing the South through the use of force began to change quietly in the early 1990s. Pyongyang accepted the idea of simultaneous membership for the two Koreas in the United Nations which it had so strenuously opposed over the last forty years; and similarly accepted the existence of two political entities on the peninsula.[4] Although it was not realized due to Kim Il Sung's death, the two Koreas even agreed to a summit meeting in 1994—the very first since 1945.

North Korea will not easily avoid the changes at this point. The guarantee of its security by the Soviet Union and China have been shaken to its foundations, and it has become nearly unavoidable for North Korea to reconcile its erstwhile relations

---

History and Strategies for National Unification (Na-eui Kil Na-eui Sasang: Saegaesa-eui Dae-jun-hwan kwa Minjok Tongil-eui Bang-ryak) (Seoul: Hangilsa, 1993) pp. 191-234.

[3]If the two Koreas continue the present state of confrontation and conflict, while all four major powers (the United States, China, Japan, and Russia) maintain relations with them, they will surely be the unwitting victims of an unending war of attrition in which the Korean nation will suffer the ultimate sacrifice. This obviously is the intangible cost of national division.

[4]The two Koreas recognized each other as legitimate political entities through the signing of the "Agreement on Reconciliation, Non-Aggression, and Exchanges and Cooperation between the South and the North" [The Basic Agreement] in December 1991.

of utter hostility with the United States as well. Economically, also, North Korea is faced with a serious crisis owing to the sudden and general collapse of its export market and the technology and capital sources in Eastern Europe as a result of the collapse of the Communist Bloc. The only way for North Korea to restore its critically battered economy would be through the opening of trade relations with the West and capital import from the outside.

In reality, North Korea seems to be pursuing the open door policy with some acumen. As seen in the establishment of Special Economic Zones in Najin and Sunbong in 1991, the enactment of the Foreign Investment Law in 1992, and in the Joint Venture Law of 1994, the open door policy is now becoming the focal point of North Korea's external economy strategy.

South Korea, too, has changed. To suppress the democratic and progressive political forces, the military governments in the past resorted to creating and maintaining heightened political tension through the falsified climate of security threats against vital national interests—the perpetual exaggeration and reproduction of fictitious alarm and vigilantism against security threats. As a legitimizing process, too often, they have deliberately provoked and promoted inter-Korean tension and conflict. However, at last with the advent of a civilian government, we can look forward to a new horizon in inter-Korean relations.

North Korea's nuclear issue, hitherto the origins of tension on the Korean Peninsula, was settled through the Geneva negotiations in October 1994, while the problems surrounding the lightwater reactors were resolved in June 1995 in Kuala Lumpur. This series of negotiated settlements has finally put a decisive end to the Cold War conflicts in Northeast Asia, and enabled hopeful future vistas on the possibility that North Korea can be expected to follow the general rules of the international society in Northeast Asia and eventually become a suitable member of that society.

To be sure, a longer period of time will be required before there is a fundamental solution to North Korea's nuclear issue. However, considering the basic interests of the two Koreas and their neighboring states and the general flow of world history, we can presume that the future development will not go against the tide of general tension reduction. The North Korean-United States agreement to open their respective liaison offices in Washington and Pyongyang, whose authorities extend to political and economic functions with the temporary exception of consular duties, duly give rise to the reasonable expectation that the liaison offices will eventually extend to normal diplomatic relations. These developments and their likely consequences reinforce the possibility of the visions of a rosier future all around. The regional extension of such track records thus far could conceivably extend to the diplomatic normalization between North Korea and the United States and North Korea and Japan; these twin developments would be sufficiently powerful incentives to draw North Korea out of the ideological conflict into a new arena of "normal competition." Based on this set of objective factors and reality, we can dare to expect the gradual improvement of inter-Korean relations.

As the circumstances and environment change over and around the Korean Peninsula—from division and confrontation to unification and peace—what would be the optimum means for Korea's unification? Logically, it will have to be one of peaceful process that also promises national prosperity; and we believe that "Kim Dae-jung's Unification Plan (The Three-Stage" Formula) offers such a vision and possibility. Our purpose in this chapter is to present exactly how the economic exchanges and cooperation ought to proceed under the Confederation—the first stage of Kim Dae-jung's three-stage unification.

"Economic exchange," defined for our purpose in this chapter, means the simple movement of goods and services; "economic cooperation" means not only the movement of capital and labor but also (the joint) investment that accompanies the movement of goods.[5] As mentioned earlier, the two Koreas have already agreed "[to] promote an integrated and balanced development of the national economy, the welfare of the entire people, and the two sides shall engage in economic exchanges and cooperation, including the joint development of resources, the trade of goods as domestic commerce and joint ventures." [Article 15 of the Basic Agreement] We shall present here our considered plans for the desirable direction of inter-Korean exchanges and cooperation under the Confederation as well as the methods of implementation—all designed to establish the national economic community and its healthy development.

Our methodology shall transcend the traditional declaratory and self-assertive mode and shall be based on a more neutral and impartial stance, founded upon a realistic understanding of the factors involved, and hopefully present highly feasible guidelines for the solution of this problem. To this end, we shall comprehensively re-examine the history of the past economic exchanges and cooperation between the two Koreas; the structural idiosyncrasies of the two economies, their developmental

---

[5]As the exchange of goods between the two Koreas is an internal exchange between our own people, the two Koreas agreed during the drafting of the Basic Agreement to use the expression, "the trade of goods as domestic commerce," rather than "economic trade" which could mean an international exchange between two different countries.

level and sophistication, and the effects of the exchanges and cooperation.

II. The Processes of Economic Divergence between the Two Koreas and the Realities of Exchanges and Cooperation Today

The purpose of this chapter, as mentioned earlier, is to present specific plans for facilitating and expanding inter-Korean economic exchanges and cooperation for the ultimate purpose of creating and developing a national economic community under the Confederation. In this section, we shall focus on the need for the economic exchanges and cooperation and their possibilities. We will, therefore, carefully examine the opening processes of exchanges and cooperation and their current situation in order to lay the groundwork for the next section, in which the discussion will be on the plans to expand the economic exchanges and cooperation between the two Koreas.

1. The Necessities for Economic Exchanges and Cooperation

Why are inter-Korean economic exchanges and cooperation necessary? The reasons for it are, first, the two Koreas will gain great economic benefits from the economic exchanges/cooperation. North Korea will gain as the industrial production base and as the supplier of natural resources and a labor pool; while South Korea will gain through the supply of its capital and technology. Specifically, the benefits that North Korea can derive from the economic exchanges/cooperation will be: capital, technology transfer, utilization of its labor force, development of its resources, and attraction of foreign capital by raising its credit worthiness. However, it must be pointed out that the inter-Korean economic exchanges/cooperation are not beneficial solely to North Korea as a kind of charity. South Korea will obviously benefit enormously from it as well. Today, under the conditions of increasingly cutthroat internal and external market competition, more than 10,000 South Korean small and medium businesses go bankrupt each year. On the other hand, North Korea has several enviable potential assets to offer: cheap industrial sites, a quality labor force, relatively rich natural resources, and most of all, common linguistic and cultural identity. Accordingly, South Korean investment in North Korea will bring life back to its declining industries by greatly extending the life cycles to its increasingly less competitive products; facilitate joint South and North Korean economic advances to the northern hemispheric markets of Siberia, Central Asia, etc.; and greatly relieve the problems of the supply and demand of capital.

Second, to raise the level of the North Korean economy through economic exchanges/cooperation is the best possible means available to reduce the ultimate cost of national unification. In this regard, German unification offers us many valuable lessons. If unification were to occur with the current enormous economic gap between the two Koreas, even if that were to occur gradually, it would create a host of extremely difficult economic and social problems for us all—such as massive unemployment, social unrest, and the imbalance in industrial structure and infrastructure. Enormous resources and time would have to be spent to resolve these explosive problems. As the world turns more and more to economic regionalism, and there is increasing competition in the Northeast Asia to attract foreign investment, Korea's expected downturn in economic growth after the unification is the kind of problem that would seriously impede our efforts to provide the enormous expenses necessary to finance the national unification. Accordingly, the optimal ways to limit and/or to reduce the cost is to invigorate the inter-Korean economic exchanges/cooperation so as to change and improve the North Korean economy both quantitatively and qualitatively.

Some would, however, raise the possibility that the North Koreans could exploit the fruits of economic exchanges and cooperation to preserve and prolong their existing system, thus ironically pushing back further the prospect of unification. In the short run, one cannot entirely rule out such a possibility. But what we should not overlook is the fact that North Korea will evolve through acceptance of the open door policy, the market economy and a form of democracy—albeit very gradually per-haps—if for no other reason than mere survival now that the entire Socialist Bloc has collapsed. Such a development, inevitable for North Korea in the long run, could indirectly result in facili-tating the unification process. In the long-term perspective, it is not too unreasonable to predict that the fruits of economic exchanges and cooperation which North Korea will surely gain can finance the cost of unification well in advance of the actual-ization. In this context, we believe our judgment that the eco-nomic exchanges/cooperation will in fact be an effective and realistic way to reduce the cost of unification, is borne out by the facts.

Third, the economic exchanges/cooperation will be the valuable means for the restoration of a common social identity between the two Koreas. For the past half century, South and North Korea have led wholly different lives under capitalism and socialism. Hence, the process of integration into one com-

mon society will be difficult to say the least. In order to minimize the undesirable side-effects which will surely surface during the unification process, the scope and depth of mutual
understanding must be enlarged in all areas of society between
the two countries—well in advance of unification. Viewed in
this context, it is expected that the economic exchanges/cooper-
ation will naturally accompany the human and cultural
exchanges as well as those of information/intelligence, and this
will in turn expedite and facilitate general exchanges and cooperation. As such the economic exchanges and cooperation will
have significance far above and beyond mere economics: it
should portend the integration of the whole society. That the
policies of general exchanges and cooperation between the two
Germanys under Chancellor Willy Brandt of the Federal Republic since the inception of his *Ostpolitik* in 1969, contributed
immeasurably to the buildup of mutual trust and confidence
between West and East Germany has much to suggest to us in
our approaches to Korea's national unity.

Fourth, economic exchanges and cooperation will smooth
the way for the eventual transition to a Federation by naturally
nudging North Korea towards a market economy and the democratic elements and environment. What we seek most under the
Confederation is to effect a fusion of inter-Korean economic systems into a market economy. We have learned from the collapse
of Eastern Europe in the 1980s that the obvious and inevitable
choice between a planned economy and a market economy is
the latter. Hence, it is desirable to form the general environment
through the introduction of the elements of a market economy
into North Korea during the Confederal Stage so that North
Korea would ultimately be able and willing to accept a market
economy. The establishment of a market economic system will

be an important pre-condition for democratic development, and for this reason the inter-Korean economic exchanges and cooperation are matters of the highest political significance.

Fifth, inter-Korean economic exchanges and cooperation will facilitate and expedite reconciliation between the two Koreas and will consolidate the foundation for national unity. Once economic exchanges and cooperation begin, they will be unstoppable. In fact, although the South Korean government tried to control and limit inter-Korean economic cooperation over the issue of North Korea's nuclear weapons project, it eventually had to abandon its efforts because it realized that it could not scotch the robust business interest in investment. On the other hand, once North Korea experiences the undeniable benefits of economic exchanges/cooperation, its general attitude can be expected to undergo substantial change. It is clear and evident to us that the actualization and vitalization of the inter-Korean economic exchanges/cooperation will lay a veritable highway towards national unification.

2. The Processes of Economic Divergence and the Possibilities of Economic Exchanges/Cooperation between the Two Koreas

If the inter-Korean economic exchanges/cooperation are so essential to the general interest and prosperity of the entire Korean nation, then one could ask if they are in fact feasible. In this section, we shall look for the possibility of mutual complementarity between the two different economic systems by re-examining the history of the evolution of heterogeneity between the economic structures of the two Koreas; and attempt a comparative analysis of the respective economic development.

Because of geographic factors and the Japanese policy of

imperial expansion and aggression against the Asian continent, light industry and agriculture were the principal economies in the South while heavy industry and mining dominated the Northern economy. Comparing the industrial production in southern and northern Korea prior to the National Liberation in 1945, the [Chart 4-1] below shows that chemical and metal industries formed the backbone of the northern economy, while light industries such as textile and food processing predominated in the south.

As for the distribution of the mineral resources at the time of the Liberation in 1945, 90% of the metal ores, 87% of anthracite coal, and 98% of bituminous coal were concentrated in North

[Chart 4-1] Comparison of Industrial Production in
South and North Korea in 1940.

(Currency Unit: ¥100, %)

	South Korea		North Korea	
	Total Production	Ratio	Total Production	Ratio
Heavy Industry	138	20	549	80
Chemical Industry	91	18	411	82
Metal Industry	14	10	123	90
Machine Industry	33	69	15	31
Light Industry	171	85	30	15
Textile Industry	214	65	115	35
Food Industry	177	65	96	35
Others	177	65	96	35

Pre-Liberation statistics; numbers in this chart were adjusted by the division along the 38th parallel line.

Source: Board of National Unification, Republic of Korea, *Comparison of Two Koreas' Economic Power by Segments, and Long-Range Estimate* (Seoul: 1972), p. 54.

Korea. Utilizing rich water resources, North Korea produced 1,078,000 kw of electricity, 92% of the total Korean output of electricity.[6] On the other hand, the arable land for rice production in the south was about three times that of the northern region.

With the division, capitalism entered South Korea, while socialism overtook North Korea. Soon thereafter, the economic structures of the two Koreas' began to diverge significantly as they pursued mutually opposite development strategies. The seeds of serious heterogeneity began to take root in both halves of the peninsula. The basic principles of economic management in the Socialist North were based on the national ownership of the means of production and on highly centralized planning. All economic activities, therefore, including production, distribution, and consumption were wholly and totally dependent on state planning and directives, a system that is a world apart from the capitalist market economy.

As shown in [Chart 4-2], North Korea was able to achieve rapid economic growth in the early phase of its political existence based on the socialist system of economy, self-reliant rejuvenation, and the Stalinist developmental strategy of heavy industry orientation. The North Korean style planned economy chalked up high results in transforming the post-colonial agrarian society into an industrial one and in overcoming economic contradictions born of the Japanese policy of military logistics industries and the war of national division. By the early 1960s, the North Korean economy was able to achieve a degree of self-reliance.

However, as the economic dimensions became more com-

---

[6]Yeon Ha-cheong, *North Korea's Economic Policy and Its Operation (Bukhan eui Kyungjae-jungchaek kwa Un-yong)* (Seoul: Korea Development Institute, 1986), p. 144.

*[Chart 4-2] Average Annual Growth Rate in Industrial Output
in North Korea and Eastern Europe*

(Unit: in percentage)

	1951-1955	1956-1960	1961-1964
Bulgaria	8.4	12.7	8.2
Czechoslovakia	4.6	9.1	1.9
East Germany	11.2	7.2	4.1
Hungary	9.0	5.5	8.2
Poland	9.6	8.1	7.3
North Korea	6.6 (1949-56)	36.0 (1956-59)	7.8 (1960-63)

Source: Maurice Ernst, "Postwar Economic Growth in Eastern Europe (A Com-
parison with Western Europe), " in *New Directions in the Soviet Economy*,
Part IV (Washington, D. C.: Joint Economic Committee, Congress of the
United States, 1966), pp. 878-916. Cited from Lee Bong-seog, "The Gross
National Income and Industrial Growth during the Period of North
Korean Economic Construction," in Hwang Eui-gak, *et al.*, *The Political
Economy of North Korea's* Socialism Building (Seoul: The Kyungnam
University Press, 1993), p. 202

plex and as the horizontal relations among the industries
became increasingly more important; and due to the built-in
contradictions of obsessive quantitative growth, the North Korean economy began to show signs of inefficiency and decreasing
utility in its economic policies.

Moreover, several major external developments and internal South Korean upheavals radicalized North Korea's policies:
the flexing of United States military power through active intervention in Vietnam and the Cuban Missile Crisis; the Sino-Soviet conflict and the discontinuation of Soviet assistance to North
Korea; and the political upheavals in South Korea such as the
April Revolution in 1960 (against President Syngman Rhee) and

the May military coup in 1961 (by General Park Chung-hee) and other developments. In the wake of these events, in September 1961, North Korea decided on an aggressive policy line against the South—the policy line of the "National Liberation Democratic Revolution"—and commenced the major political campaign for "Four Military Lines" and the policies for the "Consolidation of Three Revolutionary Capabilities." The adoption of these policies for military buildup inevitably drew the funds away from economic sectors, and became an added reason for the serious stagnation of the North Korean economy.

Totally subservient to the personality cult of Kim Il Sung and based on the misguided strategy of mass mobilization through political and ideological agitation,[7] North Korean economic management style supplanted economic rationale for political goals; and by stifling the creativity of its society, it distorted and undermined the economy.[8]

To solve the dilemma, beginning in the mid-seventies, North Korea tried to open trade and economic cooperation with the West. Due to the political and economic rigidity of its system, and the low competitiveness of its products, however, it failed to achieve any results. Compounding the crisis, North Korea was completely cut off from its technology sources and export market after the collapse of Communism in Eastern Europe. Faced with both external and internal crisis, the North Korean economy showed a consistent trend of minus growth in

---

[7]For the discussion of this issue, see, *inter alia*, Charles E. Lindblom, Politics and Markets: The World's Political-Economic Systems (New York: Basic Books, 1977), passim. Cited from Lee Jong-seog, "The Substance and Limitation of 'Socialism Our Style'," in Hwang Eui-gak, *et al., Stagnation of North Korea's Socialist Economy and Response* (Seoul: Kyungnam University Press, 1995), pp. 206-208.

[8]Lee Jong-seog, *ibid.*

the 1990s, and as of 1993, its foreign indebtedness is estimated to be US $10.32 billion.[9]

Today, in capital, technology, light industries and trade, North Korea's backwardness is pronounced. However, following the general nature of the socialist system, North Korea's educational level is generally high, its labor force is well trained and low cost,[10] and it has relatively rich and cheap mineral resources.

On the other hand, the capitalist South embarked on a policy of building up industries to replace imports. However, due to the saturation of the domestic market and decline of profitability, it switched to a new developmental strategy of export driven industrialization based on cheap labor in the mid-1960s. Copying from the Japanese model of economic growth, concentrated investment was made in selected businesses to form strategic industries. Such strategies, although they contributed to rapid industrialization, ultimately resulted in serious long-term damage through the tight control of labor, stunted growth of democracy, and the widening income gap between classes, professions, and regions.

After years of rapid growth, South Korea finally undertook the task of reorganizing its industrial structure in the 1980s, and in the process had to face the thorny problems of declining industries. The competitive edge of the labor-intensive export industries had suddenly disappeared owing to the increases in

---

[9]Bank of Korea, *Comparison of Key Economic Indicators in South and North Korea in 1993* (Seoul: Bank of Korea, June 1994), p. 7.

[10]Although graded differently depending on job categories and experience, the average monthly wage of the North Korean worker is said to be around US $150. Cf. Chun Hong-taek, "The Investment Environment in North Korea and Strategies for Investment in North Korea," *Korean Development Studies* (Hankuk Gaebal Yunku) (Seoul: Korea Development Institute, 1993), p. 105.

wages and land prices, and failure and/or slow development of indigenous technology. Faced with the problem of aging product-life cycle[11] in some areas of its declining industries, South Korea has been expanding and quickening the pace of transfer of the labor intensive production facilities and low technologies overseas.

As shown above, under the heavy industry oriented economic system, North Korea enjoys relative high ground in terms of its labor force and mineral ores, and other natural resources, including land; and South Korea enjoys the upper hand in capital and technology while it suffers a relative handicap in light industries and trade. Be that as it may, South and North Korea have economic structures which can be mutually complementary. If the economic exchanges and cooperation can be handled skillfully and wisely, it is clear that they could have a greatly enhancing synergic effect to both. Especially their geographic propinquity, linguistic-cultural homogeneity, high educational standard, and work ethics are all powerful incentives for investment in North Korea, unavailable elsewhere in the world.

3. The Economic Exchanges Today

Immediately after the National Liberation in 1945, there existed, although it was severely limited, inter-Korean economic exchanges in goods and human movement under the format

---

[11]The "aging or maturing" of the product-life cycle occurs when the profit margin from a line of products based on a certain technology is wiped out and/or drastically reduced when a specific technology spreads widely to other users. In such a case, the use of that technology no longer guarantees the kind of windfall profits that were once available when the technology in question was the monopoly of its originator.

popularly known then as "the 38th parallel secret trade" and "US Military Government trade." These exchanges were stopped after the armistice, but resumed again in October 1988—following South Korea's "Special Declaration on National Self-Existence, Unification, and Prosperity" of July 7, 1988 and the legal provision for the inter-Korean exchanges through the October "Directives on inter-Korean Exchanges of Goods." In August 1990, the "Law of Inter-Korean Exchanges and Cooperation" was passed, and to support this legislation, the "Law for Inter-Korean Cooperation Fund" was enacted, and the inter-Korean "Basic Agreement" went into effect in 1992, thus beginning the exchanges between the two Koreas.

[Chart 4-3] The Yearly Records of South Korean
Export & Import with North Korea

(Unit: US $1,000, based on Customs clearance)

| Year | Import (from N. Korea) | | Export (to N. Korea) | | Total |
	No. of Items	Value	No. of Items	Value	Value
1989	24	18,655	1	69	18,724
1990	21	12,278	3	1,187	13,465
1991	50	105,722	17	5,547	111,269
1992	81	162,863	24	10,563	173,426
1993	77	178,166	21	8,425	186,591
1994	83	176,298	42	18,248	194,546
Total	157	653,982	74	44,039	698,021
Jan. 1995	23	10,787	13	8,081	18,868
Feb. 1995	30	19,477	19	2,417	21,894
Total	37	30,264	24	10,498	40,762
Grand Total		684,246		54,537	738,783

Source: Board of National Unification, Republic of Korea (1995)

Aided by these systemic steps, the volume of exchanges increased consistently through 1994 as shown in [Chart 4-3], and particularly in 1990-1991 with an explosive 730 percent increase in trade volume. Below [Chart 4-4 and 4-5] show that in these exchanges, South Korea imported mainly primary industrial goods and intermediate materials such as iron and steel, iron ores, farm and fishery products, and other minerals; while the exports to North Korea were mostly textiles and textile fibers

[Chart 4-4] The Yearly Record of South Korean Imports from
North Korea

(Unit: US $1,000, based on Customs clearance)

Year	Farm/Forestry Products		Fishery Products		Minerals		Iron/Metals	
	Value	Ratio	Value	Ratio	Value	Ratio	Value	Ratio
1989	414	2.2	174	0.9	1,094	5.9	15,073	80.8
1990	4,391	40.1	392	3.2	1,599	13.0	4,529	36.9
1991	4,600	4.3	3,053	2.9	6,619	6.3	86,046	81.4
1992	10,435	6.4	5,085	3.1	14,579	8.9	125,416	77.0
1993	9,674	5.4	878	0.5	1,371	0.8	154,263	86.6
1994	9,916	5.6	2,723	1.6	1,448	0.8	136,340	77.3

Year	Textile		Chemicals		Others		Total	
	Value	Ratio	Value	Ratio	Value	Ratio	Value	Ratio
1989	1,311	7.0	–	–	589	3.2	18,655	100
1990	204	1.7	–	–	623	5.1	12,278	100
1991	1,588	1.5	1,672	1.6	2,144	2.0	105,722	100
1992	3,683	2.3	1,248	0.8	2,417	1.5	162,863	100
1993	8,945	5.0	663	0.4	2,372	1.3	178,166	100
1994	18,500	10.5	954	0.6	4,272	2.4	174,153	100

Source: Board of National Unification, Republic of Korea (1995).

[Chart 4-5] The Yearly Record of South Korean Exports
to North Korea

(Unit: US $1,000, based on Customs clearance)

Year	Farm/Fishery Products		Textiles		Electric/Electronic Products		Iron/Metals	
	Value	Ratio	Value	Ratio	Value	Ratio	Value	Ratio
1989	–	–	69	–	–	–	–	–
1990	–	–	–	–	–	–	1,094	92.2
1991	1,607	29.0	25	0.5	447	8.1	–	–
1992	64	0.6	496	4.7	–	–	22	0.2
1993	6	0.1	6,274	74.5	463	5.5	–	–
1994	151	0.8	12,856	70.5	–	–	38	0.2

Year	Chemicals		Steel Product		Others		Total	
	Value	Ratio	Value	Ratio	Value	Ratio	Value	Ratio
1989	–	–	–	–	–	–	69	100
1990	83	7.0	–	–	10	0.8	1,187	100
1991	3,468	62.5	–	–	–	–	5,547	100
1992	7,932	75.1	1,957	18.5	–	0.9	10,499	100
1993	1,096	13.0	34	0.5	552	6.6	8,425	100
1994	1,349	7.4	243	1.3	3.610	19.8	18,247	100

Source: Board of National Unification, Republic of Korea (1995).

and chemical products. What is noteworthy here is that most of the exports to the North were textiles and textile-related products. The reason for this is that there was a steady increase in supplies of production materials for consigned processing in North Korea. Today, although the amount of processing on commission in North Korea is still around 12 percent of the total manufacturing industries, in 1994, the monetary value of such processing amounted to about US $30 million, a remarkable increase of 257 percent over the previous year.

But the increase in economic exchanges has not met expectations since the visit to Nampo Industrial Park by a South Korean Delegation in October 1992. The reasons for the stagnant exchanges between the two Koreas are as follows: first, the economic exchanges and cooperation to date has been directly affected by the negative impact of political frictions between the two Koreas including that of the North Korean nuclear weapons project. Second, fearing the detrimental effect on their system that the exchanges and cooperation could cause, North Korea has been extremely hesitant and defensive about the general exchanges and cooperation. Third, there was an imbalance of trade against the North because it had very limited export capabilities. Fourth, indirect trade has several major problems: the difficulty in verifying the quality of goods being exchanged, the complexity of procedures, and the long time lag between the completion of exchanges.

That the inter-Korean economic exchanges are still on the upswing despite these various obstacles is a very encouraging sign. Undoubtedly, this demonstrates, albeit indirectly, that the economic exchanges and cooperation are an important bridgehead in untangling the knotty relations between the two Koreas.

III. The Basic Principles of Economic Exchanges/ Cooperation Under the Confederation

The economic exchanges and cooperation under the South-North Confederation will not only be conducive to political confidence-building between the two Koreas, but also play a vital role in realizing all other forms of exchanges and cooperation. The inter-Korean economic exchanges and cooperation, therefore, ought to be attempted under firm and consistent principles, and carried out effectively, systematically, and deliberately adjusting fully and skillfully to internal and external factors that affect inter-Korean relations. We shall now look at the systemic background of the Confederation under which the economic exchanges/cooperation will take place and discuss the basic principles and specific plans for economic exchanges and cooperation.

1. Economic Exchanges/Cooperation and the Significance of the Confederation

The "Three-Stage Unification" Formula, seeking gradual and peaceful unification, proposes the formation of a Confederation as a deliberate mechanism to materialize "dialogue and cooperation" between the two Koreas. Unlike the South Korean government proposal, we do not consider the intensified form of reconciliation and cooperation as the necessary pre-condition for the Confederation. A minimum political trust and confidence such as through the settlement of North Korea's nuclear weapons program can in fact be enough for the establishment of a Confederation, which, once established, can be the vehicle for active pursuit of inter-Korean reconciliation and cooperation. Therefore, the Confederation, envisioned under our unification formula, is *not the result* of prior exchanges and cooperation, but a clearcut consequence of the "political decisions" [of the two Korean political authorities] and the "consensual agreement" [between the two Koreas]; and shall be, once established, the facilitator/expediter of inter-Korean reconciliation and cooperation.

As the first stage of our unification plan, the South-North

Confederation, as a state-to-state confederation, signifies a fusion of two independent sovereign states into one confederation. First, under the Confederation, the two existing republics in both Koreas will continue with their respective authorities as independent states in the areas of foreign relations, defense, and internal affairs.

Two, the Confederal Summit Conference, composed of the two leaders of the South and the North, will discuss and decide the general policy directions based on the three major policy guidelines of Peaceful Coexistence, Peaceful Exchange, and Peaceful Unification. Functioning as the legislature, the Confederal Council will decide on the specific measures to actualize the guidelines through "listening to the views and opinions of the citizens of both republics" and discussions in the Council, then refer the decisions to the Summit Conference.

The decisions reached at the Summit Conference will in turn be referred to the Ministerial Council for conversion to policy decisions, while the Confederal Committees, consisting of the officials of the two governments, decide on the specific measures for final implementation.

Third, the Confederation is expected to last approximately a decade or so until the time for the Federation, the second stage of the unification process, is reached. Once under the Confederation, we can expect gradual changes in the North Korean system—the changes that would become inevitable through North Korea's diplomatic-economic-cultural contacts and exchanges with South Korea and the Western world. The ultimate outcome of these exchanges will gradually allow a market economy to take root in North Korea. Even political freedoms will go forward, resulting someday in a multi-party system and free elections. The prospect of changes such as these is not the mere fantasy of an idle dreamer, but is a realistic picture of the future, brought on by the indisputable march of economic factors unleashing inevitable historical changes. While such changes are taking place in North Korea, there will also be a great transformation in the South as well: the firm establishment of national self-reliance and self-determination and the realization of social justice. With these changes, the two Koreas will finally be in a position to make the next transition to a Federation.

Under the Federation, composed of two "autonomous regional governments," foreign relations, national defense, and important internal affairs related to the operation of the Federation will fall under the jurisdiction of the Federal Government. The two republics that will have existed as independent states under the Confederation will be transformed into two autonomous regional governments.

Thus far, we have discussed and examined the schematic locus of the Confederation within the large framework of the "Three-State Unification" Formula. What, then, would be the significance of the Confederation for the inter-Korean economic exchanges and cooperation?

The economic exchanges and cooperation under the Confederation will have quite a different meaning from the exchanges and cooperation that existed prior to this period. The main difference would be from the fact that the Confederation, representing all of Korea, will be a systemic mechanism for the eventual transition to a Federation. Accordingly, the inter-Korean economic exchanges and cooperation in the early phases might be implemented in the respective interests of the two Koreas. Gradually, however, as time goes by, the exchanges and cooperation will be more concerted and systematic, under the growing impact of the Confederal organizations, and their operations and recommendations.

Besides, the Confederation will provide favorable conditions and a rationale to accept inter-Korean trade as "domestic commerce" between the Koreans themselves. Until now, inter-Korean trade has been conducted without customs duties and with quiet acquiescence on both sides. However, under the new economic order of the World Trade Organization, such customs duty free commerce will be in direct contravention of the "most-favored-nation" principle. To be sure, even under the Confederation, such a problem will exist as the two Koreas are considered to be sovereign and independent states. But if and when a new cooperative structure is formed through the confederation of two states, customs duty free commerce will have greater relative rationale.

In the final analysis, therefore, the inter-Korean economic exchanges and cooperation will have much greater dynamism than any time before under the institutional mechanism designed for greater harmony and cooperation between the two Koreas—namely, the Confederation. In the next section, we shall examine and discuss how the economic exchanges and cooperation should proceed as one of the means to achieve a common national economic community as well as ultimately the peaceful national unification.

2. The Basic Principles of Economic Exchanges/Cooperation

The economic exchanges and cooperation under the Confederation ought to be conducted under the following five principles.

First, the inter-Korean economic exchanges and cooperation ought to proceed with the purpose of forming common "national economic community" and its successful operation. To be specific, the goal set for the economic exchanges and cooperation under the Confederation is to reach the following targets: the abolition of mutual limitations on inter-Korean trade; the guarantee of the free movement of goods and capital; and the implementation of common trade policies with the outside world. The ultimate goal would be to achieve economic integration through the coordination of each other's economic policies on finance, currency, social welfare, and others. In that context, South Korea's economic exchanges and cooperation with the North should not be carried out selectively on a short-term basis and with myopic considerations of cost-effectiveness or chance opportunities, but rather with the long-term post-unification perspective of balanced national economic development and its continuing prosperity. It is here that the inter-Korean economic exchanges and cooperation are fundamentally different from that of Western companies, whose sole motive is the maximization of their profits. Nevertheless, the pursuit of the goal of the common national economic community is not an act that is necessarily "economically irrational." On the contrary, what is needed is to maximize the exchanges and cooperation in areas from which both Koreas could draw real benefits, while assuming the posture of making strategic investment for the future so that unified Korea could have high international competitiveness.

As a part of this operational principle, for example, it would not be advisable to transfer to North Korea only the declining industries. In accordance with the simple logic of the "international economic cycle," early in the economic exchanges between the two Koreas, it would be natural for South Korea's labor-intensive, export-driven industries to move into North Korea. Based on the "product-life cycle," the declining industries of the advanced economies could often play the role of a vital engine for early phase of industrialization in developing economies. Recognizing, especially, North Korea's present level of economic development and the trend of industrial reorganization in South Korea, the Northern transfer of the declining industries of South Korea would be a reasonable proposition.

However, it is imperative to note the possibility of foreign domination of dynamic industrial sectors in North Korea.[12] There are high possibilities that Japan and the United States would attempt to seize the structural center of North Korea's economy and monopolize its market by: 1) in Japan's case, provide considerable loans/credits and assistance in return for diplomatic normalization with North Korea; 2) while the United States may offer a huge capital investment. Headed by Germany, the European countries are also seriously considering capital investment in North Korea. We can include China, Russia, and even Taiwan among the interested states. We have no reason to be alarmed by their interest. On the contrary, we should welcome and encourage their interest. But, in response to the likelihood of the Western countries' entry into the North Korean economy, it would be advantageous for the two Koreas to heighten their economic cooperation and coordination in order to take the initiative and leadership for Korea's own future—a future under the principles of "by our people and for our people." It would be imperative that the South Korean government first draw up a broad blueprint for the economic development of a unified Korea for the sake of the independent growth of the national economy, followed by a carefully laid out strategy for economic cooperation

---

[12]The "dynamic industrial sectors" are the economic areas like electronics and tele-communications in which the technology development is very rapid with high added values.

with the North to effect further economic development and for industrial reorganization/rearrangement.

In the process of forming the common "national economic community" through the inter-Korean economic exchanges and cooperation, there are several tasks for North Korea as well. North Korea ought to depend on "domestic" national resources as China did during the early stage of the "special economic zone." Since the 1984 enactment of the Joint Venture Law until mid-1995, North Korea has legislated some thirty laws concerning the opening of the country to the outside world, demonstrating its will and intent for the open door policy. If North Korea is serious about the tangible results of all these preparations, it will have to offer favorable investment conditions for South Korean businesses, and take steps to actively seek their investment, thus making it clear that South Korean businesses can be confident of business relations with the North. Such confidence, once established, could be contagious to other potential Western investors. Without question, this will be the shortcut to North Korean access for Western investment in North Korea.

Second, the inter-Korean economic exchanges and cooperation will be based on the principle of the separation of economics and politics. Although there would be at least minimum political confidence between the two Koreas at the early phase of the Confederation, we can be certain that the hardened state of hostility and distrust built up and reconfirmed during the half century of division will not have been completely dissipated. Under the circumstances, it is evident that the Confederation itself would be the means to build up the necessary trust and confidence between the two. No one can predict when and how serious political conflict would reoccur, given the conditions of political confidence in the duration of the Confederation. What is important, however, is that we should not let unexpected political events sour the economic exchanges and cooperation. The economic exchanges and cooperation must be continuos and consistent based solely on the economic principle. Needless to say, our advocacy of the separation of economics and politics does not at all mean that there are no inter-relations between the two. We believe in the truism that improved economic relations could very well be an effective means to overcome the political obstacles. In that context, the principle of the separation of economics and politics is simply a utilitarian statement meaning that economics must not be made subservient to politics.

The case of China and Taiwan tells us how important the principle of economic-political separation is in economic exchanges and cooperation. Since 1988, around the time of Lee Teng-hui's assumption of the presidency, Taiwan began to change its previous hardline policy—the "Policy of 3 Nos: No negotiation; No Contact; and No Compromise—and began to take a more realistic line of policy toward the mainland. This allowed active participation of Taiwan's private businesses in China. Under this new policy, by 1994, some 10,000 Taiwanese businesses entered the mainland market with the total investment in excess of US $12 billion. That both sides have reaped economic benefits from it and that the growing economic ties have contributed considerably to the tension reduction is a widely recognized fact.[13]

---

[13]Since the end of 1987, Taiwan allowed the visitation from the mainland relatives to Taiwan's families. Moreover, Taiwan has decided recently to permit its civil servants, except the cabinet ministers and deputy ministers, to travel to China. Taiwan has also opened its doors to high ranking Chinese government officials—above the rank of ministries' bureau directors and their deputies. Per *Joong-ang Ilbo,* June 1, 1995.

Third, we ought to allow special assistance to medium and small businesses in the process of inter-Korean economic exchanges and cooperation. As mentioned earlier, the world has entered a new era of heated economic competition (or warfare, to be more precise), in which the winners and losers will emerge clearly.[14] The key to victory in that competition will be the "flexibility of the economic structure."[15] In this context, the growth and development of medium/small businesses that can flexibly adapt to major changes and trends—such as diversification of goods, shortening of the product-life cycle, and small quantity production of a variety of goods—will be the great source of national economic power.

If inter-Korean economic exchanges and cooperation take place mainly with the Big Businesses, the small and medium companies will suffer great damage. Most of the imports from North Korea thus far were products that South Korea's small/medium businesses already make domestically. The North Korean imports, therefore, are in direct competition with South Korea's small and medium firms. Such a phenomenon will become even more serious when the economic exchanges and

---

[14] The economist, Lester Thurow, predicted that the world is gradually transcending the "niche competition" for a "head to head competition." Thurow, *Head to Head: The Coming Economic Battle Among Japan, Europe, and America* (New York: William Morrow and Co., 1992)

[15] According to Ralph Hawtrey, "the ultimate basis of the economic strength... is the flexibility and mobility of its economy." According to Robert Gilpin, "In the long term, economic power is neither the possession of particular monopolies and/or technologies nor economic self-sufficiency, but rather the capacity of the economy to transform itself and to respond to changes in the global economic environment, such as shifts in comparative advantage or price changes." Hawtrey, *Economic Aspects of Sovereignty* (London: Longmans, 1952), *passim; Gilpin, The Political Economy of International Relations* (Princeton, N.J.: Princeton University Press, 1987), p. 77.

cooperation with North Korea begin in earnest. For this reason, we ought to make certain that small and medium businesses become key participants in the inter-Korean economic exchanges and cooperation in the interest of solidifying Korea's national economic power.

Even from the North Korean perspective, it is important to bear in mind that it can reap real benefits only through active participation in the economic exchanges and cooperation by South Korea's small/medium businesses. What is most needed by North Korea today obviously is the consumer goods manufactured by light industries. Considering, too, the technology levels of North Korea, its cooperation with the small and medium businesses would suit it far better than with the big businesses.

Participation by the smaller businesses would also be needed if only to induce "gradual changes" in the Northern economy. Since, by nature, investment by big businesses will be mostly on a large scale and thus limited to one or two sectors, its economic effect would not benefit the lower economic levels in North Korea as much as through the smaller firms' investments.

In reality, however, for smaller businesses to enter the North Korean market, there would inevitably follow the problems of capital shortage and market survey capability. To alleviate these problems, and to make the access by the smaller businesses effective, it would be desirable to link the small and big businesses. The investment contemplated by the big businesses in North Korea is on a short-term basis and confined to labor-intensive "assembling" and "processing." If the smaller businesses participate in it through the supply of the parts and raw materials, needed in the assembly and processing of the products as partners to big businesses, the difficulties and burdens in securing the necessary market and capital will be equitably divided and shared. In the medium- and long-term period, the market and the knowhow accumulated by the partnership, will be utilized by the smaller companies to expand their own independent operations in much broader and varied areas.

Fourth, to assist in the phased changes in North Korea, it is important for the South to regulate and modulate flexibly the speed and quantity of its exchanges and cooperation with the North. As the phased national unification is judged inescapable due to the history of our national division and the realities of inter-Korean relations, it is important for us to understand that the changes in North Korea will not occur overnight and certainly not in a way to change its own basic system. What South Korea can do is help to provide the conditions so that North Korea will be able to open up if it so desires, but nothing more. South cannot do the opening by itself for North Korea. If for some reason the North fears the economic exchanges and cooperation, North Korea's open doors will not be possible. Excessive expectations and impatient demands for very large scale economic exchanges and cooperation on the part of South Korea will actually discourage the Northern decision for the open doors.

Fifth, inter-Korean economic exchanges, cooperation, and economic development ought to be "environment" friendly. To be sure, the deepening inter-Korean economic exchanges and cooperation will expedite the economic development of Korea, particularly in the North, but will inevitably accompany environmental damage and pollution. In general, environmental problems occur as the result of economic growth; the truth is that the former in turn will limit the latter in a vicious cycle. Being directly related to the very survival of human race, the environmental problem is emerging as an important international political-economic issue for the future. Today, the reality of environmental pollution in and around the Korean Peninsula is already very serious, and the situation is deteriorating rapidly. Accordingly, the inter-Korean economic exchanges and cooperation must be pursued with the prudent strategy of harmony and balance between economic development and the environment.

We have thus far discussed the principles under which the inter-Korean economic exchanges and cooperation ought to be conducted. For the systematic and logical implementation of the economic exchanges and cooperation, the long- and short-term plans by periods must first be established before their implementation takes place accordingly during the entire phase of the Confederation.

Here, we shall look into the feasible strategies and plans for each period under the larger framework of the early and the later stage of the Confederation. As shown in [Chart 4-6], in the early phase, the indirect trade must be changed to direct trade. Several institutional setups must precede such a transition. Also, it is important and necessary to get international recognition of the domestic nature of the inter-Korean trade. What can be expected in the early phase of the Confederation is that the economic exchanges and cooperation will take shape without involving a huge capital investment—for instance, the processing on consignment, investment in the "free economic trade zone," joint development of tourist areas, agricultural cooperation, cooperation in some energy field, joint ventures in some third countries, urgently needed infrastructure, environmental cooperation, and others.

Investment in North Korea's infrastructure must be carried out and prioritized, in terms of importance and through stages. For instance, the investment in simple infrastructure projects

*[Chart 4-6] The Economic Exchanges/Cooperation Plans for
Different Periods of the Confederation*

	Plans for Major Economic Exchanges and Cooperation
Early Phase	transition to direct trade; domestic national exchanges; processing on consignment; investment in "free economic trade zone"; joint development of tourist areas; agricultural cooperation; energy cooperation in some areas; joint ventures in third countries; investment in urgent infrastructure; and environmental cooperation.
Later Phase	large scale infrastructure investment; active energy cooperation; and joint development of natural resources in North Korea

such as the communications systems in the "free economic trade zone" is possible even in the very early stages of the Confederation, But a very large scale infrastructure investment could not only be a great burden to the Southern economy, but could even be shunned by the North for its effect on its society; thus, it would be more appropriate towards the very later stage of the Confederal period. Other large scale projects in the later stage of the Confederation would be the construction of electric power stations and other forms of cooperation in energy areas, and the joint development of natural resources. Such large scale projects must be done in full consideration of the industrial structures in both Koreas. For the supply of the needed capital, it would be necessary to invite foreign capital participation or loans and credits.

In the next section, we shall turn to the specific measures for the expansion of the economic exchanges and cooperation.

IV. Ways to Expand Economic Exchanges and Cooperation Between the Two Koreas

Specifically, how are we to establish the common national economic community under the five principles mentioned above? Let us now turn to the discussion of the ways in which the economic exchanges and cooperation can be expanded.

1. The Means to Expand Economic Exchanges

The economic exchanges that involve merely the exchange of goods between the two Koreas is quite different from those that require investments, and can be implemented with relative ease. The transition from indirect to direct trade and the conversion of the inter-Korean economic exchanges to domestic national commerce will be the key to the expansion of the exchanges between the two sides. Let us now examine the need for and the institutionalization of the necessary mechanism.

(1) Transition to Direct Trade

What would be the effect of the transition from indirect to direct trade? For one, in the case of indirect trade, there are certain difficulties: verification of the quality of goods in advance; the cumbersome procedures in transactions; and the high transaction costs including the protracted lag for the completion of export/import. For these reasons alone, the transition to direct trade will have the effect of greatly reducing the production cost of the involved traders by alleviating the above mentioned difficulties. Especially in a situation of direct trade, there will be increased opportunities for direct contact between the businessmen of the two Koreas, thus making it easier to identify the products for exchange as well as promoting mutual trust, confidence, and understanding between them.

To establish direct trade, direct sea routes must be opened between the two sides so that the ships of both Koreas can freely navigate reciprocally. In April 1994, a direct sea route was opened between Pusan in the South and Chungjin in the North under non-governmental auspices. Although it is nominally a direct inter-Korean sea route, there still is no regular service between the two ports. It is mainly used for transporting cargo from the Yunbyun area in Manchuria through Chungjin. Besides, no South Korean ships have been allowed into Chungjin at all. Under the present conditions of irregular sea routes and services, shipping is normally delayed whenever a ship is not loaded to capacity, inflicting financial loss to the cargo owners; and/or if the cost of shipping is higher than the actual expenses because of such problems, the difference must be paid by the cargo owners themselves. When direct trade is in place, businesses estimate that about one-third of the transportation cost, will be saved. As the previous agreement demands, the two Koreas must open the ports of Inchon, Pusan, and Pohang (on the Southern side); and Nampo, Wonsan, and Chungjin (in the North) to enable the operation of direct sea routes between the two.

As for the payment methods to be used for direct trade/exchanges, Section 8 of Article 1 of the "Protocol for Exchanges and Cooperation," signed and entered into force on September 17, 1992, provides that "In principle, payments for goods exchanged between [the two Koreas] shall be settled through an open account,[16] providing, however, that when necessary other

---

[16]By an agreement between the two countries, interest-free "Open

methods of settlement may be used by agreement between both sides." Because of the serious shortage of foreign exchange holdings, North Korea prefers barter trade. In fact, under the circumstances, it would be desirable in the early phase of the exchange to accept barter trade with North Korea, under which we could send South Korean products to the North and collect the required compensation from it promptly. Once both sides get used to the exchanges, we would then convert to the open account settlement. The merits of an "open account" system will be to eliminate the limitations of the barter trade which force a decision on what and how much to trade in a short span of time.

But even when the "open account" system is finally adopted, it will still require other measures to complement it for the short term—because it would be unrealistic to expect a balance of payment between the two Koreas for some time to come. Hence, it might become necessary for the South to effectuate special loans for North Korea—a sort of a "swing" account—to enable it to settle the accounts for the exchanges. This system, sometimes called the interest-free credit arrangement, determines the limit of the "swing" in the settlement account, thus allowing the non-cash settlement of the account if the surplus or deficit remain within that determined range. Such a system existed between the two Germanys and contributed to the brisk exchanges/trade between the two.

We ought to consider also long-term interest free loans to North Korea to cover their deficits arising from inter-Korean

---

Accounts" can be established in each other's central bank, and the accounts of exchanges will be settled not on individual cases each time they occur by drawing on foreign exchange, but settled at regular intervals by merely paying in cash or by exporting additional goods to eliminate the differences between imports and exports.

exchanges as well as institutionalizing a mechanism by which long-term loans can be provided to enable the North to purchase South Korean goods. Section 5 of Article 8 in the "South-North Cooperation Fund Law"[17] provides for "loans of funds necessary for inter-Korean exchanges and cooperation that will contribute to the restoration of national trust and confidence as well as the common national community; and assistance for projects designed to promote the inter-Korean exchanges and cooperation." Thus, under this provision, some of the necessary funds can be drawn from the Cooperation Fund.

As these systems, discussed thus far, merely provide incentives for the expansion of exchanges/trade, it is necessary to activate other mechanisms to eliminate in advance those elements of uncertainty and conflict that could impede the expansion of inter-Korean trade/exchanges. As North Korea is burdened by heavy foreign debts, and the high "country risk" in the case of international exchanges and trade due to rigidity and the bureaucratism of its Socialist trade practices, the lack of understanding of international customs and practices, there would inevitably be high possibilities of disputes when the exchanges and trade commence with South Korea.[18] To solve these problems through institutional means, we ought to establish realistic procedures and mechanisms to take care of problems that may arise from the inter-Korean economic exchanges under the

---

[17]This law was enacted in August 1990 to support the inter-Korean exchanges and cooperation, and as of June 30, 1994, the Fund has secured 116.1 billion Won.

[18]Cho Chung-kon, "The Settlement of Disputes in Inter-Korean Exchanges and Trade, and in Investment through the Mediation by International Trading Companies," in *Anthology of Articles Dealing with North Korea and Unification Issues II: The Inter-Korean Exchanges and Cooperation* (Seoul: National Board of Unification, 1993). p. 198.

charge of the "South-North Joint Economic Committee." The dispute resolution bodies can be organized following the international agreements on arbitration such as the "New York Agreement."[19]

(2) "Domestication" of Internal National Exchanges Between the Two Koreas

For the inter-Korean exchanges and trade to take place actively, the system of duty-free transactions must be in place. The difficulty, however, is that even if the two Koreas cooperate under the Confederation, since the two sides are considered to be independent and sovereign states by other nations, duty-free direct trade between the two Koreas will be in violation of the "most-favored-nation" principle under the World Trade Organization, raising the problem of according similar privileges to others as well. Nevertheless, based on the precedent of the recognition of the inter-German exchanges as internal German commerce,[20] the domestic/internal nature of the inter-Korean

---

[19]The "New York Agreement"—the "Convention on the Recognition and Enforcement of Foreign Arbitral Awards"—was adopted by the General Assembly of the United Nations in 1958. Refer to Cho Chung-kon, *ibid.*, p. 216.

[20]The intra-German character of the exchanges between the two Germanys was recognized and guaranteed through the agreements in Frankfurt in 1949, in Berlin in 1951, and in Rome in 1957. Under these recognitions and guarantees, the two Germanys were able to enter into the European Community market. The reason for West German success in justifying its exchanges with East Germany as internal German exchange/commerce was based on the international law of the "Potsdam Agreement." In the Potsdam Agreement, the victorious powers in the Second World War had agreed not only to treat Germany as "eine ungeteilte wirtschaftliche Einheit" (one economic entity), but had agreed to jointly manage "Deutschland als Ganzes" ("Germany as a Whole"). Eventually, the Federal Republic of Germany (West Germany) was able to establish a link, in its agreements with the Allied Powers, between the Potsdam Agree-

exchanges can also be recognized as justifiable. The two Koreas should persuade the concerned countries to accept this important precedent.

To establish the inter-Korean economic exchanges/trade as intra-national transactions, two indispensable conditions must be met. First, there must be the will and intention on the part of the two Koreas to define their exchanges as intra-national in character. Such intent and will on the part of both Koreas have already been clearly declared and confirmed in December 1991 in the "Basic Agreement" [Agreement on Reconciliation, Nonaggression and Exchanges and Cooperation between the South and the North]: in the Preamble itself, it is declared that "WHEREAS in keeping with the yearning of the entire people for the peaceful unification of the divided land... WHEREAS both recognize that their relations constitute a special provisional relationship geared to unification;..."; and re-confirmed specifically in Article 15 of Chapter 3 that "...both parties shall conduct economic exchanges and cooperation, including the joint development of resources, trade in goods *as a kind of domestic commerce* and joint investment in industrial projects." [Emphasis added]

Second, it is important to receive international recognition of that fact. So far, however, the inter-Korean exchanges have not been recognized as internal national commerce. However, in our view, the international agreements that consider the Korean Peninsula as "a unified political and economic entity" are not difficult to find. The Cairo, Yalta Conferences, and the Moscow Conference of the Foreign Ministers of the Big Three are the his-

---

ment and the "Binnenhandel" ("internalization of exchanges/trade") and the German options in national unification. Refer to *Wortlaut des Protokolls, in "Europäische Gemeinschaft"* Nr. 2/71, S.10.

torical examples of that international recognition. The two Koreas will have to base their common positions on this issue not only on the German precedent but also on the above-mentioned international agreements in the past.[21]

Some people may feel that the simultaneous entry of the two Koreas into the United Nations will be an obstacle to Korea's later efforts to win international recognition of the internal nature of the two Koreas' exchanges. But the two Germanys

---

[21]For example, during the Second World War, the Allied Powers agreed and declared in the Cairo Conference that "...The aforesaid three great powers, mindful of the enslavement of the people of Korea, are determined that in due course Korea shall become free and independent." There cannot be any argument that the independence of Korea signifies that the Korean Peninsula is a unified political and economic entity. In this context, the Cairo Declaration by the Three Allied Powers in December 1943 can and should be presented as the historical basis of international law under which the inter-Korean exchanges of goods can be recognized as "internal national commerce." Again in February 1945, the Allied Powers met in Yalta and agreed to establish an international trusteeship for all of the Korean Peninsula for a period of time. The division of Korea along the 38th Parallel was meant to be a temporary demarcation line, drawn to enable the United States and the Soviet Union to disarm the Japanese forces in Korea. Subsequently, the Allied foreign ministers met in Moscow in December 1945 to discuss the post-war problems, and to reconfirm their earlier agreement for the independence of Korea. The agreement of the three foreign ministers on Korea was: 1) the recognition of Korea as single political-economic unit by stating, "With a view to the re-establishment of Korea as an independent state..."; 2) "In order to assist the formation of a provisional Korean government and with a view to the preliminary elaboration of the appropriate measures, there shall be established a Joint Commission consisting of representatives of the United States command in southern Korea and the Soviet command in northern Korea... It shall be the task of the Joint Commission... to work out measures also for helping and assisting... the political, economic, and social progress of the Korean people, the development of democratic self-government and the establishment of the national independence of Korea." Unquestionably, these decisions once again indicate the Allied Powers' handling of the Korean Peninsula as "one political and economic entity."

after their simultaneous entry into the United Nations in 1973, continued with their exchanges without change, as internal national commerce. No special problem arises for the two Koreas as a result of the United Nations membership.

How should we approach the problem of winning international recognition for our desired position on the inter-Korean exchanges? One way would be to seek recognition from an international multilateral body. For example, we could try to insert a written provision in the World Trade Orgaanization to the effect that "the inter-Korean exchanges shall be considered internal national commerce." However, to win individual countries' support for our position, it is highly advisable that we implement the strategy of "domestic commerce" as flexibly and prudently as possible. Despite the numerous historical and international law bases that could justify our efforts to characterize the inter-Korean exchanges as internal national commerce/ trade, our unilateral insistence or declaration on it could make it difficult to effectively amplify and expand the cooperation of the concerned countries. For this reason, it would make greater sense for all concerned if we make our case by persuading others to acknowledge Korea's right to self-determination, the special strategic position of the Korean Peninsula in the post-Cold War international relations, and the political, military, and economic benefits to the neighboring states from the expected improvement of relations between the two Koreas—rather than merely relying on the arguments for justifying our case.

Second, another way to achieve the recognition in this case would be for the two Koreas to approach the third countries independently for bilateral agreements. For example, the agreements/treaties normalizing relations between North Korea and the United States, between North Korea and Japan could contain specific provisions recognizing the inter-Korean exchanges as internal matters. Although it would depend entirely on North Korean willingness and intention, we could still expect an optimistic outcome, considering the fact that such provisions would be beneficial to both Koreas, and that it would be entirely compatible to the underlying spirit and intent of the inter-Korean Confederation.

Also if and when the Armistice Agreement is replaced by a peace agreement under the Confederation, that would also be an appropriate time for it to happen as well. The two Koreas could include in the peace agreement two specific references: namely, "Ultimately, the two sides aim for the peaceful unification of Korea" as well as "the economic exchanges between the Koreas shall be considered internal national commerce and trade."

Lastly, we believe there is a way to skirt the complex international legal procedures on this issue. Specifically, we could start the precedent of internalizing the exchanges between the two Koreas in the economic exchanges surrounding the construction of the lightwater reactors in North Korea. When such precedents are established under the conditions that South Korea supplies most of the lightwater reactor construction funds, to get the acquiescence of others for such precedents would not be too difficult.

So far, we have examined the ways to expand the economic exchanges between the two Koreas. Now we shall describe the specific means for their expansion.

2. The Means to Expand Economic Cooperation

To rehabilitate the North Korean economy and to actually produce real benefits for both Koreas, we ought to expand inter-Korean investment cooperation. As these investments are accompanied by more expansive levels of economic relations compared to those of exchanges, it must be pursued systematically and consistently if we are to achieve the intended results efficiently and effectively. For instance, the project examples for economic cooperation could include: consignment processing, investment in the "free economic trade zones," joint development of tourist areas, agricultural cooperation, cooperation in an energy field, joint ventures in some third countries, urgently needed infrastructure investment, environmental cooperation, and others. But before such projects actually begin, we ought to consider the important matters of providing the necessary institutional framework for expanding economic cooperation between the two Koreas.

(1) The Tasks of Institutionalization for Economic Cooperation

To actualize the investment in North Korea, an improved institutional set up is vital. To begin with, legislative support and/or inter-Korean agreements are necessary for the increased investment and its protection, mainly because South Korean business investment in the North will inevitably carry some risks even in North Korea does not limit the investment. For this reason, the inter-Korean "Confederal Economic Committee" will have to make arrangements for the expanded investment and its guarantee and establish the administrative procedures to prevent double taxation.[22] The Confederal Economic Committee

---

[22]Although North Korea has completely abolished all taxation at least pro forma under the pretext of achieving a complete Socialist System (Science Encyclopedia Publishing *Company, History of the Chosun War [Chosun Junsa]*, Pyongyang, 1981-1982, p. 389.

shall also deal with the issues of worker employment, repatriation of investment returns, and other related problems.

We must also provide for industrial standardization in both Koreas. At present, North Korean industrial standards are based on Russian and old Communist Bloc countries of Eastern Europe, while South Korea's industrial standards are based on the International Standardization Organization (ISO) and/or on Japanese Industrial Standards (JIS). Unless we standardize the two Koreas' industrial facilities, once the southern investment begins in earnest in North Korea, it would be impossible to use each other's parts and facilities, and would bring serious problems in our economic cooperation. The standardization ought to take place not only in industry, but also in all measurements and in "symbol/marking method standards," uniform product testing standards, and others.[23]

The uniform standardization would become difficult to achieve if some third country's investment in North Korea's industrial facilities results in different standards. As such developments could result in added cost once the inter-Korean economic integration takes place, the task of uniform standardization is an urgent matter for us.

In that context, the institutionalization, as discussed above, could be even more important than the economic cooperation plans themselves. Only when the institutional framework is established for economic cooperation can the two Koreas effectively proceed with the actual plans of cooperation as shown in [Chart 4-6] above—such as the consignment processing, "free economic trade zones" investment, joint development of tourist

---

[23]KOTRA, *Facts about Investment in North Korea* (Seoul: KOTRA, 1993), p. 211.

areas, agricultural cooperation, cooperation in an energy field, joint ventures in third countries, investment in urgent infrastructure, and environmental cooperation.

(2) Consignment Processing

Consignment processing is a form of economic cooperation in which a firm A provides a firm B the production facilities, raw material, production cost, and other resources, necessary for production so that the latter can manufacture the actual products, which are in turn handed over to the former. Such consignment processing could be usefully employed in the early stages of the inter-Korean economic cooperation.

For North Korea, consignment processing will bring excellent benefits: assistance in all forms of manufacturing facilities and raw materials without ever having to put up its own capital, and ultimately a guaranteed market for its products. Besides, since North Korea will be the sole manager of the processing operation, potential threats to its own system will be minimal—unlike other unwelcome possibilities under an economic open doors policy.

Even from the South Korean perspective, consignment processing has several major benefits compared to simple exchange/trade. The products imported from North Korea via consignment processing will be of high quality and standardized; and by producing goods of an older "product life cycle," South Korea can also extend the utility of the manufacturing machinery and technology.

Naturally, even when the general economic exchange has been affected by the prevailing political conditions between the two Koreas, the trade through consignment processing has

[Chart 4-7] Yearly Record of Approved Consignment Processing
in North Korea

(Unit: US $1,000)

Year	Number Approved	Import	Export
1991	1	23	13
1992	10	556	413
1993	44	4,385	3,611
1994	109	16,598	11,966
Total	164	21,562	16,003

Source: Bureau of Exchange/Cooperation, Board of National Unification, Republic of Korea, *Status of Inter-Korean Exchange/Cooperation* [Monthly], No. 44, 1995

increased steadily as shown in [Chagrt 4-7] below. It also has its strength in that it provides South Korean businesses with opportunities to penetrate North Korea's hinterland, albeit indirectly.

Being superior to simple exchange/trade, consignment processing carries great significance in that it helps accumulate valuable collective experience in inter-Korean economic exchanges.

(3) Investment in "Free Economic Trade Zones" and the
Strategies for their Utilization

Other than the bilateral cooperation such as the consignment processing, let us now look at the possible benefits to both Koreas from multilateral economic cooperation such as the investment in free economic trade zones. The area with the most favorable conditions for free economic trade zones in Northeast Asia is undoubtedly the Korean Peninsula. Situated in the center of six countries in Northeast Asia, Korea occupies an area with most favorable conditions for communication and transportation. Entry into the world market structure by the Socialist countries in Northeast Asia would become easier through improvement in international investment and trade; and their economic development will undoubtedly contribute to prosperity and peace in the entire region. The 1991 United Nations Development Plan (UNDP) has designated the Tumen River development project a priority multilateral regional economic development in Northeast Asia.[24] Specific measures for the project have been discussed at several international conferences thus far.

The Tumen River development project—the very first Northeast Asian multilateral economic cooperation—under the management of the UNDP has two main long-term objectives. The first is to develop the area as one of the leading world market centers; and the second is to develop in the Tumen area a raw material processing and manufacturing center for the region. Once these two objectives are achieved, the Tumen area will emerge as the regional economic center for Northeast Asia.

To capitalize on the UNDP to the maximum, North Korea has expanded and reorganized its free economic trade zone, designated in 1991, to the new free trade zones of Najin/Sunbong in December 1993—an area of 746 km². As shown in [Chart 4-8], the North Korean plan for the Tumen River area calls for: building a new city with a long-term population of 750,000 to a million, thus providing the necessary manpower for the development project; a large scale expansion of the port facilities; expansion of the electric train service and construction of multiple

---

[24]Cf. Andrew Marton, Terry McGee and Donald G. Paterson, "Northeast Asian Economic Cooperation and The Tumen River Area Development Project," *Pacific Affairs*, Vol. 68, No. 1, Spring 1995, pp. 9-33.

[Chart 4-8] Development Phases of Najin/Sunbong Area

Phase	Projects	Projects
First Phase (1993-1995)	Role enhancement as the transit transportation base for international cargo and the creation of favorable investment environment through modernization of infrastructure such as the existing rail and road system, and port facilities	•Main rail/road system link with neighboring countries for a one-day transit transportation capability •Improvement and expansion of the existing road/rail/port facilities to increase the cargo handling capacities in the ports of Najin, Sunbong, and Chungjin to 20 million tons. •Building major urban center for concentrated investment in Najin area.
Second Phase (1996-2000)	Role as the center of exchanges in Northeast Asia	•Concentrated efforts to build up export center for manufactured industrial goods for export, based on the international transit materials, utilizing the infrastructure built up during the first phase. •Improvement of cargo handling port facilities: 50 million ton cargo handling capacity by Year 2000. •Buildup of large scale export-oriented economic zones for attracting large investment via specialized centers for industrialization. •Development of the area into an international center for tourism.
Third Phase (2001-2010)	Completion of ultramodern facilities suitable for 21st century center for international exchanges	•Cargo handling capacity: more than 100 million tons •Comprehensive functions in entrept trade, export industry, manufacturing business, financial service, tourism, etc. •High degree modernization and functionalization of facilities, industrial structure, and service suitable for the 21st century.

Source: KOTRA, *North Korea's Leading Economic Indicators 1993* (Seoul, 1993) p. 124

tracks; expansion of the existing road system and the building of a super highway system; and the construction of the necessary infrastructure including the expansion of the communication facilities.

As these projects require a massive capital infusion and technology, foreign participation is absolutely essential. However, because of North Korea's low credit rating and distrust of its policy continuity in economic opening, foreign capital participation has been slow thus far. Under the circumstances, if North Korea is serious about the Tumen project, it would be vital to successfully attract South Korean capital to allay the legitimate concerns of the potential foreign participants. The important lesson for North Korea in this regard is the case of the investment in China by the Taiwanese businesses at the very early stage of China's economic open doors, causing the Western countries to begin their own investment in China in earnest. For the success of its own economic opening, North Korea must first demonstrate its wisdom and skill to attract South Korean investment for its initial projects. As for South Korea, its serious economic participation in the North Korean development project will have great significance, for its rich experiences in foreign construction projects can be usefully applied in North Korea. Furthermore, its active participation in the North could considerably reduce the chances of foreign capital domination of the North Korean economy.

At present, North Korea pursues a strategy of attracting foreign investment primarily for the Najin/Sunbong Free Economic Trade Zone. Although it is expected that other North Korean regions will gradually open for outside participation, North Korean success in Najin/Sunbong area will ultimately be the key to the expedited opening of other North Korean regions. The success or failure of inter-Korean economic exchange/trade will depend on the outcome of the Tumen River project, in the final analysis.[25]

(4) Joint Development of Tourist Areas

The most desirable joint project that the two Koreas could pursue in the early stage of the Confederation is the development of tourist areas. The tourist industry is relatively pollution free, earns high foreign exchange, and contributes to the enhancement of national prestige. Once developed and established, the tourist industry will continue to generate outstanding returns. As an industry, tourism has a high cash turnover, and for cash poor North Korea it should have special attraction.

For the specific substance of cooperation, one could include the joint investigation and study of the actual tourist assets in North Korea and the possibility of their development; and the entire spectrum from actual development to their management once established. In the early phase of investment in the tourist industry, it will be necessary to establish separate special tourist zones to allow for the impact of foreign tourists on North Korean society. One specific candidate for a special zone would be the Kumkang Mountain region. As a tourist industry asset, Mount Kumkang's natural beauty is beyond dispute. Because of its natural geographic link with South Korea's Sorak Mountains, it has all the strengths to recommend it for inter-Korean cooperation for development. Once the development project is complete, a foreign tourist itinerary could traverse both Koreas, doubling the spillover effect of the influx of foreign tourists attracted

---

[25]Although it seems that North Korea might open additional ports in Nampo, Wonsan, and Shinuiju, the development of the Najin and Sunbong regions is Kim Il Sung's last will as well as Kim Jong Il's primary interest.

independently by both Koreas. For such an eventuality, an integral linkage can and should be made between Northern Kumkang and Southern Sorak for visa exemption for the combined Kumkang-Sorak Special Tourist Zone.

(5) Agricultural Cooperation

North Korea urgently needs agricultural cooperation which can be a great benefit in that it has almost no risk factors. It is an important area of cooperation and serious investment if for no other reason than the national security of food supplies for Korea after unification.

Today, North Korea suffers from a serious food shortage. We can only guess at the enormity of its food crisis by watching its appeals for assistance to UNESCO, Japan, and other countries. Although its major causes are related to natural factors such as its climate and topography, correctable areas include its agricultural methods, the shortage/lack of farm machines and tools, and crop damage due to insects.

First, by mindlessly borrowing the model of collective farms from Stalin's Soviet Union, North Korea has seriously stifled farmers' basic incentives for production. Other Socialist countries, having understood the serious problems of the collectivization "without human factors," had adopted the system of an indefinite lease of farm land and tools, and the contract farming system.[26] North Korea, however, continued to insist on the previous system by sticking and even strengthening the so-called "Juche Agriculture."[27]

---

[26]*Inter alia*, refer to Richard Evans, *Deng Xiaoping and the Making of Modern China* (New York: Viking, 1994) pp. 253ff.

[27]Chang Meng-yul, "Problems of North Korean Economy and Its Internal

Second, although North Korea has the Hungnam Fertilizer Manufacturing facilities with production capacity of more than one million tons a year and a total fertilizer production capacity of 3.5 million tons per annum, the actual utilization is around 40 percent of capacity, due to aging machinery, lack of raw materials, an energy shortage, and others.

Third, North Korea lacks the resources and technology to prevent the agricultural damage from blight and insects. Once North Korea sought South Korean cooperation and assistance in stemming the serious damage to rice crops from a particularly pernicious insect, the ["rice (black) weevil": "Byu-mulba-gumi" in Korean] highly destructive to rice crops in North Korea.

Some of the specific plans to address the agricultural problems through inter-Korean cooperation include: cooperation for the supply of fertilizers and other farm materials, joint preventive measures against blight and harmful insects, the development and exchange of agricultural technology, contract cultivation of grains similar to consignment processing in the manufacturing sector, soil testing for major grains, agricultural technology training for farmers, and others.

As for more fundamental solutions, we ought to look at such methods as the indefinite lease of farm land and tools/machines, and contract farming which can boost farmers' incentives for heightened production. South Korea should seek ways to assist North Korean agriculture in technology assistance and cooperation through the United Nations and other international bodies, while systematically expanding agricultural cooperation by

---

Structure: Internal Approaches," in Hwang Eui-gak, *et al.*, *The Stagnation of North Korea's Socialist Economy and Responses* (Seoul: Kyungnam University Press, 1995) p. 92.

establishing a specialized body for agricultural cooperation under the "South-North Confederal Economic Committee."

(6) Energy Cooperation

North Korea suffers from frequent power outages owing to a chronic energy shortage. This, in turn, causes work stoppages even in its basic industries and creates a serious impact throughout the economic sectors. Therefore, along with agriculture, North Korea needs urgent cooperation from the South in the energy area. In fact, however, North Korea has relatively rich energy resources in coal and hydro-electric power. In reality, for some time after the National Liberation in 1945, the North supplied the South with electricity. Then, what are the reasons for the energy shortage in North Korea? We can consider the matter along the following three areas.

The first is the problem of inefficacy in its energy policy due to North Korea's reliance on the Juche ideas. North Korea's energy policy relies mainly on the internally available hydro-electric power and coal based on the principle of "autonomous-regeneration" originating from the Juche concept. But such a policy is wholly uneconomical because it does not account for the supply principles on energy and the supply stability and pricing of different categories of energy.

The heavy reliance on capital-intensive hydro-electric power and coal, despite its lower utility than petroleum, for capital poor North Korea has led to a serious maldistribution of resources and has created havoc with its economic efficiency. As a result, its economic growth has been severely retarded. Because of the long history of coal mining in North Korea, the mine pits became deeper and more difficult to manage while the mining technology remained non-mechanized and primitively backward. For these reasons, the volume of coal extraction has dropped drastically, adding to the inefficiency of energy supplies in North Korea.

Besides the problem of the misguided energy policy, the serious problems of trade deficits and the unwise waste of resources through the excessive preparations for holding the Pyongyang Festival and other unnecessary projects have rendered North Korea economically unable to undertake the necessary development of new coal mines, the construction of power generating stations and the renovation of old existing plants and facilities. In addition, there has been the serious problem of power loss and leakage because of the poor facilities in power transmission, distribution, and wiring.[28]

Consequently, only the munitions factories are being operated to capacity. Only thirty percent of other non-military plants and facilities are actually being operated, and those are running below forty percent of their capacity. The operation stoppage and/or decrease in the rate of operation has caused a drastic decline in exports and in turn has aggravated its foreign exchange holdings. Thus North Korea's import of vital raw materials has dropped, further eroding its economic performance. Understandably, the North Korean leadership considers these problems not merely economic in nature but major problems threatening the very survival of its system.[29]

---

[28]Kim Il Sung suffered from the haunting nightmare of U.S. bombing in the Korean War, which led to his decision to bury the electric power transmission and distribution facilities underground after the war. The deterioration of the underground power facilities through inattention and poor maintenance created the serious loss of power in North Korea.

[29]Chang Meng-yul, "Problems of North Korean Economy and Its Internal

In order to alleviate North Korea's energy crisis, South Korea must consider first the supply of South Korean electric power to the North. The difference in voltage between the two Koreas can be fixed by building the necessary transformer sub-stations. Southern power supply assistance to North Korea will be relatively easy as the peak demand period for power in North Korea is the winter while the reverse is true in the South.[30]

Second, South Korea should assist the North in the construction of new power generating stations. Once the two light-water reactors with 1,000 megawatt capacities are built in North Korea in connection with the solution of the North Korean nuclear weapons program, a considerable portion of North Korea's energy shortage will have been solved. However, before that can happen, there is the problem of an extended time lag. Accordingly, it would be vital for South Korea to cooperate with the North in the task of renovating and improving the existing electric power stations in the early phase of the South-North Confederation. Cooperation ought also be rendered to North Korea in the area of technical assistance in coal production as well as in the improvement of petroleum supplies. The diversification of energy sources, as well as the reduction of dependence on coal, will promote environmental protection.

Third, South Korea ought to cooperate in the upgrading of North Korea's facilities for power transmission, distribution, and wiring. However, to fundamentally improve the electric power situation in the North, the South will have to expand the eco-

---

Structure: Internal Approaches," in Hwang Eui-gak, *et al.*, *The Stagnation of North Korea's Socialist Economy and Responses* (Seoul: Kyungnam University Press, 1995) p. 78.

[30]Chang Young-sik, The Energy Economy in North Korea (Seoul: Korea Development Institute [KDI], 1993).

nomic exchanges and cooperation so as to assist the North to improve and solve its chronic trade deficits, and help them to transcend their penchant for extravagant showcase projects, fraught with uneconomic and unproductive characteristics. Considering the trend, too, that the higher the industrial structure became, the importance of petroleum became even more pronounced—not merely as the source for general energy needs but also for its pervasive impact in other industries including the petroleum-related products and for transportation—it would be a wise policy to help North Korea revise its current energy policies more fundamentally, to diversify the energy sources, and ultimately to introduce flexibility in its policies to transcend its misguided "reliance on coal and neglect of petroleum."

(7) Joint Ventures in Third Countries

The joint ventures by the two Koreas in third countries will be a promising area for the promotion of mutual interests. The Koreans are people who can easily adapt to both the searing heat of the Middle East and the arctic cold of Siberia. Besides, South Korea has the accumulated rich experience, knowhow, and technology of overseas development, while North Korea has an inexpensive quality labor force. If the two sides cooperate, they can have a competitive edge anywhere in the world.

The third country target areas which could provide opportunities for South-North joint ventures are the Middle East, Siberia, the Far East, and Manchuria. Of these, the Middle East would be a most appropriate place to start because of the relatively low demand on capital and the high on-site labor cost. Because of the fact that there is an exploding demand for construction and that numerous South Korean businesses are already there, joint ventures by the two Koreas could be started there relatively easily. There is a fairly high possibility of easy capital recovery and profit.

Siberia and the Far Eastern region is reputed to be rich in natural resources, and has been estimated to hold 80 percent of the potential economic power of the Soviet Union. However, because of the bitter cold, geographic limitations, and the labor shortage, real development has not occurred yet. But in recent years, an active development of the region is slowly but surely taking place with the participation of the United States, Japan, and China. They are all in search of an initiative and leadership in the development of the region with its immense economic potentials.

For a resource poor Korea, economic entry into the region is highly significant. The economic significance of the development of petroleum and natural gas in Eastern Siberia will be enormous for Korea, as the vastly increased energy needs of the two Koreas through the intensification of their economic exchanges and cooperation could be easily met by such regional development. Unlike the South Koreans who just began to make a feasibility study of the development of the natural gas fields in the Yakutsk region, Japan is already well entrenched in Eastern Siberian development projects. Considering this reality, joint venture projects by the two Koreas are undoubtedly extremely important and ought to be regarded as high priority goals.

Manchuria, too, is an important area to be considered for joint ventures. In 1992, South Korea's "Continental Development Company" (*Daeryuk Jonghap Kaebal Jusik-Hoesa*) signed a joint development agreement with China's Heilongjiang Province Agriculture Development Company over a portion of territory along the plains of three major rivers; and in July 1994 broke the ground for the joint project.[31]

As a great majority of the Chinese population is concentrated south of the Yangtze River, even with the monthly pay of 300-400 Yuan, it would be extremely difficult to recruit local labor for the project.[32] Accordingly, if we can somehow cooperate with North Korea for the utilization of North Korean labor in the "Three River Development Project," it would be a great help for North Korea in its foreign exchange earning, utilization of its labor force, and certainly in the amelioration of the food shortage crisis.

(8) Joint Development of Resources

The joint development of resources has been proposed by both sides since the first South-North Economic Conference in 1984. Although North Korea is relatively rich in mineral resources, their development has been retarded by inadequate indirect social capital and backward technology. For South Korea, the development of mineral resources in North Korea will save a lot in transportation costs; for the North, it will mean a significant development of minerals as well as the means for acquiring foreign exchange.

Inter-Korean cooperation is also desirable in fishery as well. Since the mid-1970s, the two Koreas have experienced a great deal of difficulty in the fishing industry due to the increased

---

[31]The vast area along the confluence of three major rivers—Argun, Amur, and Ussuri—whose total size is roughly 110 million *pyung* (Korean land measurement), 130 times the size of Youido Island in Metropolitan Seoul. The Sino-South Korean joint development project of this area will produce coal, graphite, timber, beans, corn, wheat, sugar cane, and rice. [One *pyung* is 3.3 m²]

[32]Lee Sang-man, On *"Unification Economy": North Korean Economy and South-North Korean Economic Integration* (Seoul: Hyungsul, 1994), p. 302.

fishing regulations of other states. What is needed for the joint development of maritime resources of the two Koreas is the negotiation of a fishery agreement between them and the establishment of joint fishing grounds based on that agreement. Joint fishing operations in the Sea of Okhotsk and around the Kamchatka Peninsula, an area already used by the North Koreans, will go a long way to meet the demands of South Korea's fishing industry. In all this, South Korea could provide the North the technical assistance in shipbuilding, repairs, and other fishing needs.

(9) Infrastructure

The building of social overhead (indirect) capital contributes to industrial efficiency[33] through the creation of "external economies" and the elimination of "external diseconomies," and is highly important from the perspective of balanced regional development. Hence, the innovation and/or systematization of backward and inefficient social overhead capital that interferes with industrial cycles are the essential conditions for the invigoration of the inter-Korean economic exchanges/cooperation. Such ventures would be highly significant in that they will function as the key policy means—the Keynsian macro-economic means—to absorb the idle North Korean labor force, and to

---

[33]The "external economies" denote the reduction of production costs by individual businesses within an industry through the expansion of the general industrial dimension. For instance, through the expansion of an industry, other related industries are newly created; or when the rail system is built, new benefits in transportation are created, leading further to reduction in transportation costs, thus ultimately reducing the cost of production. The "external diseconomies" denote the specific economic activities which lead to the increase in production costs in other industries.

minimize the chaos and confusion in the "National Economic Community's" labor market especially after the economic integration or during the latter phase of the Confederation. However, the building of infrastructure requires great amounts of funds and time. We should seek the assistance and cooperation of the International Bank of Rehabilitation and Development (IBRD) and/or the International Monetary Fund (IMF) to acquire the necessary funds. We ought to carefully prioritize necessary projects and approach them selectively. The most urgent area for cooperation in overhead social capital during the Confederal Stage would be to establish transportation and communication linkups between the two sides.

1) Means to Link Up the Transportation Network

Maritime transportation will most likely be highly utilized during the early phase of the inter-Korean economic exchange/cooperation. The primary ports that can be put to use in direct trade between the two Koreas will be, as agreed upon previously: Inchon, Pusan, and Pohang in the South, Nampo, Wonsan and Chungjin in the North.

Cargo transportation will be greatly helped by the proximity of railheads to North Korean ports. Nevertheless, none of the ports have real container handling facilities; and except for Chungjin and Nampo, the other North Korean ports are too small to accommodate the increase in cargo traffic, and must necessarily be expanded in preparation for future needs. Once the two Koreas agree to enter into a Confederation, the tensions in Korea will abate and the logic of economic principles will prevail in East Asia. Under the circumstances, and given the ideal geographic conditions of the Korean Peninsula, we can expect that it will be able to play the central role in the expanding Northeast

Asian economic cooperation. In that context, the effective linkup between the ports in the two Koreas and the improvement of conditions of these ports will have enormous economic significance.

We shall now look at the project of linking up the land transportation systems. The main characteristics of the two Koreas' land transportation systems are that while in the North railroads form the nucleus, the road networks are the main transportation means in the South. The reasons for the centrality of the railroad system in North Korea are: first to control the movement of people; second, under the planned economy, cargoes rather than people are the main concern for the rail traffic; and third, because of the mountainous geographic conditions. On the other hand, the transportation system in the South is built around the road network because of the more prominent role of distribution and service areas due to the high development of a market economy and greater movement of people. In terms of total rail tracks, North Korea is not far behind the South,[34] of which approximately 63 percent are electrified, which is far ahead of South Korea's 8 percent electrification. On the other hand, the total length of North Korea's road system is less than 60 percent of South Korea's, and its roads are generally much narrower and unpaved.[35] On the basis of these transportation systems in the two Koreas, the following principles can be offered for the linkup. First, the two governments ought to be

---

[34]As of 1991, the total railroad tracks in North Korea are about 5,060km, and 6,460km in South Korea.

[35]Roughly 8 percent of the roads are paved in North Korea. See Oh Jaehak, "North Korea's Road and Railroad Systems Today and the Proposals for the Linkup of the two Koreas' Land Transportation System," *North Korean Studies* [*Bukhan Yunku*], Summer, 1994 [Seoul: Daeryuk Yunkuso], p. 36.

allowed room for more strict government control over the flow of men and material in the early stage of the Confederation because of the low level of mutual trust and experience. Second, as the project for linkup between the two transportation systems will require a great deal of expense and manpower, the project must be undertaken on a manageable piece by piece basis that will require minimum monetary and time expenditures. Third, since the primary object for inter-Korean transportation under the Confederation is expected to be cargo, the linkup must begin with the system that is best suited for the task.

Top priority, therefore, must be placed on the linkup of the maritime transportation system, while the land transportation should be linked up on a phase by phase basis. The maritime transportation system can be linked up more easily as it also has the edge in bulk carrying capability. Besides, since the North Korean social overhead capital is in an inadequate state and its industrial sites are close to coastal areas, the improvement and expansion of the maritime transportation network will be far more efficient and economical for the growth of North Korean industry as well. And as the innovation and repairs, and standardization (for compatibility) of the ground transportation systems such as the road network and railroads will require huge expenses, these tasks should be undertaken gradually over time.

As mentioned earlier, the ground transportation system ought to be structured around railroads. Since the primary transportation need for inter-Korean traffic is logically expected to be long-distance cargo hauling, the railroad would be far better suited for the task than the road network. As far as the railroad linkup is concerned, there are already rail lines which were built long before the national division, and the railroad system is relatively better than the roadways in North Korea. Additionally, it must be pointed out that the railroads are more easily controllable in terms of people's movement, making it a "better system" to allay North Korean fears of "the penetration of capitalism" into its system. The road network, on the other hand, can be utilized for short-distance internal relays of cargo.

The major rail networks that can be activated for the inter-Korean linkup will be the Seoul-Shinuiju Line ("the Kyung-eui Line"), linking Kaesong, Panmunjom, and Munsan and the Seoul-Wonsan Line ("the Kyung-won Line"), linking Chulwon, Pyunggang, and Bokgae. These main axis lines can be restored and opened in a relatively short time. The restoration of the "Northern Eastern Sea Line," linking Kangnung, Sokcho, Kosung, and Wonsan, will take a longer time as Wonsan-Kosung section has been removed. For the rail networks to function properly, there must be suitable facilities for the transfer of cargo/passengers, such as warehouses and open storage facilities; and as most of the North Korean rail system is electrified, the exchange of trains will have to entail the exchange of the locomotives and the adjustment of voltage on both sides.[36] In addition, being outdated and inefficient, the North Korean rail system is too slow. These problems will have to be corrected first, along with the laying of multiple tracks.[37] The inter-Korean rail linkage and improvement of the rail system are expected to bring tremendous economic benefits to export-oriented South Korea by considerably cutting the transportation costs for exports bound for China and Europe.

Of the major trunk road networks linking the two Koreas,

---

[36]*Ibid.*, p. 39.

[37]The average running speed of the South Korean trains is 100 km per hour while it is merely around 40 km per hour in North Korea due mainly to weak track foundations.

one can point to National Route 1, linking Munsan, Panmunjom, and Kaesong; National Route 3, linking Chulwon-Pyunggang in the central region; and National Route 7, linking the eastern coastal cities of Kansung and Changjun. But considering that most of the roads in North Korea are unpaved, its rectification is an urgent business that has to be attended to. Along with the plans for road building, plans for compatible standardization must be provided for traffic signals and road signs. Once the North Korean system becomes more flexible after a lapse of time under the Confederation, there will arise the need to build a super highway system connecting the two Koreas. A super highway linking Chayuro (the Liberty Road), Munsan, Panmunjom, Kaesong, Pyongyang, and Shinuiju will be eventually linked to China, Central Asia, and Europe, contributing enormously to the increase in trade volume and human welfare—along with the rail system.

If the two Koreas manage an aviation agreement, the establishment of an air cargo link between the Kimpo International Airport and the Sunahn in Pyongyang will soon follow. However, the problem of the use of the air link will have to be approached more cautiously with a longer-term perspective as it would have accompanying sensitive military implications.

2) Means to Link Up the Communications Network

For the speedy exchange of ideas and information/intelligence, indispensable for economic exchange and cooperation, there will have to be a linkup of the communications networks between the two Koreas. The definition of the communications network ought to include: mail, covering letters and parcels; electronic communications such as telegraph, telephone, telex, and others; and other modern public communications systems such as digital communications, radio and television electro-magnetic waves, and others. Of these, the most essential means of communication in the economic exchange and cooperation will be electronic communication. However, considering the great pervasive impact of this particular communications net-work, the use of it could be limited in terms of areas, affected groups, and its application to accommodate the North Korean situation in the early phase of the Confederation. To wit, in the early stage of economic exchange/cooperation, we can consider the idea of exchanging information/intelligence by initially establishing the communications network in the Free Economic Trade Zones. Communications through the specially established lines can begin anytime with technical agreements on the estab-lishment of the lines as well as their use.

3. The Build-up of the International Environment for
the Promotion of Economic Exchange/Cooperation between
the Two Koreas

What is needed for the active pursuit of inter-Korean eco-nomic exchange and cooperation is not merely the effort of the two Koreas, but also the effort to create a favorable international atmosphere for it. In this context, we shall now examine the sig-nificance of enhancing the roles of the Asia-Pacific Economic Cooperation (APEC) and the "Northeast Asian Economic Zone."

APEC, established originally for the increase of economic exchange and for the firm establishment of free economic order in the Asia-Pacific region, can be defined as the collective response of the Asian-Pacific states to the global trends of rising regionalism. APEC was established to meet the needs of the regional states in the Asia-Pacific for economic consultation and cooperation in accord with the trends, since the mid-1980s, of the global rise of economic regionalism; the economic decline of the erstwhile hegemon, the United States; the expansion and intensification of economic interdependence.

Officially begun in 1989, based on an Australian proposal, with South Korean support, and with the participation of the United States and twelve states, including ASEAN, APEC has been gradually consolidating its organizational unity through several conferences. In accord with the Bogor Declaration, by the years 2010-2020, the developed states and the developing states in the region will respectively complete the required phased steps for liberalizing trade and investment practices. The high level APEC official meetings in February 1995 in Fukuoka, Japan, and in April of the same year in Singapore began specific planning for the realization of the agreements for free trade arrangements for 2010-2020 as spelled out in the Bogor Declaration adopted at the APEC summit.

However, there are conflicting views among the APEC member states due to their varied interests. For example, while the United States and Canada, citing APEC's general speed of economic growth, wish to see APEC bring visible results faster, the ASEAN states and China desire slower growth, citing the great economic differences that still exist in the region and the need for adjustment in the industrial structures of their respective states. The member states also revealed the differences in their views on such issues as technology transfer. Believing that the technology transfers will occur naturally as a side effect of increased direct investment, the developed states do not wish to consider technology transfer as a major organizational issue for APEC; while the developing states, believing the technology transfer to them is an important means to narrow the developmental gap

within the region, are demanding more active technology transfers as part of APEC's project for increased cooperation.[38]

Besides, several ASEAN nations with Malaysia leading the
way are pushing for the East Asia Economic Caucus (EAEC)
without the United States. To be sure, APEC will be a part of the
important international environment for Korea's economy; however, it will be difficult for it to be a concrete force in a short
span of time.

On the other hand, although much smaller than APEC, the
concept of the Northeast Asian Economic Zone offers potentially
greater possibilities in terms of directly affecting the inter-Korean economic exchanges and cooperation. The Northeast Asia
Economic Zone should include China's three Northeast Provinces
(Manchuria), Russia's Siberia and the Far East region, Mongolia,
the Korean Peninsula, and Japan. Again compared with APEC,
the countries in the Northeast Asia Economic Zone enjoy geographic propinquity to each other, share a great deal of common
culture, and possess a high degree of economic complementarity. The concept has high feasibility as China, Russia, and North
Korea express deep interest in it.

Therefore, when and if the Northeast Economic Zone is
established, it is generally estimated that the zone will have
unlimited potential for development due mainly to the fact that
all the nations in it possess the necessary natural resources and
labor, and a high degree of complementarity in the capital and
technology, needed for production. Because of the diverse geo-
logical structure, embedded in the vast continental expanses of

---

[38]Roh Jae-bong, "Vision for Asia-Pacific Economic Cooperation and the
Direction of Its Development," in Lee Jae-sung, ed., *New Direction in Asia-Pacific
Economic Cooperation* (Seoul: Korea Institute for International Economic Policy &
Korea Committee for Pacific Economic Cooperation, 1993), p. 79.

Northeast Asia are great quantities of coal, petroleum, natural
gas, uranium, iron, and other important minerals; the rich labor
pool in China and North Korea can easily be harnessed to the
development of natural resources in nearby Siberia and
Manchuria; and capital and technology from South Korea and
Japan can be the moving force in the economic development of
the entire region.

However, in reality, the formation of the Northeast Asian
Economic Zone would be difficult without including the United
States. The reasons are, first, the Northeast Asian countries alone
do not yet have the adequate economic power and drive to initi-
ate regional economic development. Second, considering the
economic dependence of South Korea and Japan on the United
States, the exclusion of the United States from the Northeast
Asian economic considerations could actually detract from the
significance and benefits of the economic cooperation. Besides,
the likely rivalry or competition between Japan and the United
States for economic hegemony could reduce the possibility of
excessive economic domination from either side. Third, we can
not entirely rule out the political and military factors, such as the
political and military ties of South Korea and Japan with the
United States; the increase of the American influence in North
Korea; and the global strategy of the United States that perforce
deters China and Russia. Consequently, the formation of the
Northeast Asian Economic Zone without the United States is
simply unrealistic. Hence, it would be far more desirable as well
as feasible to form the Northeast Asian Economic Zone as a sub-
group under APEC with the participation of the United States.[39]

---

[39]The establishment and development of the Northeast Asia Economic
Zone could be the catalyst for the ultimate establishment of a multilateral security cooperation in Northeast Asia, like the CSCE in Europe.

We shall now focus on the study of the impact on the inter-Korean economic exchange/cooperation by the economic cooperation of the Northeast Asian countries. First, one immediate result will be the reduction of burden and/or dangers in the inter-Korean economic exchange and cooperation. Although the economic exchanges and cooperation have gone forward steadily between the two Koreas, no South Korean investment in the North has yet materialized. The South Korean government has not allowed it, while North Korea has not been too forward looking for fear of its collapse. As the Northeast Asian economic cooperation under these circumstances will mean the transition from largely bilateral ties to multilateral relations, the role of China as a friendly ally to North Korea is expected to be highly significant and important. Consequently, North Korea's political and economic apprehension towards South Korea will be visibly reduced. That the multilateral economic projects will be governed by economic logic rather than by non-economic factors should assure greater security and stability for South Korean investments in the North, especially when the latter is expected to avoid a new round of international isolation.

Second, the Northeast Asian economic cooperation will expand the opportunities for North Korea's external economic contacts thus ultimately expediting its eventual opening. Because of the geographic centrality of the Korean Peninsula, a great bulk of human and material movement would have to pass through it. Even if such movement affects only North Korea, it should indirectly enlarge North Korean residents' contacts with the outside world, and help enlighten them on the merits and principles of the market economy. The important thing is that the two Koreas will have to coordinate their joint efforts to vitalize the Northeast Asian economic cooperation. In this, South Korea's primary role should be to try to create a cooperative international environment to assist and enable the North to become a part of international market structure, and to help it join the regional economic cooperation in Northeast Asia as a full-fledged member of the international community. The important thing is for us to realize clearly that we would not only benefit substantially from economic cooperation in the Asia-Pacific region and/or in Northeast Asia, but by expanding the inter-Korean economic exchanges and cooperation, we will be contributing materially to the smooth process of Korea's own national unification.

V. Cooperation on Environmental Issues

There is an intimate connection between economic growth and environmental issues. Although the environmental problems are created by economic development, they in turn become the limiting factors against further economic growth. Globally, too, the environmental issue is intimately related to the survival of the human race, and as such is emerging to be one of the greatest international political and economic issues of our times.[40] In that context, the problem of balancing development

---

[40]The environmental problem has great implications in international economics. As the international society not only limits the use of environmental pollutants and emissions but also regulates the products made of pollutants, nations of the world will now have to take comprehensive measures on these problems. For example, of international agreements on environmental protection, the "Montreal Protocol on Substances that Deplete the Ozone Layer" will have direct impact on automobile and electronic industries; the agreement adopted by UNCED on global climatic change will have a direct impact on the general energy use and on all industrial activities; and the agreement on biodiversity will

with the environment must be dealt with as the primary agen-
dum in the policy decisions concerning inter-Korean economic
exchange and cooperation.

We shall now scrutinize the environmental status of Northeast Asia and the Korean Peninsula and present appropriate
plans for environmentally sound and sustainable development.

1. The Realities of Environmental Issues in Northeast Asia and in the Korean Peninsula

The environmental problems have risen to a serious level
because of the high population density, rapid paced urbanization, and the process of industrialization in Northeast Asian
countries. What must be noted with emphasis is that the environmental problems in this region, because of the geographic factors, cannot be confined to one's own state, but create a serious
case of transnational pollution. The most serious case is China's
rapid industrialization and the pollution that accompanies it. The
major cause of China's atmospheric pollution is the ubiquitous
burning of coal that emits sulfuric acid and particle matters. Of
the total 1990 energy production in China, coal production was
74.1 percent, while the use of coal in the total energy consumption is 76.2 percent.[41] Chinese coal is known to contain a high sul-
fur content. China depends on heavy use of lignite coal and peat,

---

have impact on oil resources and industries related to life sciences. The Environmental Protection Agency, Republic of Korea, *White Paper on Environment* (Seoul,
1993), p. 11. See also, Gareth Porter and Janet Welsh Brown, Global Environmental Politics (Boulder, Colorado: Westview Press, 1991); Stephen Rainbow, *Green
Politics* (Auckland, Oxford, New York: Oxford University Press, 1993).

[41]Korea Institute for International Economic Policy, *The Study of Korean-
Chinese Environmental Cooperation* (Seoul. 1993), p. 44.

and the sulfur-dioxide (SO_2) and dust from the burning of these become the main cause of the atmospheric pollution.

China's pollution of the sea also impacts negatively on the Korean Peninsula. The economic development is most noteworthy all along the Chinese coastal regions, from which 5-7 billion tons of waste water and garbage are being emitted into the sea annually.[42] Despite the fact that the Yellow Sea and the East China Sea are closed and semi-closed areas, and limited in their scope, China and Korea lie astride these areas. In oceanographic terms, because of the big tidal differences in this area, the sea water circulates fast there. The sea pollution, therefore, in this region spreads rapidly to all adjoining waters. China denies that the pollution caused by them affects the Korean Peninsula and other countries.[43] In addition, although the dumping of the nuclear waste by Russia and Japan in the Eastern Sea seriously threatens the environment in Northeast Asia and the Korean Peninsula, they either deny the dumping itself or are completely indifferent to the serious issue of their own making.

The atmospheric pollution in the two Koreas has now reached a truly serious level. Logically speaking, the capitalist states which seek maximum profits should experience much more serious cases of environmental pollution than the socialist states with their planned economy. For the capitalists, to deal with the externalities of their productive activities through

---

[42]*Ibid.*, p. 261.

[43]In a "Meeting of the High Level Officials for the Environmental Cooperation in Northeast Asia" held in Seoul in February 1993, China flatly denied that its atmospheric pollutants were affecting other countries in the region, and expressed displeasure over the very discussion of the problem of atmospheric pollution. Bureau of International Economics, Ministry of Foreign Affairs, *The Final Report of the High Level Officials on Environmental Cooperation* (Seoul, 1993), p. 21.

social cost would be far more logical from their own personal perspective.[44]

However, as seen in the report by the Club of Rome, the reality is that the population increase and industrialization under any economic system are bound to inflict damage on the environment. The realities of pollution in Russia and Eastern European countries are the irrefutable proof of that. It is judged that North Korea cannot be an exception to this. On the problems of pollution in North Korea, there are not yet any publicly available reliable data.[45] But based on the following several factors, it seems that North Korea's environmental damage has gone far enough. Under the principles of self-reliance, North Korea has actively developed its mineral and energy resources. Especially, to raise the level of self-supply, North Korea has relied mainly on its own coal production rather than on imported petroleum, causing serious air pollution. Besides, North Korea's environmental pollution is judged to have been particularly serious for the following reasons: North Korea's industrial structure is centered around pollution inducing industries such as steel and iron, metal refineries, metallurgical works, and

---

[44]For example, in the process of manufacturing a product, water around the factory can be polluted—the "externalities." But for the capitalist manufacturer, whose sole purpose is to maximize his profit, the installation of facilities to prevent pollution using his own funds would be far less desirable than by using the public taxes (the social cost).

[45]However, one report that combines all the available information in Korea as well as abroad indicates that the water quality of the Tumen, Yalu, and Daedong Rivers has fallen seriously, and that the water and air pollution in the waters around Wonsan harbor and industrial centers around Hamhung and elsewhere are serious. Nam Young-sook, "The Inter-Korean Environmental Cooperation and the Study of Plans to Integrate Environmental Policies" in *Proceedings of Baedal Green Federation Symposium* (Seoul, 1995)

chemical industries; while overly stressing the quantitative growth, designed to meet the arbitrarily set production quotas, North Korea could not have spared the necessary investment on pollution prevention measures.

In South Korea, the problem of environmental pollution has surfaced as a major issue ever since the first Five Year Economic Development Plan went into effect in 1962; not until 1967, after the implementation of the Second Five Year Plan, did South Korea establish an administrative mechanism to deal with the pollution problem. Because of the sustained industrialization and urbanization founded on the economic policies of growth first principles, the severity of environmental pollution has now become a major social issue. According to the reports of the World Health Organization (WHO) and the United Nations Environmental Programme (UNEP), the air pollution in Seoul is ranked second in the world after Mexico City. But particularly through the recent automobile explosion in Korea, a dangerous level of carbon monoxide emission has created the fear of the phenomenon of "photochemical smog" in South Korea.

Once North Korea's open door policy becomes real and investments from South Korea and others begin in earnest, North Korea will become an area of economic development and growth. As in the early stages of South Korea's industrialization, most of the foreign industries which will enter North Korea will be the ones in decline elsewhere and all of them will be pollution prone ones. As a result, it would not be too difficult to imagine greater and accelerated environmental damage in North Korea. Let us now discuss measures to counter this problem.

2. The Means to Effect Inter-Korean Cooperation for the Environment

To deal with the environmental pollution in the two Koreas, what is needed first is the collective effort by the regional states to institutionalize multilateral cooperation in Northeast Asia. Considering the political realities in the region, it would be be conducive to the solution of the problem if the meeting for all the concerned countries were called under the sponsorship of an international body to discuss the problems of pollution. Either the Northwest Pacific Action Plan (NOWPAP) of which the two Koreas, Russia, Japan, and China are already members, or the Economic and Social Committee for the Asia-Pacific (ESCAP), to which South Korea has been making annual contributions to its fund for cooperation, could be an excellent venue for multilateral negotiation.[46]

Second, we ought to hurry with an inter-Korean agreement for environmental cooperation. The two Koreas had participated in the United Nations Conference on Environmental Development (UNCED) held in Rio de Janeiro, Brazil in 1992, and joined in the "Rio Declaration" [which established the basic principles for the prevention of artificial environmental destruction and for sustainable economic development] and other international agreements. It is necessary, therefore, to agree on specific measures for mutual cooperation in order to implement the above agreements and commitment.

Third, we should begin a joint investigation of the realities

---

[46] A multilateral Northeast Asian environmental cooperation could either expedite a multilateral security cooperation or could be discussed as a part of multilateral security cooperation.

of environmental pollution. Needless to say, the identification and collection of reliable data on pollution would be an essential step prior to working out appropriate solutions to the problem. Hence, it would be vital for the two sides to publish a "South-North Confederation White Paper on the Environment" based on the realities of area-by-area pollution; the ecological study of the Demilitarized Zone; and the impact on the Korean Peninsula from the emission of pollutants from neighboring countries.

Fourth, purification technology must be transferred as soon as possible. Although in international standards, South Korea's environmental technology is relatively behind its industrial technology, even this limited level of pollution reduction technology must be owned jointly with North Korea. Technology to prevent air pollution and water purification knowhow ought to be shared promptly in order to assist in environmentally sound and sustainable industrialization. We must learn from our own experiences of environmental pollution in the process of our industrialization, and apply it in North Korea to assure its environmentally sound and sustainable economic growth.

Fifth, a policy-making body for the development of environmental management and the mid- to long-term policies for the problem should be established under the Confederal Economic Committee. This body should be empowered to participate in and to oversee the policy-planning for economic growth, while minimizing the environmental damage. Joint inter-Korean research ought to be encouraged by establishing a combined economic and environmental research center, linking all the major regions of the Korean Peninsula through an electronic communications network to enable round-the-clock supervision and collection of relevant data.

VI. The Transition to a Federation

We have thus far discussed the basic principles and methods of inter-Korean economic exchange/cooperation and environmental cooperation under the Confederation. In this section, we shall examine the prospect of economic conditions, anticipated during the very final stage of the Confederation, and present our views on the process of economic integration and the most desirable policy direction for economic management in the post-integration period.

Once the inter-Korean economic exchange/cooperation is upgraded under the Confederation, we expect that the North Korean economy will show the following changes. First of all, North Korea will overcome to a considerable extent its capital shortage and technological backwardness through economic opening to the outside world; and its external economic relations will pick up momentum. Along with the economic opening and transition to a market economy from its planned economic structure, North Korea should experience rapid economic growth, thus reducing somewhat the economic gap between the two Koreas. At that point, along with the improvement of economic living standards and the changes in popular consciousness towards the outside world, there will come a time when North Korea will be faced with rising popular demand for changes in its political system, quite possibly resulting in the acceptance, or at least, the acquiescence of a multi-party system and some form of free elections. Without a doubt, through the process of economic exchanges and cooperation, the two Koreas will enlarge the scope of their mutual understanding and realize the importance of mutual interdependence.

Before the two Koreas' economies could be integrated, however, there are a few tasks which the South Korean economy must fulfill. Through the process of economic integration, the South Korean economy must lead the Northern economy towards a market economy. But because of the twisted characteristics of South Korean "capitalism," it is doubtful that the Southern capitalism can in fact perform the role of leading the Northern economy towards the needed transition. The problem is that the South Korean economy is riddled with difficulties owing to the intensification of inequities among regions and social classes and the consequent rise of the popular feelings of deprivation; and the pervasive human alienation through the uncontrolled mammonism and the omnipotence of materialism. Accordingly, inter-Korean economic integration ought to be seen as a rare opportunity for the Southern economy to elevate itself to a higher plane. It should mean changes for the better in the South Korean economy in advance of the integration. The integration of the two economies ought to take place only after the completion of an internal purification and rectification of the South Korean economy. Only then will the process of integration be smooth and efficient, and the integrated national economy be truly significant in an historical context.

When the conditions are rife for entering the Federation, the Second Stage of the "Three-Stage Unification" Formula, the two Koreas will have to prepare themselves for economic integration: namely, they ought to begin the main tasks of sorting out the operating principles of the economy. The primary task of this will be the establishment of a rational currency exchange structure as well as policies for common currency. Since cooperation in currency policy will not be possible without cooperation in financial policies, these issues will have to be dealt with by the Confederal Economic Committee. Along with the task of handling and coordinating the policies and principles for economic operation, the Confederal Economic Committee will have to make the necessary preparations for the establishment of the Central Federal Bank and currency integration.[47]

The Confederal Economic Committee will have to come up with a master plan for the development of the national economy after unification. The master plan ought to include developmental strategies for the realignment/reorganization of the industrial structure suitable to an integrated and balanced national territorial development of the integrated national economy. The strategy, however, ought to be based on a "specialized economic developmental strategy." Considering the differences in economic structures of the two Koreas and the economic "customs/ habits" due to these differences, economic relations between the two under the Confederation could not be a complete economic integration but rather a transitional one. Thus, the economic structure in the process of integration should be understood as the "specialized integrated national economy" to accord with the nature of the fluid transitional period. In a large sense, the integrated economy could constitute a single economic entity; however, in specifics, specialized strategies must be applied and implemented to account for the different developmental stages and historical legacies of the two Koreas.[48]

---

[47] According to Balassa, this period can be seen as one of economic alliance. Whether or not, however, his theories can be applied to an integration between two wholly different systems is in question. Hence his frame of conceptual reference—namely "from the free trade zone → to customs union → to common market → to economic union → to a complete economic integration"—is not being used here as the basis of integrating the two Koreas' economies. Bela Balassa, *The Theory of Economic Integration* (Homewood, Illinois: Richard D. Irwin, Inc., 1961), pp. 1-7

[48] We shall cite the examples of the "specialized policies" or the "policy of

The historical significance of the economic integration to be accomplished with the establishment of the Federation can be described as follows. First, the economic integration has the significance of laying the economic foundation for the modern nation-state in our history. Historically, we developed early our brand of nationalism based on a powerful ethos of national unity. Unfortunately, however, we degenerated into a Japanese colony before we could ever attempt to establish a modern nation-state. Although the National Liberation in 1945 finally put an end to the unfortunate interlude, the division of Korea again forced the two Koreas to develop into different and opposing systems despite the fact that we are one homogeneous nation. Indeed, despite the long history of a powerful sense of national unity, we have yet to experience the joy of establishing a modern nation-state. Accordingly, we as a nation have been carrying the burden of settling the question of national division and establishing a modern nation-state. The economic integration between the two Koreas will lay the foundation for that

---

special assistance for North Korea" that will be implemented by the central government under the Federation. Since the stage of Federation signifies national unification, the free movement of workers cannot be limited by any law. But judging from the experience of unified Germany, the free movement of labor has the potential of greatly disrupting the labor market under the unified economy. Therefore, as a matter of judicious compromise between the principle and the reality, we could instead depend on the policy of massive investment in North Korea's overhead social capital. This policy will not only guarantee the principle of free movement of labor, but also have the effect of absorbing excess North Korean labor force. Providing subsidies for the privatization of state-owned enterprises and for the improvement of society and welfare areas can be cited as examples of the "specialized policies" or "specialized assistance." However, as a strategy to accelerate the establishment of a single unified economy, the "specialized strategies" should also consider the idea of combining specific areas of the two Koreas into a single unified industrial zone as an experiment.

very modern nation-state.

Second, the economic integration will mean the formation of a huge internal market of seventy million people. The existence of an enlarged internal market will lead to an increase in production and the accompanying cost reduction for businesses, demonstrating the beneficial effect of the "economies of scale."

Once the economic integration is complete, the Federal Government will undertake the task of institutionalizing the plans established prior to the integration, and will implement gradually the specifics of the plans. The tasks for the economic integration ought to be carried out carefully and wisely under the guiding principles that ultimately it will lead to the creation of a common national community with economic justice for all. To wit, it should mean that South Korea would not attempt to reorganize the North Korean economy arbitrarily in the process of integration. Because the economic integration is not only for the establishment of a unified state, but to enhance the quality of life for North Korean residents, the economic integration ought to take place through the process of the voluntary consent of the North Koreans; and with the overall philosophy that the integration will assure equality and reciprocity for all North Korean regions and social classes so that ultimately they will become an integral part of the unified national economy.

VII. Conclusion

In this chapter, we have presented the plans for the inter-Korean economic exchange/cooperation under the South-North Confederation, the beginning stage of the "Three-Stage Unification" Formula. We shall now conclude the chapter by restating and emphasizing its central points.

First, we have tried to project the processes toward unification under our "Three-Stage" Formula from the economic perspective, and have focused on presenting the specifics of the main direction of the process. We have particularly tried to inject our will and hope into every aspect of the economic exchange and cooperation so that they will be implemented peacefully and gradually—in every phase and detail. We have tried to make sure that all the means that we employ and all the plans that we envision are systemically integrated and consistently harmonious to the ultimate goal of peaceful and gradual unification.

Second, the direction of the economic exchange and cooperation discussed in this chapter is important not only in terms of its short-term significance and individual goals, but highly significant as a project leading to the formation of the common "national economic community." For this, we have presented the principle that the inter-Korean economic exchange/cooperation is to be implemented systematically throughout the entire phase of the Confederation and in accordance with the principle that its long- and short-term plans are justifiable by their necessity and feasibility. For instance, the reasons for the efforts to effect cooperation as a common community rather than merely working for maximum profits and the reasons to actively assist the medium/small businesses in the South are examples derived from the principle stated above.

Third, this study also addresses the external effects of the principle of "Economic Exchange and Cooperation Firstism"—namely, that development and progress ought not be allowed to contradict the goal of environmental protection but should rather be harmonious with that goal. The importance of the genuine value of economic exchange and cooperation should be that it remains true to the concepts and principles outlined above.

Fourth, in view of the dynamic nature of the Confederation in the unification process, we have offered our visions for institutional needs for smooth economic integration. In this context, we call attention to our self-deprecating and realistic position that in order to transform the Northern economy to a market economy, South Korea will have to undergo a series of vital changes itself.

Today, the great tide of world history is moving away from division and confrontation towards unification and peace. Even in the Korean Peninsula, the waves of unification and peace are quietly, yet powerfully rising to the surface. We firmly believe that the principles and plans for inter-Korean economic exchange and cooperation presented in this study are absolutely necessary economic preconditions for the gradual and peaceful unification of Korea and the future prosperity of our common national community.

CHAPTER 5

SOCIAL-CULTURAL EXCHANGE AND COOPERATION UNDER THE CONFEDERATION

Summary

The purpose of this chapter is to present the plans for social and cultural exchange and cooperation under the Confederation.

Despite innumerable foreign invasions owing to geopolitical factors, we have persistently maintained and preserved our cultural identity. Today, however, because of the prolonged division, South and North Korea seem to exhibit a considerable number of differences in all areas of society. However, these superficial differences could provide a foundation on which to fashion new culture in Korea. We could in fact metamorphose the differences into a higher level of creative diversity for the ultimate design of a new culture. The goal of the social and cultural exchange and cooperation that we seek under the Confederation in our "Three-Stage Unification" Formula is the epitome of such a plan. For such a goal, the "Three-Stage Unification" Formula posits the Confederation as the first stage of the unification process. The Confederation means the "union" between the two independent states, under which the two governments continue to function as before but institutionalize the cooperation between the two.

The search for plans to realize the social and cultural exchange and cooperation under the Confederation will be conducted in two separate periods—the early and late phases of the Confederation. The early phase of the Confederation will be a period for establishing the basis for exchange/cooperation; a period in which the ideological differences are set aside to activate the exchange in areas where the mutual agreement is the easiest. Recognizing the differences that have accumulated in the two societies under division, efforts should be made in this early period to reduce the social and cultural differences between the two and to identify and enlarge/expand the common factors, still extant underneath the social/cultural fabric of the two societies.

To establish the foundation for exchange and cooperation, the efforts in the early period should be focused on settling the institutional framework for the task. The institutional framework ought to be based on the "South-North Confederation Charter" and the agreements for exchange/cooperation should be dual in nature: one for comprehensive across-the-board exchange/cooperation and the other for specific individual areas. To facilitate and expedite the human exchange, an "agreement on travel/passage" ought to be signed, while a separate "cultural agreement" should be made to regulate the exchange and cooperation in different areas or sectors; and more detailed and specific supplementary agreements to cover the above-mentioned agreements.

In the latter phase of the Confederation, the best possible efforts must be made to minimize the differences and to maximize the common national characteristics based on the foundation created in the early phase, so as to create a basis for social/cultural integration later. Additional effort should be focused on the development of creative diversity. The projects for separate areas in the latter phase of the Confederation should transcend the simple nature of exchanges, but should be aimed at a higher level of cooperation for effecting joint programs and projects.

Once these programs are implemented systematically, the gaps created by the division will eventually be gradually filled; while the shared social and cultural similarities will expand and deepen, thus facilitating the eventual transition to a Federation. Hence, the programs/projects in the later stage of the Confederation will, in fact, be the necessary preparations for the Federal structure. When all these programs/projects become concrete, the realistic foundation will have been laid in all areas of society and culture for the integration of the two Koreas.

The Federal State that will develop from the Confederation will mean much than merely the reunion of the Korean people, but actually will mean the creation of an entirely new state. As the integration—which will be the foundation for a Federation—of the people, and the society and culture will be established on the different ideologies and political systems of the two Koreas, it will of necessity show the diversity. Once the stage of the Federation is entered, originating from the social and cultural integration, a new identity for the unified state should emerge, giving rise to an open and creative "cultural state."

I. Introduction

The unification of the Korean Peninsula—a notion which was once only a dream—has now entered the world of reality due to the demise of the Cold War. The economic war that has replaced the war of ideologies under the Cold War conflict makes national unification a task of great national urgency. The purpose of this chapter, as stated earlier, is to present the methods and plans for the social/cultural exchange and cooperation under the South-North Confederation (the Confederation of the Two Republics), as envisioned by the "Three-Stage Unification" Formula—a unification proposal that has increasing credibility and promise as the unification environment becomes more favorable and the necessities greater.

Human life does not depend solely on bread; rather than material needs alone, it depends more on freedom and equality, self-development, national pride, and cultural heritage. Industrial production, science and technology, and independent national defense play very important roles as the means of life for the community, but they are not the purpose of life itself. The meaning and purpose of life derive from the cultural system. The cultural system binds the members of the national community together through the common sentiments of belonging and shared feelings. In a high level modern society with rapid circulation of information and intelligence, wherein the roles of knowledge, information, and education become increasingly more vital, the ability to create "culture" will have decisive import in strengthening and consolidating a nation's economic competitiveness in the international arena. Thus, culture has become an indispensable factor for strengthening competitiveness in the international market place. Under the circumstances, and particularly on the crossroads to national unification, it is imperative for us to critically examine and study the cultures of the two Koreas, and ultimately to overcome the differences, in order to prepare for the creative vision for the future.

Superficially, South and North Korea seem to exhibit many

cultural gaps and differences. However, there is a fact that we should not lightly dismiss. Under more than 2,000 years of Chinese cultural influence, we were not Sinicized; on the contrary, we demonstrated our superb cultural prowess by co-opting the Chinese culture and assimilating it as our very own.[1] In that context, the national division of mere fifty years and the processes of differentiation thereunder can not have uprooted the firm basis of the common cultural heritage of our homogeneous nation.

Hence, if we can manage to integrate the superficial differences into a common existence based on diversity, it can be elevated to a significant historical achievement of the culture creation processes not merely as the simple accommodation of the systems themselves. Therein lies the real meaning of our study for the realistic plans and methods for social and cultural exchange and cooperation as well as for the creation of the common social and cultural community.

The South-North Confederation under the "Three-Stage Unification" formula is only the beginning of a long journey towards Federation and complete unification. It is, indeed, a kind of fusion of two independent states. Under the Confederation, the two Korean governments will continue to maintain their respective authority while institutionalizing their cooperative relations. Therefore, the urgent task under the Confederation will be to systematize and institutionalize the efficient exchange and cooperation for coexistence and coprosperity. The two sides ought to make preparations for integration in all areas of society and culture through the peaceful management of the

---

[1]Kim Dae-jung, *My Way and My Ideas: The Great Transition of World History and Strategy for National Unification [Na-eui Gil Na-eui Sasang: Saegae-sa eui Dae-junhwan-gwa Minjok Tongil-eui Bang-ryak]* (Seoul: Hangilsa, 1994), p. 26.

national division, and work toward *de facto* unification.

What is the exact status and role of the social and cultural exchange and cooperation under the Confederation, and how can they be managed for effect? To be sure, the most important yardstick for such exchange and cooperation is its realism and feasibility. To put it differently, the central question is how realistic and feasible are the plans for exchange and cooperation in the world of specific realities, and through what means should they be implemented?

In discussing the plans and methods of social/cultural exchange and cooperation in this chapter, we shall consider our tasks for the early and latter phases of the Confederation. Our task in the early phase will be, while recognizing the expected differences, to identify the specific areas in which there still remain intact common characteristic between the two Koreas. For this, the two sides should try to understand and evaluate each other's society and culture with an open mind, and concentrate efforts to overcome their differences.

Our task in the latter phase of the Confederation ought to be to face the differences not as an obstacle to social integration, but to tolerate them as useful diversity to be harnessed as an important foundation in building a more advanced form of a cultural community. Such an objective, being distinguishable from the traditional state goals of "rich nation, powerful military," should signify our purpose of moving towards an open democracy based on the cultural capabilities that can enable us to carry on with the creative legacies and traditions of our culture. Such national efforts must be preceded by and based on the careful and systematic understanding of the changes in world order. Now our ultimate goal is to emplace the diversity and richness of life in the great framework of the "cultural state" armed with the spirit of peaceful exchange and coexistence—all within the context of the great East Asian cultural identity and moving forward to the new civilization of the twenty-first century.

The social-cultural community should be differentiated from a political community, based on political sovereignty, which covers a specific territoriality and designates legal qualification of citizenship; and in its basic characteristics, still different from a market-related economic community, established through human and material exchange as in the case of the European Common Market. It is a community that is based on a long accumulated national identity based on history and tradition; the cultural identity that binds the group through common linguistic and sentimental ethos; and the folk lore linking the past to the future, the collective national memories and experiences.

To restore social and cultural community under the circumstances of national division will not be easy by any means. There are still too many gaps and conflicts unresolved in the belief systems of the two Koreas, originating from the Cold War experiences, in all areas of society and culture. The Cold War of the last fifty years has made it impossible for Koreans to experience genuine national community. There were only mutual distrust, recrimination, and vilification. Nominally homogeneous, the Koreans in fact have become aliens to each other—the "others" who were out of bounds and off limits. Mutually exclusive taboos, oppression and persecution prevailed, resulting in the collective loss of historical awareness. Instead of a "reflective life" based on the correct understanding of the past as well as preparation for the future, life has been uni-dimensional, obsessed only with the moment.

The fact is that we, as a nation, have been deprived of our pride and self-esteem in the international community as a result

of national division and confrontation. Our international standing has been both minimized and distorted. Instead of focusing
and concentrating the national energies of both Koreas, we have
been split asunder, forcing us to bear the heavy material and
spiritual burden internationally.

The investigation and research, therefore, of the social and
cultural exchange/cooperation under the Confederation will
have to first reinstate the integrative symbols of the nation as the
foundation of the future ventures in social and cultural area. To
be sure, this will not happen naturally and by itself. Without
mutual cooperation in nurturing the common cultural roots and
soil, we will not be able to accomplish the task. It is vitally important that we employ all the available social and cultural means
to draw out mutually supportive and complementary experiences and self-esteem while at the same time we strive to overcome unhappy memories of the past and ossified images of each
other.

What can be done under the Confederation? For more
detailed discussion, we would categorize the three areas of
social/cultural community for the purpose of analyses. [Chart 5-1]
below shows the three areas and their inter-relations.

The first is the area which is related to the basic cultural values. The basic cultural values can be categorized as "cognitive
values" that both recognize things and search for the truth;
"normative values" which provide the rules for action and
behavior and value systems; and "esthetic values" which are
related to feelings, sentiment and esthetic experiences.

These cultural values can be implemented through specific
societal systems. The "Cognitive Values" reflected in the objective knowledge are managed through education. Through education, cultural and scientific development occurs; knowledge and

[Chart 5-1] Three Areas of the Social and Cultural Community

Areas of the Social and Cultural Community		Social System
Areas of Fundamental Values:	Cognitive Value Normative Value Esthetic Value	Educational & Scholarly System Religious System Art System
Areas of Implementation		Mass Media Sports Separated Families
Requirements for the Building of New Community	Expansion of Social Welfare Elimination of Gender Discrimination	

information accumulate; and the accumulated knowledge and information are passed on from generation to generation. The "Normative Values" are reflected in morality and ethics, and the instrument for their custody and management is religion. Religion causes the search for the ultimate meaning of life, and transmits the values of brotherly affection, love, benevolence, and justice as the moral bases of social-cultural community. Religions play a very important role in establishing the organic ties between the social groups and the larger framework of the community. The "Esthetic Values" cultivated by arts are experienced through joy and sorrow, beauty and ugliness, and so forth. These values are extended widely through artistic activities; but when such activities are appreciated and enjoyed by the masses, the quality of life becomes more abundant and richer.

Second, in discussing the ways for direct exchanges in the restoration of social-cultural community, we could consider the performing arts to transmit and to implement the cultural contents as separate from the areas of cultural values themselves. These areas can again be categorized into three fields; the first of which can be the role played by the mass media in expediting the mutual exchange, utilizing the means of language/words, cinema and television. The mass media, without question, is the most important valued means for the transmission of knowledge and information in a modern society of highly advanced information/intelligence. The second area is the role of sports in enhancing communal consciousness by means of festivals and sport events. Sports will take up an important part of the "performative" function to create national cohesiveness and unity while rejecting the political aspect.

The third "performative" area could be the reunion of the separated families. Few places in the world can one find a family structure so deeply rooted as in Korea. We are a nation in which there routinely occurs massive migration of people to their places of family roots on all major national holidays; and yet, the inability to come and go, and see one's close family members—so near and yet so far away—is an unendurable pain and sorrow not only in terms of basic human rights but also in fundamental human feelings. The problem of the separated families has been dealt with overly politically thus far. As in the case of the mass media and/or sports, the time has finally come now for us to deal with the issue from a purely humanitarian perspective; it ought to be handled as the simple issue of restoring family ties— the ties that form the basis of social-cultural community.

The third is the area of the social requirements that are needed in the process of our search for a new social-cultural community. If we are to build an open and creative "cultural state" in the Korean Peninsula, we will have to meet a series of

new social requirements along with the development of a fundamental social and cultural system. The essence of the new social
conditions and/or requirements will be to realize "democracy
that accompanies justice." There is an attempt here to overcome
several social frictions and fissures that have influenced our consciousness and actions. These frictions/fissures can be classified
as the conflicts between regions caused by regional disparities
and imbalances; the conflicts within the hierarchy and among
social classes from social and economic causes; the generational
conflicts over different values; and the gender conflicts over discrimination of women. The minimization of these differences
will be the preconditions for just and fair democracy.

In this chapter, we shall begin first with the objective understanding of the realities of the two Koreas by investigating the
processes of divergence in the social-cultural community as the
result of the national division. We shall also review the past
exchanges and cooperation between the two sides thus far, and
identify the problem areas so as to search for more suitable
modalities for future exchange.

Following that, we will address the detailed tasks in setting
up the specific plans for social-cultural exchanges after the Confederation is established. These specific plans that we envision
will be presented in the three categories, discussed above, namely, the areas of fundamental values, implementation, and the
requirements for building a new community. Here, the emphasis will be placed on meaningful methods—also both realistic
and feasible—that will contribute to the establishment of a new
social-cultural community under the Confederation.

Towards the end of the chapter, we shall re-examine the
role of the social-cultural area in the expected process of transition from Confederation to Federation. What we seek to achieve

in all this is to transform the divergence and differences into a new creative diversity so that our nation will be able to form a social-cultural community befitting the new century—ultimately to enhance the "quality of life" for all.

II. The Processes of the Social-Cultural Community Divergence and the Realities of Exchange Today

1. The Processes of Divergence in the Social-Cultural Community

After fifty years of national division, it is easy to understand why there are striking differences between the two Koreas not only in political, economic, and military systems, but also in people's ideas and thoughts, and values as well as modes of behavior and actions. No one, however, can be certain exactly to what extent the level of differentiation has progressed in the two societies. Here, we will investigate the level of differentiation and its processes in order to avoid simplistic optimism in our future task of restoring the common social-cultural community for all of Korea.

Without question, South and North Korea were a single social-cultural community until the national division in 1945. When we ponder on the fate of other neighboring peoples who were absorbed by the Chinese, and lost their own identity, the long tradition of our own existence as a unified state evokes in us all a renewed national pride in our accomplishment and its timeless significance. To be sure, we had to suffer the consequences of internal division due to serious contradictions in the Chosun Dynasty's bureaucratic society in the late nineteenth century and the heavy burden of legacies from the Japanese colonial rule in the early half of the twentieth century, but we were still able to preserve and maintain our cultural identity, necessary for the establishment of an independent nation-state. Nevertheless, contrary to our own wishes, our people were divided, which resulted in serious divergence, including the areas of politics, the economy, the military, society, and culture.

The causes of divergence can be examined on two levels. One is what we would call the structural cause. In the global order of Cold War confrontation, the two Koreas established mutually hostile systems based on wholly divergent ideologies—under which the process of differentiation began and gained momentum, armed with opposing ideologies and mutually exclusive developmental strategies. As a frontline state or a bridgehead in the Cold War world order, South Korea was to adopt capitalistic economic principles and North Korea socialistic ones. An intense conflict/confrontation and the dichotomous logic of "us against them" have come to prevail between the two sides. Ideologies of total conflict in which coexistence is ruled out in principle, stymied any flexibility and utilitarian thoughts. Interacting with the conflicting systems of society and culture, the long process of divergence began its relentless march.

The other cause is cultural. While a highly competitive and wholly self-centered climate prevailed in the South, the North was ruled by an extreme case of collectivistic thinking and highly accentuated values of autonomous identity. Although such a difference may be explained by the structural causes, there were still other reasons: to wit, there were two other potential possibilities in our very own social-cultural community. The typical difference in thoughts and actions of southern and northern Korea were not necessarily the result of outside influences but were to be found to an extent in the inherent national cultural community. The potentials for both an open and competitive cultural pattern and those of collectivistic and autarkic cultural heritage have existed in us throughout history.

The overall characteristics of the process of divergence in the two Koreas through the complex interaction between the structural and cultural factors can be summarized as follows:

While South Korea showed aspects of a pluralistic society based on a clear societal division of labor, North Korea was characterized by a society managed and controlled centripetally from top to bottom. While the ability to adapt flexibly to the changing environment increased in South Korea, the North became a society under centralized control which could force collective adaptation to surrounding circumstances. While South Korea has developed as an open society by actively accepting new ideas and new material culture from the West under the slogan "Let us also live it up," North Korea has stood on the policy of completely self-reliant development by cutting off all contacts with the outside world under the slogan "Let us live our own way." While South Korea has revealed its seamy sides in its process of modernization such as the enormous gap between the rich and the poor, social ills and conflicts, North Korea despite its equality in poverty, has implemented a more equitable social welfare system. The difference, however, is that through an effort for institutionalization, South Korea is in the process of seeking political solutions to the conflicts surrounding labor-management relations, gender discrimination, environmental pollution, and other contentious social issues. North Korea, on the other hand, lacks the institutional mechanism to peacefully resolve various social conflicts, including the important issue of human rights.

We are curious about to exactly what degree the process of

divergence and differentiation in various areas of the social-cultural community in the two Koreas has occurred. Let us therefore look at the real conditions of divergence in different areas, using the yardsticks provided in [Chart 5-1] above.

(1) Divergence in the Areas of Fundamental Values

We shall first look at the conditions of divergence and differentiation in the educational area—an area that reflects the cognitive values. The role of education is to "internalize" basic knowledge, modes of behavior and actions, and the value systems that are needed for the members of the society to be able to assume their roles as adult social beings. The determination of curricula for the future generation should be intimately related to the society's basic vision of what sort of societal members it intends to have. On this point, the two Koreas reveal a great deal of difference. In South Korea, the basic purpose of education is to realize what Korean philosophy has referred to as *"Hong-ik Ingan"*—a utilitarian concept of spreading welfare/ benefits to a wide circle of human beings—based on the principle of citizenship training with individualism and liberalism. North Korea, on the other hand, aims to "educate revolutionary workers with creative minds."

In educational systems, there are a great many differences between South and North Korea. The North Korean educational system consists of 2 years of kindergarten, 4 years of "People's School," 6 years in "High" Middle School (the "Middle Class" of 4 years and "High Class" of 2 years), 4 to 6 years in College, and Research Institute and others. One of the characteristics of the North Korean education system is that in addition to the regular education structure, it also developed various "social education systems" such as the "Factory College," "Fishery College," "Farm College" and so forth. In comparison with the South Korean system, the striking difference is in the higher development of the social educational structure for pre-school children, such as the nurseries and kindergarten. In South Korea, on the other hand, the educational system is organized around the traditional school systems.

On the contents of education, we should confine our study here to the differences that are evident in history and Korean language education, which are directly related to the problem of restoring the common national identity between the two Koreas. As to the purpose of historical education, there is a real gap between the two sides. In South Korea, the primary purpose of history education is to "plan properly for the future based on the correct understanding of the present through the study of the past" and "to develop and promote historical abilities to deal correctly with present and future problems based on the correct understanding of our national history, and to lead our present life independently by confirming our national capabilities."[2] On the other hand, North Korea's educational goal is that "the national history must be understood properly for greater success in Korea's revolution"; and "to realize the great Socialistic prospect for Korea and the promising future potentials of the fatherland through the study of Korea's history."[3]

On examination of the periodization in the history textbooks in the two Koreas, one can find considerable ideological differences. While South Korea periodizes by dynastic historical

---

[2]Ministry of Education, *History in High School*, 2 vols. (Seoul: Korea Textbooks Co., 1993), vol. 1, p. 1

[3]Educational Books Publishing Co., *The Korean History: For the Third and Fourth Grades in High Middle School* (Pyongyang, 1983).

account—the pre-historic period→Ancient Korea→the Three Kingdoms→Unified Silla and Balhae→Koryo Dynasty→Chosun Dynasty→Modern Period (from the Taewonkun Regency to Japanese Colonialism)→Contemporary History; North Korea's periodization is based on the Juche concept—the pre-historic period→Ancient History→the Middle Period (from the Three Kingdoms of Kokuryo, Baekjae, and Silla periods to the mid- and late-19th Century)→Modern Period (from the mid-and late-19th Century to the early 1920s)→Contemporary History. The historical account in North Korea, founded on the Juche historiography stresses the history of the class conflict and the mass struggle based on the "People-centered Historiography." The combined problems of the historiographical and periodizational differences make up the stark divergence in historical education in the two Koreas.

Along with history education, Korean language education also has great significance since language constitutes the nucleus of the social-cultural community. The fact is that even in the language education, one finds a great difference between the two. Under the most recent educational process in effect in South Korea, the purpose of Korean language training, despite some differences whenever there is a revision in educational processes, is specified as follows: it is defined as "the effective expression and comprehension of ideas and feelings through speaking and writing; the correct use of the Korean language through the systematized knowledge of languages in general and the Korean language in particular; and the comprehension and appreciation of literary works and the broad understanding of human life through the systematized knowledge of literature." On the other hand, North Korea, based on the concept of "language as the instrument" as the foundation of its Korean language education, stresses the importance and function of language as the manifestation of the assured self-reliance of the Koreans as well as the means for development in the economy, culture, science and technology.[4]

Second, we shall now look at the divergence/differences in the religious field that reflect the "normative values." Before the National Liberation in 1945, there were profound religious influences on the North Korean consciousness and life/life style because of the earlier arrival and dissemination of the Protestant and Catholic religions from the West, while traditional religions such as Buddhism and *Ch'ŏndoism*,[5] and others were also highly active. However, after 1945, while the total religious population increased dramatically in South Korea because of the guarantee of religious freedom, there was a drastic decline of religion in North Korea because of government hostility.

The religious situation in South Korea is characterized by the existence of multi-religions, multi-denominations, and multi-sects. In the big picture, Buddhism, Confucianism, Protestantism, Catholicism, "Won Buddhism"[6], *Ch'ŏndoism*, and others co-exist; while Buddhism is divided into eighteen denominations and Protestantism into 94 denominations. In addition, there are also numerous new religions and syncretic types of traditional religions coexisting in a complex quilt. The existence of numerous religions and the rapid growth of people with various

---

[4]Chun Soo-tae & Choi Chul-ho, *Comparative Study of the Languages in South and North Korea: For the Unification of National Language in the Era of Division* (Seoul: Nokjin, 1989), p. 21.

[5]Also known as *Ch'ŏndo* religion, founded in southern Korea by Choi Che-wu in 1859. This was the religion which was responsible in part for the Tonghak Peasant Rebellion in Korea in 1894-95.

[6]One of Korea's highly influential indigenous Buddhistic sects.

religious faiths in South Korea are unprecedented and unparalleled world wide. Such a massive surge of religion in South Korea occurred through the 1970's and the early 1980's. At the time, those who professed a religious affiliation accounted for 78 percent of the whole population.

On the other hand, there has been a rapid decline of religion in North Korea. At the time of the National Liberation in 1945, Ch' ndoism accounted for 1.5 million believers (16.4% of the North Korean population), Buddhism 500,000 (5.5% of the total North Korean population), the Protestantism 200,000 (2.2%), and Catholicism 53,000 (0.6%)—totalling nearly one quarter of North Koreans. Of the four major religions in Korea, *Ch'ŏndoism* and Protestantism had a greater proportion of followers in North Korea, while southern Korea had more Buddhists and Catholics. It was, therefore, impossible to ignore the weight of the religious population in the North, and the religious elements were the most powerful single organized force in North Korea. Besides, the Protestant Church in the North was the center and focus of North Korean intelligentsia.

Today, it is almost impossible to find data to study the real religious situation in North Korea. According to statistics released by the North Korean Alliance of Christians, there are roughly 10,000 Protestants and 1,000 Catholics; about thirty Protestant Church officials exist in North Korea—a number that has increased from only five ministers in early the 1980's—and not a single Catholic priest. The North Korean Alliance of Buddhists revealed that there are some 10,000 believers, and a great many non-believers attend their religious rites. The Buddhist Alliance reports that there are some three hundred monks in North Korea, but the number cannot be independently verified. *Ch'ŏndoism* had a powerful sway in north Korea before 1945, and because of its highly nationalistic nature, it is expected to have preserved its existence since then, although it is impossible to be certain. In the final analysis, therefore, the total religious population in North Korea, according to its religious groups, does not exceed 50,000 with a total of ecclesiastics at less than 500 for all religions. In comparison to the total North Korean population of approximately twenty-one million, the religious population amounts to a pitifully insignificant 0.2 percent. Without question, North Korea is in a near total religious vacuum.

However, even in North Korea, there seems to have been a gradual change since the 1980's. One such change has been the increasing activities of North Korea's religious organizations. Almost all of the existing religious groups were organized after 1945 under government sponsorship and supervision, and their activities came to a halt after the Korean War. However, in the 1970's, there was a partial revival of their activities, and since the eighties, they have come to the foreground, with their activities being more frequently reported by the North Korean press. The new constitution of 1992 restored partial freedom of religion by deleting the provision on "the freedom of anti-religious propaganda" in the 1972 revision of the constitution.

Third, let us now look at the process of divergence/differentiation in the field of the arts which reflects the esthetic values. Supporting pure arts, the concept of art for the art's sake without ideological overlays, is recognized in South Korea. Along with the guarantees of freedom of speech and the press, the South Korean Constitution also guarantees freedom of scholarship and the arts. Accordingly, there is freedom for creative artistic activities, and all sorts of expressions are allowed to exist depending on literary and artistic trends of thinking. Needless to say, the cultural and artistic activities are limited and/or regulated by the National Security Law in the South, with the result that it is impossible to find works that show any pro-Communist aspect or exhibit a "soft" stance on Communism, and certainly no pro-North Korean bent.

In North Korea, following Kim Il Sung's directives, the arts are defined as revolutionary weapons to educate the masses in the Communist revolutionary spirit. Artistic expression is based on "Socialistic Realism"[7]—the combination of the Nationalistic form and Socialistic substance. The most notable characteristic of the Socialistic Arts a *là* North Korean style is the inculcation of "mass patriotism," for which culture and art must create a "model human being"—a model created from the mold of the Great Leader. North Korea's cultural and artistic policies emphasize evolutionary development based on the critical inheritance of the national cultural legacies, condemning pure arts without the concept of purpose or goal, and the impressionistic Western culture as the product of nihilism. At the same time, considering the upper class culture and arts of the past as the culmination of the reactionary trends, North Korea condemns and opposes both their revival and/or inheritance. Engaged in "creative" activities only within the narrow confines of the North Korean system and structure, North Korean cultural artists are entirely different from their Southern counterparts, engaged in individual acts of creation based on the market principle.

---

[7]Accordingly, under the overall principles of party loyalty, integrity as ["socialistic"] citizens and class/hierarchical qualities, the "Socialistic National Culture" is based on the specific concepts: the "Correct Seeds—the combination of Juche, Ideology, and Story Line—for Literary Art," the "Arts based on Juche Ideology," the "Blitzkrieg," "Art for the Masses," "Art based on Eternal Ideas of Juche," "Model-building based on the 'class and mass line' policies," and "Routinization."

(2) Divergence in the Area of Implementation

In the area of implementation, we shall look first at the divergence in the mass media . Being used mainly as the instrument, or weapon, if you will, of political propaganda, the process of divergence/differentiation has been particularly rapid. We will discuss the differences in the mass media in the two Koreas by examining the ownership, structure, function, contents, technology, and others.

As for the differences in ownership structure, the South Korean media is divided between state- and public-owned, on the one hand, and private media, while all the mass media in North Korea is state-owned. North Korea's press, as a lower echelon organization, discharges the tasks given to it by the state and the party; it is owned solely by the centralized authority, which exerts the complete control and management.[8]

On the differences of function, South Korean mass media play the following functions: providing information and entertainment, the accumulation of media capital through sales, the formation of public opinion through editorials and commentaries, and the expansion of capital and the promotion of reproduction through advertisements. On the contrary, the function of North Korea's mass media is the propagation of the party policy line, the ideological indoctrination of the people, the organizational mobilization of the masses in revolutionary construction, and pushing for revolution in South Korea.[9] Thus, the functions of North Korean broadcasting can be summarized as the

---

[8]Han Kyun-tae, "On North Korea's Broadcast Policy and System," *Study of Broadcasting* [*Bang-song Yunkoo*] (Seoul: Broadcast Committee, 1989), p. 204.

[9]The Korean Broadcasting Institute, *On the Technological Tasks for the Inter-Korean Broadcasting Exchange* (Seoul, 1992), p. 144.

implementation of propaganda, agitation, organization/mobilization, and cultural education.

As for the differences in the substance of the mass media, in the case of the newspapers, the Southern ones consist of all sorts of reading materials in sections dealing with politics, economy, culture, daily life, sports, society, and so forth, with nearly half of the pages crammed with information on products and advertisements. The North Korean papers, on the other hand, are far simpler in contents, and are dependent almost entirely on the Northern press agency [Korean Central Press Agency/*Chosun Choong-ang Tongshin*], and have neither society pages nor advertisements. The heavy reliance on the press agency is clear evidence of its role as the power censor of the newspapers in North Korea. That North Korean papers do not have any pages on social events, involving key events and/or accidents, and others, are what set it apart from their Southern counterparts; and that there are no advertisements is generally characteristic of all the papers in "socialist/communist" countries.

In the case of broadcasting, South Korean broadcasting works towards diversified programs, and allows relatively free criticism of the government. The Broadcasting Law sets the ratio of program organization to be 40, 20, and 10 percent each for education, entertainment, and news reporting. North Korean broadcasting concentrates on propagating the Juche Ideology and revolutionary activities, party policies; organizing and mobilizing the people into production activities by encouraging productive endeavors, and propagating and enhancing the international status of the Great Leader and North Korea through reporting on domestic and foreign news. Using music and drama programs, it advances the cause of people's unity; criticizes capitalism through the interpretation/explanation of socialism and the Juche Ideology; and levels criticism against the imperial states, including the United States.[10]

The part that cannot be ignored in dealing with the differences between the two Korea's mass media is the technological gap between the two. First in television broadcasting, the two sides cannot tune in to each other's programs because of the difference in standards.[11]

South Korea's color television broadcasting is based on the NTSC system and the "M" method of 525 "lines per frame" and the frequency and spectrum of 6MHz, while North Korea's color television broadcasting is based on the PAL (the German method of "phase alternation line") system and the "D" method of 625 "lines per frame" and the frequency and spectrum of 8 MHz. In radio broadcasting, the people on both sides cannot listen to each other's broadcasts because of the total and absolute fixing of the allowed channel and the confiscation of the radio receivers in North Korea, and the jamming by South Korea.

Now let us examine the process of the differentiation in the field of sports. Although sports, completely non-political in nature, are meant to achieve a certain result through physical exercise, the concepts, goals, and policy direction can differ depending on the characteristics of a specific society. Reflecting political ideology, sports can be turned into the means to pursue democratic ideals in capitalistic societies and socialistic goals in

---

[10]Chung Hyung-soo, "The Realities of North Korea's Broadcasting," in *North Korea's Newspapers and Broadcasting* (Seoul: Board of National Unification, Republic of Korea, 1979), p. 163.

[11]North Korea's television broadcasting from the city of Kaesong, being equipped the same as South Korea's NTSC (National Television Systems Committee) system, is a propaganda station mainly aimed at South Korea. However, because of South Korean jamming, it cannot be seen in South Korea.

socialist/communist states. Because of the intense political, military, and emotional conflicts under wholly different ideologies between the two Koreas, there inevitably occurred notable differences in the field of sports as well.

In South Korea, sports, through personal life and physical training, aim for the development of the all around person. The "Juche sports" of North Korea, on the other hand, aim for the education/indoctrination of "warriors/fighters" for the success of the Communist revolution and the construction of the Socialist State. Politically, however, both sides look at sports in a very similar fashion. Since the Liberation in 1945 and through the experiences of the Korean War, both Koreas viewed sports not only in the context of justifying their respective political ideologies, but also viewed the confirmation of superiority in the sports arena as an important state goal. The significance of this is that both sides acknowledge the political effects of sports in unifying and mobilizing divergent and unsophisticated citizens for their respective cause. Hence, sports in both Koreas have greatly deviated from the original value of the improvement of national health and/or the constructive use of leisure; and misused it entirely for the justification of each other's political system and ideology as well as for ensuring political and social unity and mobilization.

(3) The Divergence in the Requirements for the Building of New Community.

One of the goals that we wish to achieve for unified Korea is the establishment of a just and fair society through the equitable enhancement of people's livelihood and the improvement of welfare. The social welfare and the status of women in general are of great significance in eliminating the structures of inequality in all areas of society in the overall process of building a new social and cultural community for the nation.

Until now, the people of both Koreas have had to postpone a good part of their aspirations for the improvement of the quality of their lives, due mainly to excessive military outlays and mutual hostility. Moreover, under the system of authoritarian political culture, it has been extremely difficult to argue for the ideals of gender equality.

Now we shall examine the process of divergence/differentiation between the two Koreas in the area of social welfare. Since the problem of social welfare is directly related to the very nature of the social system as a whole, it would be helpful to trace the process of divergence/differentiation in the systemic changes and evolution of social welfare in both Koreas based on the ideology of capitalism in the South and socialism in the North.[12] In terms of the chronological examination of the social welfare systems in the two Koreas, the period from the National Liberation in 1945 to the 1960's was a time of the most notable divergence. At the time, South Korea was in a state of complete vacuum as far as the social security system was concerned. The major focus then was placed on the work of assisting the North Korean refugees and others who were displaced by the war; practically all of the social welfare organizations were private in nature, or were operated by various religious or foreign assistance groups as the government's function in this area was practically non-existent.

---

[12]Chung Kyung-bae, *et al., The Comparative Study of the Social Security System in South and North Korea* (Seoul: Korea Institute for Health and Social Affairs, 1992), passim.

During the same period, however, North Korea completed at least the basic framework for a socialistic social security system, albeit of very low standard. As for the measures taken for the income guarantees in North Korea, all workers and office employees and their dependents were paid subsidies and annuities as part of a social security system under the "Labor Law" and the "Social Insurance Law," enacted in 1946; and the system of insurance for state support of military families was in place from May 1949. As for the medical insurance system, North Korea provided general medical service as well as payments for illnesses. North Korea also took legal steps for the protection of women's rights and for the provision of health and medical services for children. It must be pointed out, however, that despite the outward appearance, the substance of the program is reported to have been less than adequate.

Entering the 1960's, various social welfare legislation was enacted in South Korea while North Korea continued to consolidate its existing social security system. After the military coup d'etat in May 1961, South Korea began its first Five-Year Economic Development Plan and various social welfare laws and regulations were enacted as part of that Five-Year Plan. The trouble was that the laws were provided without any substantive follow-up. In fact, the role of private welfare organizations was still basically far more prominent than that of the state; thus the welfare model in place was one of combined public and private systems with mutual complementarity.

In the same period, North Korea began and developed the system of free medical care with emphasis on preventive medicine along with the system of the regional assignment of doctors—thus expanding the system of free medical care, established in the 1950's. In the area of social welfare service, upgraded service was provided to women and children in order to fill the labor shortage caused by the socialistic industrialization program.

Concerning the changes from the 1970's to the present, we are witnessing the rapid narrowing of the gap in social welfare provisions between the two Koreas because of the active adoption of all sorts of welfare programs by South Korea. Since 1973, for instance, South Korea has begun to include social development strategy in the national developmental program; and since the 4th Economic Plan, an active and systematic program of social development has been pursued under the overall principles of growth, efficiency, and equity, resulting in several changes in the social security area. A series of social welfare laws were passed along with the overhauling of the system itself under the Fifth [the Chun Doo-hwan government] and the Sixth [the Roh Tae-woo government] Republics.

North Korea's social welfare policies in the early seventies were characterized by the factors of labor incentives as well as balanced growth. It was a period when there was a labor shortage for industrialization in North Korea. The expansion and systematization of the welfare measures for children, therefore, were, in part, the reflection of the ideological/policy goal, designed not only to attract more female workers, but also to nurture children as the warriors for Juche Revolution.[13] Simultaneously, medical services for the farm sector were also expanded as a part of the policy to accentuate the "Three Major Technical Revolutions," designed to narrow the significant gap between industrial and agricultural labor.

For North Korea, the period since the late seventies to the

---

[13]Yoon Mi-ryang, *North Korea's Policy on Women* (Seoul: Han-ul, 1991), p. 100.

present can be considered the time in which the structural framework of social welfare was being completed. For instance, in 1978, various policies were systematized for guaranteed income through the enactment of the "Socialist Labor Law"; and in 1985, the social security system, subsidized by the state, was expanded to include the farmers, hitherto excluded from the national social security system. A similar structural framework was provided for state supported medical coverage by the passage of the "People's Health Law" in 1980.

All in all, the greatest divergence/difference in the social welfare systems of the two Koreas is that whereas the Southern system can largely be characterized as a sort of indirect national insurance system based on the principle of beneficiary's co-payment and managed through the combined private organizations, the Northern system is primarily state-run as one of the fundamental policies by the state for social security. As North Korea exhibits the typical Socialist State Model of "excessive development of the state and retardation of civil society," the state as the primary actor in the area of social welfare is virtually inevitable.

Now considering the problem of women as part of social welfare, one can find a considerable degree of difference/divergence as the result of the different social systems.

First, let's take a look at the economic status of women in South Korea: there is pronounced gender discrimination against women in economic activities. In fact, women in general are treated inequitably in comparison to their male counterparts in terms of job opportunities, in wages and salaries, promotion, and in assignment; indeed, most of the female workers are still concentrated in low-paid and low-skill jobs. As a result, the majority of employed women are heavily burdened by the dual/triple chores of employment, child raising, and household labor.

In North Korea, however, the value and importance of women's labor are at least officially recognized, pro forma, in accordance with the socialist ideal of gender equality and the reality of its structural need for women's labor. At the same time, North Korea has been trying to solve the derivative problems of inequality in child raising and household chores for working women through the active intervention of state policy.

But in reality, in North Korea there still are inequality in wage and salary, job position differences solely due to gender, and the continuing dual burden on women under the deeply entrenched tradition of patriarchical domination. Simultaneously, due to the failure to provide the needed means and circumstances to actualize the idealistic policy goals, a major part of the policies designed to help women has been rendered ineffectual.

Second, comparing the political status of women in both Koreas, whereas the political status remains relatively low for the Southern women despite their higher rate of economic participation and role, and educational qualifications,[14] the Northern women are said to enjoy higher status in comparison to their Southern sisters. Needless to say, it would be impossible to com-

---

[14]The statistical data on women's participation in politics show that as of 1955, there is just one woman minister in a cabinet of 24 ministers, and just six out of the total of 299 members of the National Assembly are women (about 2.0%). In the elections for the autonomous local governments, held on June 27, 1995, 72 out of 4,541 members of the local assemblies are women, while only 13 of the 875 members for the provincial and city government assemblies are women, amounting to 1.06% and 1.5% respectively. The ratio of women taking part in the policy-making process, above the rank of the "third level" (comparable to an "assistant secretary" in the U.S. Federal Government) in the South Korean bureaucracy is only around 1.1%.

pare the actual status of the two sides merely based on statistics, because, in reality women are being excluded from the major decision-making process, and it remains to be seen if the Northern women will be able to preserve and maintain the present level of status without the active system of quotas.

Third, in terms of "consciousness" for women, one can find the most stark differences between the two sides. Southern women have become conscious of the reality of their oppression, through the acceptance, albeit partially, of the influences of the Western women's liberation movement, and are in the process of making an effort to change things legally, systemically, and in consciousness and value systems. The women in the North, on the other hand, seem to have internalized without much difficulty the conflicting images of women under the patriarchy as well as the revolutionary socialist type as an ideal model.

Fourth, as for the family systems, the two Koreas still maintain the tradition of the patriarchical family, which continues to affect the status of women in the family. On this score, one can argue that the two Koreas still retain a great similarity. By the traditional division of labor between the sexes, the two sides still assign the primary responsibility of household chores and child raising to women. Of particular significance is that North Korea, by defining the society in its entirety as the "Socialistic Family," tries to justify and legitimize the "one man dictatorship" and the principle of succession from father to son based on the tradition of patriarchy. On the other hand, a notion of strong preference for male children still prevails in South Korea, while complete gender equality is yet to be achieved in terms of the legal systems concerning the family.

The family system, being the foundation of Korea's social and cultural community, is an area where we will have to focus our major attention. Thus, the tradition of the Korean family must be considered to have several commendable strengths, as it provides the sense of stability to its component members as well as the basis for social integration. However, it ought to be pointed out that because of the entrenched tradition of the patri-archical system based on blood lines, the status of women in general has to remain relatively inferior to their male counter-parts. Therein lie the serious social limitations in Korea.

We have thus far examined the processes of divergence/dif-ferentiation between the two Koreas' social-cultural communi-ties. We believe that the objective understanding of the differ-ences between the two sides in this area will be able to provide us with the ability to determine the basic policy directions for the ultimate social and cultural exchanges and cooperation between the two Koreas, and to determine the realistic starting point of that historic attempt.

2. The Realities of Social-Cultural Exchange Today

The process of divergence/differentiation in the social and cultural community since the national division has been consid-ered a serious national issue both by the citizens and the rulers in the two Koreas. To decelerate the process, the two Koreas have made occasional attempts for exchanges. The first discus-sion since the Armistice Agreement for inter-Korean exchanges took place on August 30, 1972: the Red Cross Talks. From this point until July 1973, seven Red Cross Talks took place in Seoul and Pyongyang in rotation. The main agenda for these talks was to seek a solution to the separated families in both Koreas. The Southern demands were: the confirmation of life or death of the separated family members and their addresses; the right to communicate with them and the arrangement for their reunion; and the exchange visits to family grave sites during traditional holidays such as *Chusuk* (Thanksgiving Day). The North Korean response was that South Korea must remove all factors which inhibit the realization of free exchange of visits between the separated families such as the legal limitations and other social atmosphere unfavorable for the purpose of exchange. The talks, however, were at an impasse as the two sides' demands were irreconcilable, and were eventually stopped entirely without any result through all of the 1970's.

The inter-Korean exchanges were renewed once again in the mid-1980's, although they were confined to a very limited form of human exchanges. When South Korea suffered from serious flood damage in September 1984, North Korea proposed sending emergency goods for flood assistance. The Southern acceptance of assistance from the North opened the new door for inter-Korean dialogue, resulting in the resumption of the Red Cross Talks in May 1985 to continue the discussion of the issue of the separated families. The two sides eventually agreed on the exchange of the "First Inter-Korean Visits by the Separated Families and the Art Performing Troupes." Under this agreement, the first visits were exchanged during September 20-23, 1985.

The first visiting delegations were composed of a total of 151 persons from both sides: 30 North Koreans met with 51 separated family members and relatives in Seoul, while 35 South Koreans met with 41 separated family members and relatives in Pyongyang. During the exchange visits, two separate performances were held for the visiting members in the National Theater in Seoul and the Grand Theater in Pyongyang respectively. Through this affair, the first official exchanges took place under an inter-Korean agreement with great symbolic significance in the relations between the two sides. Hopes were high for the continuation of similar exchanges. To the disappointment of all, nothing came of it. An agreement was reached in 1989 for the second exchange visits to occur between December 8 and 11 in the same year; however, because of the serious disagreement over the scheduled performance of a revolutionary drama—"The Flower Girl"—by North Korea, the exchange visits never took place.[15]

Finally, however, high-level talks resumed between the two Koreas in 1990, resulting in inter-Korean soccer matches, a "pannational" music festival for national unification, and a year-end traditional music festival for the same purpose—held in Seoul and Pyongyang in turn. Through these events, an increasing number of people on both sides began to visit the opposite side. Following what transpired in 1990, the exchanges increased even further starting in 1991, when along with the continued high-level talks, there were the world youth table tennis tourna-

---

[15]Although the two Koreas reached another agreement in June 1992 to exchange "delegations of old parents of the separated families as well as performing arts troupes" from August 25 to 28, this too never materialized over the controversy involving the case of the "Repatriation of Mr. Lee In-mo." Mr. Lee In-mo, born in 1917, was a North Korean war correspondent during the Korean War. As the United Nations forces crushed the North Korean forces in late 1950 and marched north into North Korea, Lee stayed behind the line and served as a guerrilla fighter until he was captured in December 1952. Serving a 7-year prison term, he was released in January 1959, and was rearrested as a North Korean agent, and given another 15-year prison term. He was kept in prison under the "Societal Security Law" (now the Security Surveillance Law), enacted in 1975 during the Park Chung-hee government until 1989, having served a total of 34 years; and because of severe torture under South Korean detention, he was sick through most of his prison term. He was 72 years when he was released as an "unrepentant hardcore Communist." After a great deal of controversial debate in South Korea, he was finally repatriated to North Korea by the Kim Young-sam government as a part of the Southern gesture to improve inter-Korean relations.

[Chart 5-2] The Exchange Visits between the Two Koreas

Number of persons (Number of cases)

Year	Visits to North Korea	Visits to South Korea
1989	1 (1)	
1990	183 (3)	291 (4)
1991	237 (10)	175 (3)
1992	257 (8)	103 (3)
1993	18 (4)	6 (2)
1994	12 (1)	
Total	708 (27)	575 (12)

Source: Bureau of Exchange/Cooperation, Board of National Unification, Republic of Korea, *South-North Korean Exchanges and Cooperation Today* [Monthly] (March-April, 1995, pp. 3-4)

[Chart 5-3] The Exchange Visits by Categories

Number of persons (Number of cases)

Categories of Exchange Visits	Actual Cases of Exchange Visits
Separated Families	650 (726)
Scholarly Functions	69 (935)
Cultural Exchange	20 (393)
Religious Exchange	27 (260)
Sports Exchange	14 (60)
Economic Exchange	244 (704)
Journalistic/Publication Exchange	23 (88)
Tourism & Transportation Area	26 (79)
Others	43 (718)
Total	1,116 (3,963)

Source: Bureau of Exchange/Cooperation, Board of National Unification, Republic of Korea, *South-North Korean Exchanges and Cooperation Today* [Monthly] (March-April, 1995, pp. 3-4)

ments, the world youth soccer matches, the IPU conference, the UNDP Conference in Pyongyang, and others. These important symbolic events took place in Seoul and Pyongyang, and in third countries.

To reinforce and accentuate the atmosphere of mutual recon- ciliation and the exchanges and cooperation, sporadically pur- sued between the two Koreas since the late 1980's, the two Kore- as took additional measures: the Southern "Directives for the Inter-Korean Exchanges and Cooperation" were issued in June 1989 and the "Law for the Inter-Korean Exchanges and Coopera- tion" was passed by the South in 1990; and in 1992, the so-called "Basic Agreement" between the two Koreas went into effect, thus providing a structural mechanism for sustained relations.

The statistical data on the inter-Korean exchanges from June 1989 when the Southern Directives on the Exchanges/Coopera- tion were issued to July 31, 1994 are provided in [Chart 5-2 and 5-3] below. As shown in [Chart 5-2], the inter-Korean exchanges since 1993 have been drastically reduced, caused mainly by the interruption of the inter-Korean government level talks over the nuclear issue and by the cancellation of the planned visit to North Korea by Southern businessmen.

[Chart 5-3] describes the number of official applications by Southern citizens to the government for permission to contact/visit with their family members/relatives in North Korea and the number of permissions given by the government; and the exchanges by categories. This chart, indeed, indicates that there have been frequent exchanges in all areas.

As shown above, the inter-Korean exchanges thus far have been generally unremarkable.[16] One of the most important rea-

---

[16]In Germany's case, the human and material exchanges never stopped

sons for the meager record of exchanges between the two Koreas has been the structure of Cold War confrontation. However, besides this fundamental limitation, there have been several additional problems inherent in the attitudes of the two Koreas which placed extreme inhibition on the whole business of exchanges.

Most of all, there is the fundamental difference in the way the two Koreas approach the issue of unification strategies. Whereas South Korea prefers the "functionalist approach" of the economic exchanges—the easiest approach with the greatest possible ripple effect, North Korea takes the position that once the fundamental problems in the political-military area are settled, the exchanges and cooperation in other areas will naturally follow. Because of this fundamental difference in the policy positions of the two sides, it has been almost impossible to expect full scale exchanges between them.[17] Nevertheless, there have been signs that the basic positions of the two sides are changing in many respects under the changing regional environment around the Korean Peninsula. As it turned out, today

---

after the country was divided. Particularly, the accelerated exchanges with the signing of the Basic Treaty [*Vertrag über die Grundlagen der Beziehungen zwischen der Bundesrepublik Deutschland und der Deutschen Demokratischen Republik*] between the two Germanys in 1972 laid the foundation for the eventual unification. Between China and Taiwan, too, the human exchanges have rapidly grown since the Taiwan government permitted its people to visit the mainland for the purpose of meeting with their family members and relatives in November 1987. Today, the exchanges across the Taiwan Strait have expanded to such a level that the realities of the national division themselves are blurred. Consequently, compared to the cases of Germany and China, our situation can only be described as "pathetic."

[17]Kang Jung-koo, "Policies for the Establishment of the Inter-Korean Social-Cultural Community," in *In Search of Rapid Restoration of Common National Identity* (Seoul: Board of National Unification, Republic of Korea, 1993), p. 135.

whereas South Korea is more reluctant to move ahead with the economic, social, and cultural exchanges, insisting that the two sides ought to address the nuclear and other security issues first, North Korea has shown a greater willingness for contacts between the leaders of the political parties and/or religious leaders, and for economic cooperation via contacts with South Korea's big businesses.

Second, there are vast gaps between the two Koreas in terms of the political motives behind their respective unification policies. South Korea's emphases on the social-cultural exchanges in the past under the successive governments has been their conviction that these exchanges could bring demonstrable effects, which then in turn could be pointed to in their propaganda campaigns to the people as the tangible achievements of their unification strategies. On the other hand, North Korea wanted to avoid the exchanges at all cost as it felt that they were corrosive and detrimental to its political system. As the economic gap between the South and the North widen more seriously, it is understandable that North Korea will attempt to hide the fact to its own people and that it will desperately try to prevent the exposure of its true conditions to the South. For these reasons, unless South Korea discontinues its "exhibitionistic" exchange policy and strategy towards the North, and unless the two Koreas convert together to a posture of peaceful coexistence, reconciliation, and cooperation, it would be very difficult to expect more active implementation of the human exchanges between them.

Third, the unification policies of both Koreas have inherent weaknesses as they are completely controlled by the respective governments. If we are to achieve more active social and cultural exchanges, the role of the government will have to be minimized and the initiative and role of the private sector will have to be expanded. However, independent participation by the private sector has been systematically discouraged and even suppressed by the government thus far in the inter-Korean exchanges; while the government completely monopolized the entire process. Consequently, the exchanges and cooperation between the two sides were not pursued as they should have been; and degenerated into a competitive contest between the two opposing systems.

In the case of North Korea, the role of the private sector has been understandably weak because of the very nature of its system; and even the so-called "private organizations" are the logical extension of the government itself. Cognizant of this inescapable fact, South Korea has been insisting on contacts through a "single [designated] channel" and persisted in its position to apply the National Security Law to closely regulate the entire process. As long as such practices and logic continue, it will not be possible to expect the enlargement of the exchanges any time soon. The alternative has to be that although the negotiating channel must continue to be the government, the contacts and exchanges themselves will have to be diversified and multi-faceted through the abolition of various regulations, while ultimately, the private sector must be allowed a proper role not only in the initiation but necessarily in the participation of the exchanges themselves.

III. The Basic Principles of Social-Cultural Exchange/ Cooperation Under the Confederation

1. The Significance of the Confederation and the Need for Social-Cultural Exchange/Cooperation

As discussed earlier, the South-North Confederation is simply a form of cooperation between the two sovereign states, both maintaining their respective governmental functions. It is an institutionalization of mutual cooperation between them, designed to manage peacefully, effectively, and efficiently the process of integration so that ultimately the two sides can progress towards unification.

In this phase, the two Koreas are to remove the threat of war and maintain the conditions for peaceful coexistence; to restore mutual trust and confidence through a greater degree of exchanges and cooperation; and finally to form the "realistic environment for national unification" through the re-establishment of the common national community of compatible national sentiment. It is also a stage in which actual integrational processes will be laid out through providing assistance to North Korea to help in the gradual change of its system.

The major task for the Confederation in the social-cultural area is to restore the homogeneous social identity of all Koreans through the expansion of the inter-Korean exchanges and cooperation. The ultimate goal, however, is to establish an "open and creative cultural state" for Korea. To achieve these goals, it would be necessary to develop abilities to embrace all the differences—caused by the experiences of ideological conflict and confrontation between the two Koreas—under the umbrella of diversity and plurality. In the process of grand national integra-

tion, we ought to be vigilant against the potential rise of chau-
vinistic and close-minded nationalism in Korea, which could
compel the neighboring powers to interfere with our efforts for
national unification. As a nation with a long tradition of culture,
it is our responsibility to reconfirm the national identity, inherit
its mantle and develop it further, and to carry on with the active
exchanges and cooperation with our neighboring states to help
develop the common cultural community for all of Northeast
Asia and ultimately for the coexistence and coprosperity of all
human kind, and for world peace.

With these goals in mind, the primary purpose of the social-
cultural exchanges and cooperation under the Confederation is
to firmly recognize the presence of mutual distrust, prejudice,
and cultural disparities in order seek proper ways to transcend
the existing conflicts and frictions between the two Koreas; to
enlarge, expand, and further develop the common roots that
have bound us together through the centuries so that ultimately
we could fully restore a common social and cultural community
for the whole country. These, indeed, are the fundamental
premises of the national, social, and cultural integration under
the Confederal structure.

2. The Basic Principles and Tasks of the Social-Cultural
   Exchange/Cooperation

The following "exchange and cooperation" projects are the
means to achieve the above mentioned goals. There are expected
to be not only political and technical limitations in agreeing on
these means, but also a certain aspect of turf warfare among policy priorities and frictions. For this reason, it would be vitally
important to approach the subject systematically as well as

strategically. Especially since the Confederation will be set up with the general assumption that it will run roughly a decade, it will be particularly important to push the necessary policies in systematic progression in order to achieve a smooth transition to the next stage—a Federation. Thus, we shall divide the Confederal stage into two periods—early and late—and present our policy proposals for each phase.

The early Confederal period is one of consolidating the foundation for exchanges and cooperation, fully recognizing the mutual differences/divergence between the two Koreas; therefore, a period in which the selective exchanges shall be made only in areas where mutual approaches are the easiest. Attempts should be made to set aside the ideological differences as much as possible, and the policy programs ought to be one of mutual complementarity. The later phase of the Confederation is one of expanding and intensifying the mutual exchange and cooperation in order to lay the foundation for smooth transition to a Federal stage. The foundation laid earlier will have to expanded and intensified further during this later stage, while the two Koreas shall concentrate more on joint projects in different areas so as to help restore the common homogeneous identity between them; and to seek ways to transform the divergence/ differences into harmonious diversity.

The exchange/cooperation in the social-cultural area shall be pursued under the following principles in order to, first, overcome the problems that have been revealed in the exchange process thus far as well as to accomplish the goals set for the inter-Korean exchanges and cooperation.

First, there ought to be a principle that the two sides mutually recognize each other's autonomy or independence in the social-cultural area. As pointed out earlier, the South-North

Confederation is to be established between the two equal sovereign states, on the firm premise that the two sides recognize each other's system: the capitalist system in the South and the socialist system in the North. Accordingly, the most important principle in this Confederal stage ought to be the recognition of each other's system; and all exchange and cooperation projects in all areas will have to reflect that fundamental principle. Therefore, these projects ought be pursued on the basis of plurality/diversity, and neither side should try to impose on the other its own ideology, values, and/or systems unilaterally.

Second, the mutual benefits and complementarity ought to form the next basic principle. The programs/projects in social-cultural areas ought to proceed as a "positive sum game" wherein the two sides could ensure and increase mutual benefits through the joint implementation of the projects, designed to restore their respective cultural pride as well as the common historical consciousness and perception. A one sided "zero sum game" ought to be avoided at all cost. The ideal form of exchange/cooperation will be to develop exchange and cooperation projects that could both supplement and/or complement each other's weaknesses. To do this, it would be imperative for each side to approach the subject with an open mind—a willingness to accept each other's social/cultural strength. Despite the superficial differences between the two, what is needed is to explore and discover the historical/cultural assets common to both, and build on these commonalities.

Third, to maximize the effect of exchange/cooperation, the effort will have to be supported through political institutions. Priorities will have to be determined first in the establishment of common programs or projects so that they could be maximally supportive to Confederation. The priority projects will have to be the ones that could inspire the people of both Koreas to feel that they are members of a common national community. Only such a process will enhance mutual benefits and relations, which in turn will assist materially in the institutional operation of the Confederation.

Fourth, for more active exchange and cooperation between the two Koreas, the private sectors must be allowed greater leeway and freedom. Government interference ought to be limited to a minimum. It is highly desirable that the government abandons its arbitrary position as the sole monopolizer in relations with the other side if we are to ensure greater leeway and freedom in private sector exchanges. There is also the need to change or abolish various restrictions that have so far impeded the inter-Korean exchanges. For instance, despite the alleged intent, the existing "Law for the South-North Exchange and Cooperation" actually makes it very difficult for the inter-Korean exchanges to go forward because of the extra complex system of the government recognition and permission processes, and excessive penalty provisions. Moreover, there is ample room for the law to be abused for political purposes; and it has, in fact, been used for purposes other than the original legislative purposes of encouraging and expediting the inter-Korean exchanges and cooperation.[18] For these and other similar reasons, if we are to realistically promote exchanges and cooperation between the two sides, these restrictive regulations and laws ought to be done away with first.

---

[18]Lee Chang-hee, "The Problems in the Promotion of Scholarly Exchanges between University Professors of South and North Korea," in *The Reality and Prospect in the Scholarly Exchanges of the Professors and the Students between South and North Korea* (Seoul: Committee for the Promotion of Scholarly Exchanges of University Professors between South and North Korea, 1992), p. 72.

To increase and expand the multi-faceted exchanges in the social and culture area, we should begin with the direct humanitarian exchanges, which in turn would require a greater open door policy. The scope of contact with the North Koreans will have to be expanded, and the present system of government "permission/license" will have to be changed to one of simple notification, ultimately to be of completely open procedures.[19]

In the final account, what is needed is institutionalized and financial backup for the activation of exchanges and cooperation. First, for the institutional backup, the Confederation will be the outcome of the "South-North Confederation Charter,"[20] all exchanges and cooperation in the social-cultural area as well as their coordination and control functions will be performed under the same Charter.

---

[19]Doh Hong-ryul, "Proposal for Information and Human Exchanges between the *Two Koreas*," in *The Opening of the Era of Reconciliation and Cooperation and Inter-Korean Relations* (Seoul: Board of National Unification, Republic of Korea, 1992), p. 145.

[20]The transition to the Confederation will occur only after the Confederal Charter is signed with the fulfillment of the political conditions as discussed in Chapter 2 above. Here, a question can be raised as to whether or not a preparatory stage of "reconciliation and cooperation" is necessary before the Confederal Stage is agreed on between the two Koreas. As explained earlier in some detail, in our "Three-Stage Unification" Formula, we have not set any such preparatory phase. We do not believe that the phase of "reconciliation and cooperation" by itself can legitimately be a stage of the unification process. Besides, if such a preparatory phase is set, we fear that there may be temptation to use it as a means to prolong the status quo as long as possible, resulting in the indefinite prolongation of this stage, thus unnecessarily delaying the process of unification. However, the actual transition to Confederation will have to be preceded by the satisfaction of all the needed political conditions or requirements as well as the fulfillment of at least a rudimentary level of exchanges in cultural-social areas following the activation of the "Joint Committee" as defined by the "Basic Agreement" and its attached "Protocols."

Two problems can be considered relating to the Confederal Charter. The first concerns the agreements between the two Koreas: how to deal with the problem of the "Joint Committee" under the "Basic Agreement" and its "Protocols" that together define the issues of exchange and cooperation. This problem, however, may be resolved smoothly without difficulty under a "Social-Cultural Committee" of the Confederation to be established under the Charter and which will automatically inherit the mantle of the "Joint Committee."

The second is the issue of specification of the contents of the Charter. It is our view that the Charter ought to be divided between a "comprehensive" one and specific ones dealing with individual areas. To wit, the establishment of the Confederation and the framework of the Confederal institutions will be under the "comprehensive" Charter, while the necessary bodies in each different areas can be created under more specific "Charters" dealing with different areas of common concern.[21] Hence, in the social-cultural areas, some form of "Traffic Agreement" is needed to promote and expedite all sorts of human exchange as well as a "Social-Cultural Agreement" for exchanges in different areas. More specific sub-level agreements will also be needed for the necessary regulations for the increased activities as a consequence. At the same time, a "Confederal Social-Cultural Committee" can be established as a permanent body to handle the

---

[21]In the case of Germany, the general framework of inter-German relations was set up under the 1972 "Basic Treaty," while the two Germanys later on added individual agreements on specific areas. For instance, on the social-cultural area, they signed a "Traffic (Verkehrs) Treaty" in October 1972 and a "Cultural Agreement" in may 1985. The Traffic Treaty caused a major increase in human exchange and the Cultural Agreement was responsible for active exchanges in all areas.

affairs of the social-cultural exchanges, and under it "executive bodies" for individual areas as well as other "joint research organizations" can also be established.

As for the financial problems, one can be sure that a great deal of funds would be needed to execute the exchange and cooperation projects in different social-cultural areas. Although it is desirable to leave the exchange and cooperation projects, including the sharing of the financial burden, in the hands of the private sector, government support would, nonetheless, be vital for the active implementation of the various exchange and cooperation programs between the two Koreas. As seen in the West German precedent, South Korea will have to put up a great amount of resources if it wishes to actively promote and take the initiatives in the human exchanges. In the West German case again, all the expenses incurred in the process of the exchanges with East Germany were paid from the Federal and State budgets. As we are in the process of building up a national fund for inter-Korean cooperation, it would be helpful if we also consider the establishment of a separate "exchange and cooperation fund" to actively support the activities in individual areas—along with the guarantee of private sector freedom in this whole area.

IV. The Modalities of Social-Cultural Exchange/Cooperation

Social-cultural exchange and cooperation under the Confederation is aimed at the social-cultural integration and the achievement of genuine national union of all Koreans under the Federal Stage that follows it. For this reason, the exchange and cooperation during the Confederal phase will have to be carried out more comprehensively and systematically.

To investigate the processes of divergence/differentiation between the two Koreas, we shall now look at the problem specifically through the three categories that we discussed earlier: the areas of "fundamental values," the "areas of implementation," and in the area of "requirements for the building of new community"; and discuss the specific ideas and plans for the exchanges and cooperation.

1. The Modalities of Exchange/Cooperation in the Area of Values

(1) Education and Scholarship

Because of the flexibility, the educational and scholarly exchanges will have great significance. Causing no political confrontation or conflict, yet capable of breaking the deadlock in the inter-Korean exchanges, the educational and scholarly area could perform a salutary role. These areas could also be important as they can be both observant and critical of the reality. Although they can not exert decisive influence on politics or on the actual political process, they can be the conscience in the formation of social legitimacy as well as its critical rectifier. As such, the educational and scholarly field could provide answers or at least direction in seeking the solution to the problem of overcoming the divergence or differences between the two Koreas. In that respect, their role could truly be valuable.

Let us now look at the modalities of exchange and cooperation in these two vital areas during the early and late periods under the Confederation.

First, in the early period, the two sides need to have free access to material and a free exchange of information, for which the posture of open doors would be needed on both sides. Only the free collection and exchange of information will enable the compilation of reliable data; which in turn will assist in the determination of the priorities in the exchange projects. Accordingly, there is the need to establish a jointly operated "Inter-Korean Scholarly Exchange Center" for the promotion of the free and efficient collection and exchange of the research material. The main function of the center should be the overall management of the educational and scholarly exchanges and joint research projects, as well as the publication of periodicals introducing the scholarly information from each side.

In the early stage, priorities should be placed on the most approachable areas or on areas with the least divergence/difference, or on areas which urgently require cooperative scholarly efforts. To expect a positive response from North Korea, we will have to select and consider only those areas which will bring tangible benefits to North Korea,

Second, a common scholarly basis must be established in order to reconfirm the common national identity. For example, the areas of possible joint research would be the history of Ancient Korea and Balhae, the Three Kingdoms, and Korean-Japanese relations of the early period. In the area of language, a common denominator can perhaps be found in the projects dealing with the "streamlining of the Korean language," "research and agreement on Korean grammar for unification," and the "compilation of a new Korean language dictionary for unification" and other such related projects for the ultimate national unity. In science and technology, a joint research can be established in the investigation of ecology in the Korean Peninsula and natural resources, the energy problem, high-tech science and technology, science education, and others.

Third, there is a need for joint research of the various problems related to the educational systems of the two Koreas such as the role of education and its social function, the educational systems and curricula, textbook contents, the relationship between the teachers and the students, and other such issues related to school education programs. For these and others, we believe there is the need to establish a joint research organization.

Fourth, an active exchange of educational personnel, including students, teachers, and educational officials, ought to take place. The personnel exchange can be either in groups or by individuals: however, in the early period of the Confederation, group exchanges would be both preferable and easier than personal/individual ones. Needless to say, exchanges in this area will play an important role in preparing for the educational system of the unified Korea by generating a greater understanding of each other's educational system, educational process and contents, purposes, instructional methods, and others.

Fifth, we shall seek exchanges between all levels of schools between the two sides. The establishment of sister-relations between the two Koreas educational institutions—between the elementary, middle/high schools, and specialized educational institutions—will help not only in the exchange of information but certainly in building up the necessary knowledge of each other's systems. The "specialized colleges/universities" developed in North Korea such as the "factory university," "farm and fishery university," and others may and can be applied in South Korea to make the connection between the schools and industry, and theory and practice. The system of "communication college" is already being used in both Koreas. Its joint operation can perhaps be easily accomplished under the Confederation, although the scope may have to be limited to only certain types of subjects.

Sixth, we propose that steps should be taken to effect an expansion of common scholarly bonds between the two Koreas through holding of joint seminars on individual disciplines via active exchanges between individual scholars and/or scholarly associations; and hold "Conference of All Korean Scholars" including those who are overseas. The exchange and exhibition of historical artifacts from both sides could also help restore the common national identity.

When the exchange and cooperation projects in the early stage of the Confederation make expected progress, additional programs can be undertaken during the later phase to consolidate the gains already made: such as the establishment of a "unification school" or an "institute for political education," designed as a specialized institution for citizen orientation/education on political matters which are judged to be useful for ultimate national unification. The function of these special bodies would be to enlighten the public about the existing divergence/differences in the realities of the two sides, particularly in the area of interpreting and comprehending the national history of Korea, thus introducing and reinforcing their understanding of the great necessity for common consciousness and perception as a unified people. These institutions can provide the necessary milieu for the discussion of specific tasks needed for attaining unification by holding joint research projects in language and in history so as to enlarge the scope of consensus between the two sides; and to investigate the possibility of establishing new concepts for the future of Korea as well as for unification.

The next concern is the construction of educational facilities for North Korea. Just as China induced capital investment from Hong Kong and Taiwan in the building of university facilities in China, South Korea, too, if North Korea wishes, should be involved in the construction of facilities for North Korea's elementary, middle/high school, college/university institutions, and other social educational systems. The same should be permitted for North Korea, if it so desires. A better mutual understanding of each other's educational system, methods, and curricula can be obtained through the implementation of this project along with the exchange of necessary information.

Also, ideally, whenever possible, regular periodic meetings between the scholars of the two Koreas should be held to lay the foundation for the integration of the scholarly associations of the two Koreas; periodic and non-periodic journals and magazines should be set up and published; and joint research centers and associations ought to be formed.

Last, but not least, an attempt should be made to devise common textbooks to be used jointly, although the essential substance of North Korean education will be very difficult to harmonize with that of South Korea because of the vast gap in the ultimate purpose of the two systems. Nevertheless, whenever and wherever there is a chance to set aside the different ideological values in favor of the restoration of common national identity, such as in areas of mathematics, science, and the natural sciences, as well as in language, geography, customs, etc., an attempt should be made to publish common textbooks for the two sides.

In conclusion, it is our expectation and hope that the educational and scholarly exchanges can and will go a long way towards reconfirming our common national heritage and tradition, and ultimately contribute to the inculcation of national consciousness for the desirability and necessity of the unification of all Korea.

(2) Religion

From the South Korean perspective, a question can be raised as to whether or not religions do actually exist in North Korea. However, what we ought to consider is the possibility that if we evaluate the religious situation in North Korea solely by our standards and minimize or undervalue it, or try to impose our values on the Northern situation, all doors to exchanges will be shut tightly.

If we are interested in useful exchanges in the field of religion, we will have to first recognize the reality in the North as it is, and devise feasible programs on that basis. Because of the Juche philosophy, the religious foundation in the North is bound to be different; and under the circumstances, the religions in North Korea which have survived thus far, could not have been different in their forms and substance because of the circumstances. And we have to recognize the differences as they actually are. However, once we realize that there is still common ground due to the inherent nature of religion, we will be able to discover ways for exchange and cooperation with North Korea in this respect.

Unlike the other areas, the religious exchange and cooperation require even greater leeway and freedom, and for this reason, we ought to make certain that government intervention is minimized in this area, while insuring maximum leeway and freedom.

In the early phase of the Confederation, emphasis will be placed on laying the foundation for the exchanges between the two Koreas as in other fields discussed above. The religious organizations in the South will have to form a unified consultative body to carry on with the task of implementing the exchanges with North Korea with efficiency and results. Because of its nature, the activities of religious persons and organizations in North Korea are under unified control; consequently, the channels of communication and dialogue are also organized through their individual organizations. The numerous religious denominations, sects, and organizations in South Korea, on the other hand, individually try to make contact with North Korea's highly organized religious bodies on their own. Under these circumstances, these individual contacts and exchanges for their respective individual interests, could invite chaos and eventually be even counter-productive. Therefore, it would be necessary to at least establish some form of overall organizations for different religions in order to maintain close cooperation with them so as to maintain unified positions vis-a-vis the North in terms of missionary activities or in establishing exchanges.

Further, we can consider some form of material or financial assistance to North Korea's religious organizations so that they could become more self-sustaining. As it is almost impossible for the Northern religious bodies to be self-sufficient and autonomous, it might be an excellent idea for the financially well endowed Southern religions to use their individually established "unification funds" to support their Northern counterparts.

In the later phase of the Confederation, we ought to try to implement programs/projects, based on the foundation created during the earlier phase of cooperation with the North, that could ultimately achieve religious integration between the two Koreas. Examples might be: the development of joint projects, purely religious in nature; joint compilation of religious scriptures, religious doctrines, and/or catechism; joint development of common religious rituals for separate religions; organization of pilgrimages for separate religions to holy sites and sites of historical significance that are scattered around Korea; exchange exhibits of religious books and cultural artifacts; and even the joint production of religious cable television programs. Buddhism, Christianity, and other religions which already have their own cable television programs in the South could co-produce with the North religious programs containing sentiments of patriotism and national independent-mindedness.

They could even develop religious festivals that symbolize national independence, or semi-religious movements or movements with some religious contents on the "Movement to Live together in Harmony," "Movement to Preserve Mt. Kumkang," or the "Movement to Oppose Nuclear Armament," and others. All in all, programs can and should be devised and implemented to lay the foundation for ultimate religious integration between the two Koreas in expectation of the eventual transition to Federation.

Considering the roots of profound religious consciousness or subconsciousness in all Koreans, and judging that there lie dormant underneath the North Korean society entrenched elements of Buddhistic faith, other national religions, and even Shamanistic beliefs, the national task of restoring a common national religious community may not be as difficult as generally believed. The attempts to realize higher universal values on the foundation of the existing divergence/difference may even lead to a consolidation of the roots of cultural integration between the two sides.

(3) Arts

The modalities of exchanges in the area of the arts that reflect esthetic values can be considered at several different levels. The purpose of the exchanges in the arts under the Confederation will be to firmly lay the common foundation for national *pathos* so as to create a new national culture for unification—a necessary preparation for the new common cultural community for Korea. The creation of the unification culture is not merely the extraction of the integrated culture. Rather it is an activation of the multi-faceted effort to expand and disseminate the national will and determination to achieve Korea's unification through culture and the arts. The purpose of the unification culture is to cleanse the national consciousness, distorted under division, in light of the future vision of Korea's history, and to revamp and reorganize the cultural and ideological foundation in preparation for national unity for both national integration and the creation of new national culture.[22]

As for the modality of exchange in the field of the arts, one can consider the "open doors" for cultural and art works, the exchange of information/data, and exhibitions during the early phase of the Confederation. The opening of a culture/arts data exchange center, to which North Korea has shown no enthusiasm thus far, can be pursued more vigorously, while culture/arts joint research projects can also be attempted. Active contacts and exchanges can also be maintained with Korean cultural personalities and artists overseas with joint participation in international motion picture, performing arts and drama festivals.

Once the early phase of the culture/arts exchanges has made some progress, towards the late phase of the Confederation, we can then contemplate regular and institutionalized forms of direct exchanges between the cultural and artistic personalities from both sides of the Korean Peninsula. We could hold regular/periodic drama and film festivals between the two Koreas; invite the Northern artists and cultural personalities to the regional cultural

---

[22]Cho Min, "Unification Culture and Korean National Community," *The Korean Journal of Unification Studies*, Vol. 2, No. 2., 1993. (Seoul: The Research Institute for National Unification, 1993), pp. 231-252.

events in South Korea; and institutionalize the regular exchange performances by stage groups and musical groups.

In addition, there could also be joint production of films and stage plays. Because of the vast mass appeal and its spectacular impact on mass culture, the co-production of motion pictures could have wide ranging ripple effects on the entire cultural scene. The areas where such co-production can easily start would be documentaries dealing with ecology and environmental issues, advertisement of Korea's tourist assets, and descriptions of lives of the Koreans overseas.

It would also be worthwhile to push vigorously such joint projects as the protection of the ecology/environment along the truce line and the DMZ, the conversion of the same area into a joint research zone or into a "cultural zone" for the inculcation of national history and culture, towards the latter phase of the Confederation. In addition, efforts could be made to establish and develop a joint research center or a culture-arts organization to more systematically push the idea of joint research between the two Koreas in the field of culture and the arts, and to demonstrate the symbolic importance of the inseparability of mutual linkage in culture and the arts.

The basic principle of the cultural-artistic national community will have to be the universal achievement of the ideals of liberty and equality. The principle of nationalism will be the foundation for the establishment of the Korean national community, but it will have to be undergirded with democratic ideals and concepts.[23] The developmental process of overcoming and

---

[23]Kim Mun-hwan, "On Increasing the Level of Cultural Homogeneity between South and North Korea," in *The Seminar on the Means to Form the Cultural Community between South and North Korea* (Data Book) (Seoul: Association for the Promotion of Cultural Exchange between South and North Korea, 1993), p. 8.

creating a new trend of pluralistic diversity from the cultural/artistic heterogeneity between the two Koreas thus far will not be merely an effort to restore the culture of the bygone age. That in fact would be impossible. Beyond that, if the cultural community of unified Korea is to contribute to the development of world culture and the coprosperity of humanity, we will have to strive for the creation of an independent-minded, self-sustaining civil culture based on the restoration of homogeneous national identity.

[Chart 5-4] below is the summation of the modalities of inter-Korean exchanges and cooperation in the field of basic values—especially in education and scholarship, religion, and the arts.

[Chart 5-4] Modalities of Exchange/Cooperation in the Areas of Basic Values under the Confederation.

Stages of Implementation & Purposes	Areas	Modalities of Exchange/Cooperation
Early Phase: Laying the Foundation for Exchange/Cooperation	Education & Scholarship	① the negotiation of the "culture agreement" and "science/technology agreement" & the establishment of org. for exchange/cooperation. ② the establishment and operation of the "Inter-Korean Scholarly Exchange Center." ③ the creation of common scholarly basis to reconfirm the common national identity. ④ the joint research of the educational systems of the two Koreas. ⑤ active organization-centered exchanges of educational personnel. ⑥ exchanges between all levels of schools. ⑦ active exchanges between scholarly associations.
	Religion	① South Korea's missionary activities in the North through the formation of a unified consultative body among South Korea's religions.

*The transition to active, real exchanges from the pro forma ones.		② Assistance to North Korea's religious organizations through material or financial support.
	Arts	① the "open doors" for cultural and art works. ② exchange of information/data on culture and the arts & joint research. ③ the establishment of private exchange & research centers for culture and the arts. ④ active contact with Korean artists and cultural personalities overseas.
Later Phase: Period of Expansion & Maturity in Exchange & Cooperation— Preparatory Phase for Transition to Federation. *Towards the integration of education & scholarship for overcoming the heterogeneity that has developed between the two Koreas and for the development/restoration of homogeneity.	Education& Scholarship	① the establishment of a "unification school" or an "institute for political education." ② the establishment of educational facilities in each other's territory. ③ joint research & preparation for educational integration: compilation of common textbooks. ④ holding regular/periodic scholarly meetings, the publication of periodic & non-periodic journals and magazines, and the establishment of joint research centers & joint conferences.
	Religion	① the development of joint projects, purely religious in nature. ② the co-production of religious cable television programs. ③ the development of joint religious festivals, symbolizing national independent-mindedness; religious citizen movements such as the "Movement to Live Together in Harmony," etc. ④ preparation for the integration of the religious organizations of the two Koreas.
	Arts	① regular and institutionalized forms of direct exchanges between cultural and artistic personalities. ② active co-production of motion pictures and stage dramas. ③ the creation of a "culture area" in the DMZ. ④ the establishment & development of joint research centers for culture and the arts.

2. The Modalities of Exchange & Cooperation in the "Functional" Area

(1) The Mass Media

Exchanges in the area of the mass media will be both cultural and political in nature. Hence, they will depend a great deal on the progress of inter-Korean relations in the political arena. Of particular significance, the Southern side considers the broadcasting exchanges as the most effective "weapon" because of its explosive potential and its strategic importance, while the Northern side views it with trepidation since it views the problem as directly related to the very survival of its system.[24] Therefore, to discuss the issue of exchanges in the mass media without the prior improvement of political relations between the two Koreas will be meaningless. Mutual confidence building in the political area must precede before any exchange can be realistically possible in the mass media field.

The mass media exchange, more than any other area, will be an effective means to check and verify the general status of divergence/differentiation between the two Koreas.[25] The mass media will be able to demonstrate the degree of divergence/dif-

---

[24]Park Hyung-sook, "Problems and Prospect of Broadcasting Exchanges between the Two Koreas," *The Press Exchanges between South and North Korea* (Seoul: The Korean Press Institute, 1992), p. 58.

[25]To be accustomed to each other's culture and language through each other's broadcasts will be very important before the direct exchanges take place in human movement and in material exchange. The broadcasts, by revealing the divergent environments in South and North Korea, will confirm the considerable cultural differences that exist between the two sides: thus clarifying for all that the achievement of unification will have to start with overcoming the stark divergence/difference.

ferentiation that has developed between the two sides—the differentiation that can be seen and heard. On the other hand, the
mass media will also alleviate and dilute the enormous psychological shock, expected through the exchanges in all areas,
before they occur.

Considering that the restoration of homogeneity between
the two Koreas is in fact the approach to a national consensus
through the change of consciousness, value systems, and behavior patterns, there is no doubt that the mass media—through the
entire process—will undoubtedly exert tremendous influence on
the consciousness and behaviors of both individuals and
groups. Such influence will be wide in range and comprehensive. Accordingly, the mass media will be the most effective and
efficient means to help achieve the homogeneity between the
two Koreas. As clearly seen in the case of East and West Germany, the exchange in the mass media was the decisive factor in
the accomplishment of peaceful unification.

The mass media that will be involved in the exchanges
under the Confederation include newspapers, broadcasts, communications, and the new media. Of these, the most important
will be broadcasting—because of its effect, scope, and the ease of
its utility. Because of the technical aspect that the electronic
waves can easily penetrate all material obstacles such as the geo-
graphical division that separates the two Koreas, it should be
the most effective contributor to the mutual understanding and
restoration of homogeneity.

What, then, should be the modality of mass media exchange
and cooperation under the Confederation? In the early phase of
the Confederation, major efforts must be made to remove all factors that obstruct exchanges and solve the technical problems to
enable actual exchanges. The first step is for the two sides to

agree on measures to build mutual trust and confidence, and to desist from broadcasting accusations and recriminations against each other.

Second, solutions must be found to iron out the technical disparities and incompatibilities between the two Koreas' broadcasting. In case of radio broadcasting, there is no particular technical difference; however, in the case of television broadcasting, there is a real difference between the two. Finding the means, however, to overcome the differences would not be too difficult.[26]

Third, we ought to include the Koreans living overseas in areas such as China, Russia (and other parts of the old Soviet Union), Japan, and the United States, in the mass media exchanges so as to broaden the opportunities for their contribution to the cause of national unity. A new organization—"Global Korean Broadcasting Association"—can be established for this purpose.

Only after these basic conditions are met can we begin to consider other more concrete programs for implementation. Starting from the non-political areas, we should find programs

---

[26]One realistic proposal that is now being talked about is to set up a standard converter for the television broadcasts in the Demilitarized Zone. Once it is installed, it will solve the problems of the different television broadcasting systems used by the two Koreas. Since the adoption of common television broadcasting by the two sides is not realistic for the time being, we could consider producing television receivers that can be tuned into both the NTSC and the PAL systems at the same time. If we are serious about the broadcast exchanges, we ought to start pushing the solutions now to overcome the technical differences that now exist between South and North Korea. Since South Korea's electronic makers are already producing and exporting TV sets to the Middle East, compatible with both NTSC and PAL systems, there will be no technical roadblock to mass producing the same for use on the Korean Peninsula. The Korean Broadcasting *Institute, Investigation into Various Technical Problems for the Inter-Korean Exchange in Broadcasting* (Seoul: 1992), p. 127.

for co-production and co-broadcasting—programs which will reconfirm and reinforce national homogeneity. These could include sports, culture, pure arts, and science/technology. Joint broadcasting of international events should help accumulate technical knowhow on both sides, and eventually narrow the technical gap that exists in the two Koreas' broadcasting.

One interesting idea would be for the two sides to set aside specific time slots—shall we say "Unification Program Schedules"—in their broadcasting schedules for showing the co-produced programs. If not the same programs, each side could broadcast the other's productions in turn. To expedite such an exchange of broadcast programs, one could consider establishing a "Program Exchange Center."

Although the simultaneous opening of the doors for the other's programs ought to be an ideal way to begin, if such an option should prove to be impossible given the realities of division, we could in fact start first with South Korea's decision to allow its citizens to tune into the Northern broadcasts as a way to eventually induce a positive North Korean response. One way to do this would be to establish a special cable channel to receive the Northern broadcasts. Nonetheless, the reality may dictate that we approach the whole subject gradually and in phases.

Once the ground is laid for the exchange in the early phase of the Confederation, the concrete schedules for inter-Korean co-production of programs will finally materialize towards the latter Confederal period. In the case of newspapers, for instance, the two sides could dispatch resident correspondents to the other, and the whole exchange could be institutionalized. The resident correspondents should be treated the same as foreign reporters; and agreements ought to be reached between the two

sides to cover the reporters and producers to promote the concept of journalistic exchanges.

An attempt can also be made to set up and operate a special
and integrated broadcast channel—a Federal channel, if you
will—that can connect the two sides' broadcasts in general,
while still allowing each side a degree of autonomy. This idea is
modelled after Germany's case of associated public broadcast
systems—ARD [Arbeitsgemeinschaft der öffentlich-rechtlichen
Rundfunkanstalten].[27] In our case, too, it would be desirable to
reach a multi-sided agreement between South Korea's "Korean
Broadcast System" (KBS) and North Korea's Central Broadcast
System, and establish and operate a channel based on a federated system for ultimate national unification. If we are to include
in this a Korean language broadcast from Yanbian from
Manchuria—based on a special agreement/contract allowing it
a special position—it will be a considerable contribution to the
restoration of national homogeneity for all Korea.

In the latter phase of the Confederation, North Korea
should be induced to open its doors to the Southern broadcasts
and newspapers; and pursue the jointly invested operation of

---

[27]Germany's broadcast policy is based entirely and completely on the German state principle of the federated states founded on the concept of division of
power. The eleven public broadcast systems created a single federal structure of
an integrated broadcasting system based on the broadcast laws of each federal
state and on the broadcasting and state agreements. This federated structure of
broadcast systems is maintained through the participation of all federal state
broadcast systems of the old West Germany, and its operation is also collectively managed. What is important in all this is that all the federal states' broadcasting systems are assured of their independence, and enjoy what is generally
referred to as broadcast "sovereignty." The Korean Broadcasting Institute,
*Investigation into Various Technical Problems for the Inter-Korean Exchange in Broad-
casting* (Seoul: 1992), p. 134.

satellite television, newspapers, and broadcasting stations.

Information in an age of information is the source of power and influence, and will be the firm foundation of democracy. A free and uninterrupted flow of information like water will be the source of healthy social development; and the ability to absorb all sorts of information and the ability also to create new information will be the key to securing the nation's international competitiveness. Only by exchanges through the mass media will the two Koreas be able to adjust and adapt to a changing internal and external environment, build up the ability to actively adjust and adapt to the rapid changes, and thus ensure the future vision and direction for our new society.

(2) Sports

Sports can be a powerfully persuasive medium for facilitating reconciliation between the religious and ethnic entities torn asunder through friction and conflict. As such, it will undoubtedly make a considerable contribution to the alleviation of political and military feuds between the divided Korean people and to the ultimate pursuit of national unification. Until now the two Koreas have not considered sports as a proper area for exchange and cooperation. Rather they have viewed it as the means for competition between the two rival systems. With the advent of the 1990's, however, the South Korean appreciation for sports underwent a visible change. With the collapse of the Cold War order and the rise of a new environment for reconciliation, the sense of hostile competitiveness that had dominated sports began to wane, giving rise to a new collective national sentiment for its different role.

Once the political and ideological colors are removed, the

exchange in sports will become easier to attain, and such exchanges in the field of sports could induce the revival of homogeneity between the two sides. Indeed, it has been pointed out that the inter-Korean exchanges in sports will not only demonstrate the power of the unified people of Korea, but also restore national homogeneity, induce the structural changes in the political systems and social culture, excite and enhance the enthusiasm for political, economic, and Red Cross meetings between the two, while providing a healthy influence on human, communications, and other exchanges as well—not to mention their collective contribution to the development of national sports.[28] We would expect the continuation of these functions throughout the Confederal stage.

It is our belief that the ideal way for the exchanges in the sports area to take place between the two Koreas would be in the sphere with the least likely impact on politics and society. The exchanges, therefore, ought to begin gradually with concrete projects in non-competitive areas, with prudence and care. The scope of the exchanges will have to stay focused on the competitive sports; however, the exchanges will have to be transformed somehow to a new format that will enable the participation of seventy million Koreans, starting with the athletes themselves, the leaders, and the spectators.

The programs/projects that could enliven the exchanges in sports in the early phase of the Confederation could be, first, the establishment of a permanent organization for the exchanges; the exchanges of sports information and basic data (such as pub-

---

[28]Kim Sang-koo, "On the Means for the Sports Exchanges between the Two Koreas," *The Anthology of Research Articles for the Sungkyunkwan University*, Vol. 35, No. 2 (Seoul: Sungkyunkwan University, 1986), p. 52.

lications on athletics, films of sports events, and sports techniques and equipment, etc.), exchanges of sports experts and researchers, administrators and athletes through reciprocal visitations. In addition, we can also push for joint hosting of events for the traditional games, goodwill tournaments in each category of sports, and the dispatch of unified sports teams to international competitions.

The joint development of traditional games and/or competitions, co-sponsorship of an international sports meeting, joint television broadcasts of sports events held by each side, the goodwill exchange games between the national teams as well as the teams of various organizations and students, and the dispatch of joint fan groups to various international meets, and the exchange of the sports writers and commentators, and their joint coverage of sports events could all be beneficial components.

In the latter phase of the Confederation, the two sides could together establish a center for sports research or a sports training center; or an inter-Korean sports organization for joint athletic events under private sponsorship on a permanent basis or for representing all of Korea in international bodies such as the International Olympic Committee. A pan-national sports festival could be held under joint sponsorship or international sports events or games can also be considered with the efforts of the two Koreas.

(3) The Separated Families

In any debate on the issue of human exchange, there always lurks the question of the separated families—a question of enormous weight and implication. A direct consequence of the national division was the tragedy of the separation of family members. The reunion of the separated families has been con-sidered the most urgent issue, and its urgency has become ever more serious. If we are to achieve a realistic solution to the prob-lem, human exchange in general and the reunion of the separat-ed families in particular—within the context of the multi-faceted exchanges—must proceed hand in hand based on the perception of necessity and complementarity, felt equally by the two Koreas.

Let us now examine the gradualistic and phased ways to effect a free exchange between the separated families. In the early stage of the Confederation, the emphasis ought to be placed on the general exchanges, with efforts to confirm the life or death of the affected family members, their addresses, and the exchange of letters between them. Although the search for "missing persons" will have to be carried on by the government, if an agreement of sorts is difficult to attain between the two governments, or if the whole effort is not effective, the task— even in part—ought to be assumed by private organizations or by Red Cross. Considering the on-going search for "missing per-sons" through non-official channels, we believe that the exchange of letters between the affected family members will not be too difficult to manage once the whereabouts of the per-sons are fully known and confirmed.

Second, there will have to be mutual "interviews" at regular intervals. For this, an official meeting place can be established in the DMZ areas such as Panmunjom. Although North Korea may not accept the concept of "home visits" to North Korea by all of separated family members in the South for fear of inherent threats to the stability of its own system, it may still permit visits by a selected number of the separated families.

Even a resettlement of a very limited number of the affected families could be attempted, including those "unconverted left-ist" political prisoners in the South who want to be returned home to the North, or the elderly people in the South who wish to live with their families in North Korea. They could be allowed to go back. North Korea, too, should consider sending back people whom they took forcibly during the war and those others whose families are in the South. The reunion and resettlement of the separated families may have to start on a very small scale in the beginning, however, as the political confidence is being built up, the scope and dimension will also grow.

Third, while pursuing the program of allowing the elderly people to visit with their separated family members back home in North Korea, the groups of separated families could also be allowed to visit their ancestral graves during such traditional national holidays as Lunar New Year, the *Tano Festival*,[29] and *Chusok* (similar to Thanksgiving in the United States). The opportunities and scope of the exchange home visits, by groups of the affected families, should be greatly expanded and put on regular schedules; and such experimental projects ought to be implemented consistently without interruption both under governmental and private auspices. Still other projects can be considered such as the active programs of human exchanges among Koreans living overseas and/or the reunion of the separated families in third countries like China.

Towards the latter part of the Confederation, more active human exchanges ought to be pursued. For example, the expansion of mutual understanding and interest through frequent human exchanges by active joint programs such as: sister rela-

---

[29]The traditional *Tano* Festival is on the fifth day of the fifth lunar month, which has been celebrated by Koreans for centuries.

[Chart 5-5] Modalities of Exchange/Cooperation in the "Functional" Areas Under the Confederation.

Stages of Implementation & Purposes	Areas	Modalities of Exchange/Cooperation
Early Phase: Laying the Foundation for Exchange/ Cooperation	Mass Media	① the discontinuation of broadcasts of mutual accusation and recrimination. ② the installation of a TV standard converter and the production and sale of TV sets compatible with both NTSC and PAL systems. ③ the establishment of the "Global Korean Broadcasting Association." ④ the co-production and co-broadcasting of non-political programs. ⑤ Newspapers: exchange of news stories and the short-term exchange of reporters. ⑥ Permission for filming on location and the exchange of media experts/ scholars and journalists. ⑦ South Korea's "open doors" for the Northern broadcasts & newspapers.
*The restoration of mutual trust and confidence, overcoming of divergence and differentiation, and the expansion of national homogeneity. *The institutionalization of exchange and the achievement of the technical basis thereof.	Sports	① the negotiation of a "Cultural Agreement" and the establishment of a permanent org. for sports exchange. ② holding of the goodwill games in different sports categories; joint hosting of Korea's traditional games. ③ the exchanges of sports information and basic data such as publications on athletics, films of sports events, and sports techniques and equipment. ④ the exchanges of sports personnel. ⑤ the organization of unified national teams and the holding of goodwill all-sports events
	Reunion of the Separated Families	① the confirmation of life/death of the separated family members, addresses, and exchange of letters. ② the establishment of a permanent place for reunion of the separated families. ③ the resettlement of the separated families.

④ the allowance for the elderly for "home visits" and the organizations of groups to visit their family graves.
⑤ the exchange among overseas Koreans
⑥ the reunion of the separated families in third countries.

Later Phase: Period of Expansion & Maturity in Exchange & Cooperation—Preparatory Phase for Transition to Federation. *Laying the foundation for social integration.	Mass Media	① co-production of programs and joint reporting. ② the exchange of resident correspondents and the establishment of bureaus. ③ North Korea's "open doors" for the Southern broadcasts and newspapers. ④ the establishment and operation of a special broadcast channel based on a federated system. ⑤ the inauguration and operation of newspapers by joint investment. ⑥ joint operation of cable television broadcasting, ⑦ the establishment of a joint broadcasting system, entrusted with scheduling and transmission network.
	Sports	① the establishment of a center for sports research and a sports training center. ② the establishment of an inter-Korean sports organization and its representation of Korea in international bodies such as the International Olympic Committee. ③ joint sponsorship of a "Pan-National" sports festival and joint sponsorship of international sports events. ④ preparation for the integration of the religious organizations of the two Koreas.
	Reunion of the Separated Families	① sister relationships between businesses, schools, social organizations. ② grand tours of the country by students and other groups. ③ the regularization of reciprocal visits by the separated families and the expansion of the resettlement program. ④ completely free and uncontrolled visits to family members.

tions between businesses, schools, social organizations, and cities; and grand tours around the country by student groups and by other similar groups. Such programs as these are designed to promote and strengthen the national consciousness that we, in the divided Koreas, are in fact the unmistakable members of a community. By the time the transition to Federation comes around, we ought to have reached a point where there exists the general implementation of free and unfettered reciprocal visits by the separated families and resettlement based on the free will of the affected.

The aforementioned areas of implementation such as the mass media, sports, and the separated families are the actual and concrete steps to be taken for the realization of the social-cultural community during the period of the inter-Korean Confederation.[Chart 5-5] above summarizes the overall modalities for exchange and cooperation in these different areas.

3. The Modalities of Exchange and Cooperation in the Area of "Prerequisites" (for Unification)

The integration of mutually divergent systems necessarily carries with it considerable sacrifice and danger, and will require a long period of mutual adjustment and adaptation. This has been made typically clear in the two Germanys' unification processes. Thus, to minimize the likely shocks from the systemic integration between the two Koreas, we will have to consider very carefully and cautiously the social structural requirements that have to be met for the creation of the new social community of the future.

This task is not unrelated to the question of how we can overcome the phenomena of social disharmony and conflict caused by the inequitable social structures in both Koreas such as the fissure and friction, animosity and alienation, and the sense of deprivation. The truth is that both Koreas today contain in their substructure elements that obstruct and impede the national unification. In the case of South Korea, there are several serious problems: the sense of alienation and hostility between social classes due to social inequities; the intensification of regional animosities caused by the protracted and serious discrimination of certain region(s) through the highly regionalized power structure; and the generational value system conflict brought on by rapid social change. North Korea, on the other hand, is faced with serious internal and external contradictions: internally, it has imposed on its people a highly regimented, collectivistic life style in total neglect of their basic freedoms and human rights, while, externally, it is faced with the increasing internal challenges through the mindless insistence on exclusionistic autarky in a world of rapidly growing interdependence. The fact is that one witnesses in North Korea a serious case of most profound divergence between the ideals of Socialistic Goal and Purposes and the means for their achievement. Disparities in North Korea are reflected in the conflict between the party members and non-members, the individual sacrifices, the deprivation of political freedom, the right of choice, and bureaucratic corruption.

Unless and until we address these internal problems in both Koreas simultaneously with the unification processes, the integration of the two highly divergent systems will only compound each other's structural problems and could even create a new set of serious difficulties. It would be vital, therefore, to overcome the major causes of social frictions/conflicts efficiently and effectively if we are to establish a new future social/cultural community. Hence, the inter-Korean exchanges and cooperation, too, ought to be implemented with these purposes firmly in mind: to wit, the new social/cultural community will have to aspire for the achievement of a genuine social welfare state for the respect of human dignity and the enhancement of the quality of life.

In this section, we shall discuss concrete plans for exchange and cooperation in two primary areas: one, efforts in the social welfare area to deal with the vertical structure of inequity, and, two, the structure of gender discrimination to address the issues of the role and status of women in general.

Because of the very nature of the social welfare policies, under the Confederation, it would be difficult to have a direct exchange of the programs themselves and to jointly expect the effect of such policies. The reasons for this can be summarized as follows: since, in essence, the welfare policies in all cases will of necessity entail the redistribution of wealth, an additional burden on the people as well as payoffs, and efforts to limit the beneficiaries as much as possible, while the principal object of these policies could only be one's own population under its jurisdiction. Accordingly, under the Confederation—a sort of a union of states—the North Koreans cannot be the beneficiaries of South Korea's social welfare policies, and the South Koreans are excluded from the North Korean policies. The social welfare policies, therefore, cannot properly be the object of exchanges between the two sides. Hence, any exchange must begin in areas where such linkage can realistically be made by finding and expanding the common denominators, while the two sides essentially maintain their own focus.

Based on these basic premises, the direction of the bases for exchange/cooperation in the area of social welfare will be as follows: first, the early phase of exchange/cooperation under the

Confederation ought to begin with the acknowledgement of each other's strengths and merits in the social welfare area. For instance, in the case of the South, one can point to its technical, qualitative, and managerial efficiency in the social welfare field, although its coverage is limited to a specific class and/or groups. Conversely, despite its qualitative inferiority, the Northern program is superior at least in form in the universality and equity as well as in the accumulated experiences in comprehensive management. Under the circumstances, therefore, the formula for inter-Korean exchange/cooperation will necessarily be to co-opt a great deal of each other's strengths and merits.

Second, the Southern social welfare policy is, basically, oriented towards a sort of social insurance; it should eventually develop into a genuine social security system. This is the area where there is the most stark difference between the two Koreas. For this, South Korea needs a basic policy change in either turning towards a "national social security system" in individual areas in turn or applying the social security system first to segments of the people who are unable to contribute matching funds.

Third, a partial de-commercialization must occur in the means of group consumption: namely, the distribution of the means in group consumption in the areas of basic human needs such as housing, medical care, and basic food stuffs, should not be done inequitably, solely based on commercial economic principles.

The laying of the foundation for the ultimate integration of the social welfare systems of the two Koreas will to be based on these necessary efforts. Unless these foundations are laid in advance, the social integration in the Federal stage of the unification process will be a very difficult task, indeed. In this context, we will not examine the modalities of exchanges in the field of social welfare as indispensable preliminary steps towards social integration and unification of the social welfare systems.

We have to realize, first, that the inter-Korean exchange in the social welfare area can begin only after each side is fully cognizant of each other's realities. To realize and expand such knowledge, the two sides should establish a "Center for the Study of the Social Welfare Systems of South and North Korea," composed of policy-makers, concerned civil servants, and members of research centers from both sides. The Center's primary task will be to study the systemic and operational aspects of each other's social welfare systems, explore ways to complement each other's systems, and search for ways to unify selectively the social welfare policies of the two sides.

The inter-Korean exchanges in this area will have to focus on developing the specific and concrete programs/projects that will minimize the differences and maximize the similarities between the two sides. To reduce divergence/difference, the two sides will have to achieve the following: first, in the case of South Korea, it will have to provide comprehensive "social insurance," adopt an unemployment insurance system to address large scale and long-term unemployment, expansion of the medical insurance system, expansion of social welfare services for groups most likely to bear the higher-than-average burden in the process of social change and/or upheaval such as women, the elderly, low-skilled and low-income labor, the physically handicapped, and the networks of collective decision-making that include labor unions, the interest groups, and ordinary citizens.

On the Northern side, the changes will have to include: preparations for transition to a system based on the decreasing reliance on the state, increasing adherence to a free market economic system and welfare, improved tolerance to diverse life style, choice, and autonomous change without government intervention or dictation, legislative and operative methods based on democratic participation and genuine solidarity, the increased participation and role of citizen and interest groups in the social welfare administration, the strengthening of the local autonomy, the expansion of social welfare facilities for the old, the physically handicapped, and non-working population, and finally the expansion of the social welfare funding.

The two Koreas will also have to upwardly adjust their concepts of social welfare in accordance with the changing social conditions. The concept of future social welfare will be to establish a "comprehensive social safety net" that will be able to take care of and even prevent all sorts of dangers or difficulties which can be expected in the life span of an average individual.[30] As such, the concept of social welfare is clearly changing from *post facto* cure to one of prevention, and geared for the whole population rather than specific individuals or groups. For the expansion of social welfare, not merely quantitative but qualitative, the ratio of the social security portion of the national financing will have to increase dramatically. Since the role of the expansion of social security is to minimize the intensified social inequality that could happen in the unification process of integrating the two highly divergent systems, the consolidation of the social security system under the Confederation will be an important precondition for the realization of national unity.

Now let us examine the specific and concrete steps needed in the inter-Korean exchanges in the area of women which will

---

[30]Kim Tae-sung & Sung Kyung-ryung, *On State Social Welfare* (Seoul: Nanam, 1993), p. 315.

provide the necessary groundwork for the effective elimination of gender discrimination, the harmonious integration of the sexes, and genuine equality between the sexes not only in routine daily living but in social activities.

Freed from the political and ideological orientation, the exchange between the women of two Koreas will make an important material contribution to the integration of the social/cultural community in that it will visibly enhance their quality of life. Efforts to realize the genuine family-oriented national community, the review and reinterpretation of the values systems of the traditional family structure, and the joint development of policies on women for the realization of genuine gender equality, will play an important role in the formation of consensus between the women of two Koreas and lay the foundation for real social integration.

Consideration and action in the area of women will be an essential prerequisite for a "complete and total integration" from which no social group is excluded. As the very valuable lessons of German unification should tell us, the social groups that can be easily left in the lurch when two wholly divergent entities/systems become integrated, are the minority groups—including women. Clearly, the goal of a social/cultural community that is based on democracy and human dignity is to achieve a society in which no specific group is unjustly discriminated against.

Without doubt, the positive womanly qualities—patience and persistence, understanding and consideration for others, the tendency to prefer equality and cooperation—will be the important facilitator and expediter for the successful pursuit of inter-Korean exchanges and cooperation. These womanly qualities have already demonstrated their unquestioned values in the purely privately sponsored exchanges thus far between the two Koreas. If we are to strengthen and consolidate the solidarity between the women of two Koreas through broader exchanges, it will greatly help in expediting the unification processes.

To consider and explore more specific and concrete means for exchange and cooperation in the area of women, it would be desirable to begin first with sufficient information on the other side as well. The most immediate need will be to establish a permanent body "for the exchange/cooperation in the women's area," composed of government policy-makers from both sides, researchers and scholars, and women's organizations. The primary task of such an organization will be to study and exchange the data on the current conditions of women, explore ways to enhance the women's status, and finally to seek ways to make the selected policies on women uniform between the two sides.

The second is to jointly study and explore ways to alleviate as much as possible the likely phenomenon of class stratification between the women of the two Koreas as the consequence of unification. As far as the policies on women are concerned, we can point to the fact that the Socialist System has come up with more comprehensive policies for gender equality. Hence, it will be essential for the South to improve and supplement its existing policies for women; while in the case of North Korea, it will be important to heighten women's ability for self-reliance in the likelihood that the benefits that the Northern women had enjoyed under the Socialistic System might be reduced as the result of unification.

Third, efforts must be made to ensure that women will not be neglected or set aside in the unification processes by building up the power and influence of women for unification. One way to do this would be to strengthen and expand the existing government policies in the South for exchanges in the area of women so as to enable a broad scope of participation by women in all the necessary endeavors between the two sides.

Lastly, we must ensure that women can participate as major role players in the important processes for the creation of a "comprehensive and unified society for equal life experiences for both sexes"; for the establishment of a "society of the new national community based on the principles of gender equality"; and for the achievement of a "society based on fundamental respect for human dignity and a New Global Democracy."

V. The Transition to a Federation

In the section above dealing with the "basic principles for social/cultural exchange and cooperation" under the Confederation, we discussed both the principles and policy means for the goals. In this section, we shall envision the social-cultural community that can be expected in the very last phase of the Confederation, and discuss the characteristics of social/cultural exchange under a Federation (which will follow the Confederal Stage).

The social/cultural exchange and cooperation under the Confederal Stage are to proceed with the goal of overcoming the divergence/differences and restoring national homogeneity. For this, the primary emphasis in the early Confederal phase is to be placed on mutual understanding and laying the necessary foundation for the exchanges; while more active and specific steps will be taken in the latter phase to actually restore homogeneity between the two sides. If and when these processes are well advanced, we can visualize the following shape of the new national social-cultural community.

In the area of values, a great deal of homogeneity will have been restored through joint historical research and the joint study of the Korean language and through the compilation of the school textbooks of both sides, reflecting the fruits of the joint studies. Once such a stage is reached, we expect considerable narrowing of the ideological gap that now separates the two sides. And because of the progress made in understanding each other's educational systems, we will be able to present a plan for a unified educational system under the Federation, thus laying the firm foundation for the ultimate social/cultural national community.

In the area of actual implementation of various blueprints, one may cite the eventual success in the mass media exchange, facilitating the co-ownership and utilization of information and the free and uninterrupted exchange of views, helping to overcome the sense of alienation through the protracted national division. Exchanges in sports and the organization of unified national teams will inculcate the common consciousness or "one-ness," while the smooth resolution of the problem of the separated families will make the new national community of "families" possible.

In the area of requirements for building the new national community, the two sides should gradually secure the necessary conditions which will be required to alleviate to a minimum the expected shocks and confusion stemming from the social integration by way of reforming the contradictions of both systems and expanding the foundation for the ultimate integration. In addition, the two sides should overcome gender discrimination for a new community in which the equality of the sexes would be guaranteed.

Once the homogeneity in the social/cultural community is

sufficiently renewed under the Confederation, efforts should continue under the Federation to create a new cultural identity for the unified state. What is required for this under the Federation is to change the basic nature of exchanges from those between two independent states to those between "regional" governments. Once these efforts are under way, we can expect considerable integration in the areas of education and scholarship, religion, the arts, mass media, sports, and other social institutions; while specific measures will be devised for the integration of social welfare systems and for the correction of gender discrimination. More thorough and comprehensive scrutiny of social systemic problems of both sides will have to be undertaken under the Federal Government to create a new foundation for a "just society of equitable improvement in all people's lives, social welfare as well as the rule of law"; and to devise the long-term alternatives for such a society.

VI. Conclusion

The ultimate goal of the social/cultural exchanges under the Confederation is to lay the foundation for national integration as well as to form a new national social/cultural community. Tasks for the achievement of these ends would include: the eliminating of mutual distrust and prejudice, accumulated during the long national division; surmounting the cultural divergence/differentiation caused by ideological and systemic differences; and expanding of homogeneity for the ultimate creation of a new cultural community. The realization of these goals will be the foundation for the national, social, and cultural integration under the Federation, eventually resulting in a democratic and open "Cultural State." We have thus far examined and discussed various plans and programs for exchange and cooperation in various areas. What will be the shape of the social-cultural community that will eventually emerge from the aforementioned efforts? Let us re-examine the prospect phase-by-phase.

The early phase of the Confederation is a period in which the inter-Korean exchanges will be sought in the areas where such contacts are the easiest and by setting aside the ideological factors as much as possible. The exchanges and cooperation will proceed by recognizing squarely the reality of divergence between the two sides, while trying to discover the social-cultural similarities that may still exist underneath the fissure. Accordingly, the primary strategic efforts must be made to both minimize the confirmed divergence and maximize the cultural common ground as a same people, separated temporarily, albeit for a long time.

In the early phase, an institutional framework shall be established to facilitate the initiation of inter-Korean exchanges and cooperation. The social-cultural exchange/cooperation under the Confederation will be based on the "Confederal Charter," under which there will be both the "Comprehensive Agreement" and the "Agreement for Various Individual Areas." Along with them, a "Traffic Agreement" will smooth the way for human exchange, while a "Culture Agreement" and other supplementary agreements will regulate exchanges and cooperation in individual areas of common concern. The two sides will also establish a "Social-Cultural Committee of the Confederation" ("Confederal Social-Cultural Committee) for the overall management of all social-cultural exchanges and cooperation and other cooperative organs and a joint research center under it.

Ultimately, greater mutual understanding and interest will

result, and the foundation will be laid for the expanded inter-change between the two sides, if all the programs proceed suc-cessfully as planned.

The later period will be dedicated to enlarging the area of exchange/cooperation so as to reduce significantly the existing divergence/difference and to increase the level of similarity/homogeneity between the two sides. Expanded projects for exchange/cooperation will hopefully result from the foundation laid during the earlier phase; and accelerated efforts will be made to maximize the homogeneity to achieve the ultimate inte-gration of social/cultural elements. The individual projects in the latter phase will be geared to an increased tempo of joint operations/projects rather than merely the exchange/coopera-tion of the previous period. Once these programs are systemati-cally implemented, one could expect gradual dissipation of the gulf that now exist between the two sides, along with the deep-ening process of mutual assimilation—thus laying the ground for the transition to a higher process of integration—the Stage of Federation. The programs/projects to be implemented in the lat-ter stage of the Confederation will increasingly assume the char-acteristics of preparation for the transition to Federation—a stage of *de facto* unification. Because of the nature of the transi-tional stage, the programs/projects in the latter phase of the Confederation will have to be fine-tuned to reflect that particu-lar goal. For instance, if we can manage to give the projects specificity and the concreteness that they deserve, we will have succeeded in laying the necessary foundation for integration in all important areas. One final caveat: efforts must be focused on avoiding the contradictions and inequities in the ultimate state of integration that now permeate the two Koreas.

Realistically, however, it is important for us to bear in mind that we will not be completely successful in removing the gaping divergence and differences under the Confederation, which after all is a mechanism for exchange and cooperation between the two sides, free and unimpeded to preserve and maintain their existing ideologies and systems. In the long-term perspective, however, such divergence/difference may be transformed into a higher state of plural diversity—a characteristic of greater openness and creativity, ultimately conducive to the creation of a truly brilliant "Cultural State." Systematic and strategic pursuit of well-laid plans for exchange and cooperation during the Confederal Stage—expected to last roughly a decade or so—could provide a foundation for diminishing the divergence and strengthening the similarities between the two sides for the ultimate social-cultural integration.

Finally, we insist that the Federation, following the Confederation, is not merely the reunion of the separated peoples, but in fact the creation of a New State. Both the integration of the peoples of the two Koreas, and of the social-cultural sphere will also reflect the diversity and plurality as it is based on the different ideologies and systems of the two Koreas. Once under the Federation, a new identity for the unified state will emerge along with the concept of an open and creative "cultural state."

VI-1. Conclusion

Numerous ideas and formulae on Korea's unification have been floated and forgotten in the last fifty years. The majority of these failed to rise above the argument of the basic necessity of unification; while others, too removed from reality, remained in the realm of idle abstraction. Being entirely self-centered, the unification arguments put up by the two Korean governments have been used mainly as tactical instruments for safeguarding their respective status quo and vested interests.

Of late, the internal and external environment opened fresh new possibilities for Korea's unification. To benefit from the change, it is time for us to have logical and pragmatic blueprints to achieve our national unity. The primary purpose of this book is to respond to the call of the times that face us today, by providing clearer structure and specificity to the ideas of Kim Dae-jung—the ideas that have persisted and developed against all odds since the early seventies.

The main characteristic of the "Three-Stage Unification" Formula is that it is a plan that is firmly rooted in the principle of peace. Unification through the use of military force that imposes either catastrophic damage to the nation or an unbearable economic burden cannot be called a genuine unification. The "Three-Stage" Formula proposes a process, which begins with the Confederation between the two Koreas based on negotiated agreement; after a lapse of a definable period of time, a transition will occur from Confederation to a Federation, a transitional stage, before a complete unification is realized.

The second major characteristic of the Formula is that it contains elements for greater feasibility than any other plan or formula that has been proposed to date. A comparison with any of the other plans make the probability aspect even more clear. The North Korean proposal that the two sides move directly to the Federal stage is unrealistic to the extreme. On the other hand, our own government's call for a direct transition from a very loose South-North Confederation to complete unification itself has little persuasiveness. What is needed, in fact, is a period of preparation for unification, and the time and procedures to overcome the stark divergence/differences that now exist in the systems of the two Koreas. As our "Formula" has explained, the South-North Confederation is needed as a stage of preparation for the ultimate unification; while the transitional stage of Federation is essential and indispensable if we are to be successful in significantly reducing the shocks and confusion, expected from the integration of the opposing systems. In the same spirit, under the Federation, the special conditions and the sensibilities of the North Koreans are taken into account in the arrangement of providing a transitional period of regional self-governments on the two sides, while the integrated Federal Government provides special assistance to the "northern region" to assist its own efforts for the needed transition.

Third, our unification formula is a very safe and "comfortable" proposal in that it allows both sides to take the initial step with ease—and without the fear of being lured into a trap. The Confederation, as explained, is based on "state-to-state" coexistence, and is an institutionalized mechanism to promote and expedite reconciliation and cooperation between the two. Thus, even if something is amiss after the Confederation is agreed on and entered into, neither side will have to bear any burden of danger.

Fourth, the "Three-Stage Unification" Formula is a proposal that has the genuine will and desire for unification. We are only too aware of the precedents where the dictatorial regimes of the past played hostage with the issue of unification mainly as an instrument of convenience to prolong their illicit and illegitimate power. The "South-North Confederation" is a mechanism between two sovereign states, endowed with the task of seeking the best possible means for mutual cooperation without giving up any of their sovereign power. For this reason, there cannot be any apprehension of the sudden and unexpected burden once the two sides decide to proceed with the unification efforts. This should provide the incentive to try the concept.

Korea's unification will become possible only when three essential factors converge: the international environment around the Korean Peninsula; our own fervent desire for unification and the positive will and determination of the two governments; and the rational and realistic unification formula. Fortunately, for us, the latest international environment allows us a favorable climate for unification. We are in a position to achieve unification, only if there is the will and determination on our part, and provided the authorities of the two Koreas show active interest in the cause. Nevertheless, the reality for us is not entirely optimistic. Being mired in the labyrinthine depth of mutual distrust, the Koreans of the divided halves are still handicapped by the lack of precise knowledge about each other. In that distorted milieu, there are destructive elements on both sides, who, having defined the other as the mortal enemy, have no interest other than exploiting each other as a convenient strategic shield to justify and preserve their own vested interests.

It is true that our people are open-minded on the issue of unification. Their consciousness, however, has yet to be transformed into a passionate enthusiasm. The reason for this is that the basis of the unification movement is too weak to focus the vague but clear consciousness into a more potent and passionate aspiration.

We, as a people, will have to channel our national consciousness into a firm determination that national unification must be achieved and that it is possible to do so. For this task, we should be aware that while we must be on guard against the anti-unification and anti-national forces, we should be vigilant at the same time against the irresponsible actions of the radicals, detrimental to the cause of unification.

On the other hand, there are others who put up negative arguments against the unification, citing the expense and pain that are feared to ensue. We have to realize, however, that the financial burdens of unification are not wasted, but an important investment in the future reconstruction of Korea—the necessary expense for the giant leap of the nation into the future.

The changes in North Korea have become inevitable. If we are for unification, we would have to recognize the North as our partner for the cause; we ought to coexist with the North and be more forward looking in assisting North Korea's changes through a wider level of exchange and cooperation; we ought to be more broadminded, if we are genuinely interested in the task of ultimately restoring social/cultural homogeneity for a new national community.

The future of unification and peace are the undeniable and irresistible trends of the future. Our journey will be long and painful, full of travail. But we know how to get there. As the old saying goes, the beginning of the journey itself is more than achieving half of the goal; and the sooner we begin, the better it will be. We believe that now is the time to take that first step.

CHAPTER 6

SUPPLEMENT: THE EVOLUTION OF "KIM DAE-JUNG'S THREE-STAGE UNIFICATION" FORMULA

Kim Dae-jung's Unification Formula was unable to receive a proper evaluation under the military dictators because of the inordinate Cold War ideology of "Anti-Communism." On the contrary, the "anti-Communist" paranoia, in its most virulent and distorted logic, wielded its unlimited power and influence as their most effective means to fabricate the farfetched charge that all democratic and progressive intellectuals, including Kim Dae-jung, were a "pro-Communist" element; and to persecute them on that basis. Hence, no details of Kim Dae-jung's philosophies or proposals for unification, nor even their barest outline, were known to the public; therefore, his real intentions, motives, and the significance of his work were denied the justice of a fair, in-depth examination.

Now, the time has come for an objective and true evaluation of the historical significance and rationality of Kim Dae-jung's unification philosophy and formula. To do this, one has to have a proper and sufficient understanding of the historical circumstances of the times under which his proposal was made. For example, the "Proposals for Peaceful Unification" or "On the Necessity of the Cross Recognition of the Two Koreas," or his proposal for the "Security Guarantee in Korea by the Four Major Powers"—the series of proposals made by Kim Dae-jung under the Park Chung-hee regime in which he called for the recognition of the reality of North Korea and the necessity of dialogue with it. Considering the circumstances of the times when the anti-Communist security logic prevailed, these were nothing short of remarkable. To consider, therefore, Kim Dae-jung's "unification formula" in the 1990's along with the other pedestrian proposals—the proposals that have become commonplace—would be wholly improper, if we were to leave out the important historical context of its origins.

All theories or ideas will have to undergo the processes of flexible adaptation and change in tandem with the change in historical circumstances. A theory can be defined as an attempt to explain and predict the reality based on reality. The "living" theory is one that, while preserving its basic roots and principles, constantly changes its modus operandi following the contours of historical trends. Although the "Three-Stage Unification" Formula today may have the same perception of basic problems and similar foundations for its principles as when it first appeared on stage as Mr. Kim Dae-jung's unification proposal in the early seventies, in its specific policy aspects it has a new face, having fully reflected the flow and change of history since then. Indeed, we can argue that Kim Dae-jung's "Three-Stage Unification" Formula has made sufficient changes and refinement in its conceptual and theoretical framework to enhance its adaptability and flexibility and is worthy of a positive evaluation.

To objectively re-evaluate and re-assess the contributions

made by Kim Dae-jung to the history of Korea as a democrat and as an advocate of peaceful unification—in his search for transcendence of the national division and the tragic political and military conflict between the two Koreas—is in fact an historical inevitability.[1] The Formula is the fruition of his persistent and consistent efforts without ever giving up his convictions for gradual and peaceful unification of Korea despite the extremity of his personal sufferings and travails in the fight against dictatorship and for democratization. The passion and indefatigable will for Korea's unification that he has shown for so long has been both the engine of historical development as well as an effort to marry the theory with practice—and as such it is a living lesson for the future of Korea.

I. The Origins of the "Three-Stage Unification" Formula

The two Koreas, affected by the winds of the Cold War more than any other country in the world, have been in a state of unabated hostility against each other in which they not only refused to recognize each other's existence, but also avoided any contact or negotiation. In fact, both sides have consistently adhered to the policy of one-sided absorption of the other either through "liberation" based on the exercise of force or through "recovery" of the other's territory by absorption based on one's superior position.

The policy of South Korea, for instance, has changed from a

---

[1] Cf. Inter alia, Bernard Krisher, "An Interview with Bernard Krisher, former Tokyo Correspondent for Newsweek Magazine," *Wolgan Chosun (The Choisun Monthly)*, February, 1996, pp. 178-193, passim.

belligerent "March to North" in the fifties to the "Unification through Victory over Communism" through "Construction First & Unification Later" in the sixties. North Korea, on the other hand, called for the communization of all Korea through war, for which Pyongyang pursued the so-called "Four Major Military Line" policy by trying to implement the policy of "National Liberation-Democratic Revolution" in South Korea. It was an attempt to unify the country through communization by a revolutionary war "to liberate the South and to smash its puppet government."

Kim Dae-jung's proposals—the "Four Power Guarantee of Peace in Korea" and the "Gradual and Peaceful Unification of Korea through the Improvement of Relations between the Two Koreas by inter-Korean Peaceful Exchanges and Other Appropriate Measures"—were made during the 1971 presidential campaign against a background of intense political-military confrontation between the two sides. It was followed in 1972 by the presentation of the "Three-Stage Unification" Formula. Criticizing the government's lack of will for unification, Kim Dae-jung offered his plan for peaceful coexistence of the two Koreas through the relaxation of tension and the prevention of war. He went on to stress the achievement of peaceful unification through the expansion of exchanges in all social areas including the exchange of reporters as well as exchanges in sports and cultural areas.

Considering the tense Cold War confrontations in the Korean Peninsula at the time, Kim Dae-jung's ideas were nothing short of extraordinary. Nonetheless, a closer and more thoughtful look at the world also revealed that the trends in the East-West conflict already pointed to a forthcoming thaw and reconciliation. Starting with the "Nixon Doctrine" in 1969, there were already signs, albeit faint then, of the winding down of the war in Vietnam; and a series of events that indicated the relaxation of tension and detente among the great powers such as West Germany's Ostpolitik, United Nations membership for the People's Republic of China, and the improvement/normalization of relations between the PRC and the United States and Japan. Despite these clear trends, the Cold War confrontation in Korea showed no sign of abatement. It was at this time that Kim Dae-jung made the historic proposal to set peace in motion in Korea by foreseeing the inevitable impact on the inter-Korean relations originating from the global trend of relaxation, and capitalizing on that impact.

That Kim Dae-jung's unification formula was never allowed a proper hearing and evaluation in Korea under the circumstances that prevailed is well known to all of us. However, besides this generally known fact, there is one other important fact hitherto unappreciated by most. To wit, Kim Dae-jung's unification formula was both a powerful challenge to the Cold War order that blanketed the Korean Peninsula and the presentation of a viable future vision of peace for national unification—based on a most remarkable prescience of the global trends in relaxation of tension and a most precise understanding of its overall impact on Korea. Even the Park Chung-hee regime began to sense the shift in the global strategic environment, gradually revising its previous policies on North Korea: the recognition of the North Korean political entity and the lifting of its policy of opposition to the notion of North Korea's membership in various international organizations and the simultaneous entry of the two Koreas into the United Nations. It went further by declaring a new policy of "fair competition between the two systems" and making new attempts at dialogue with the North to reduce tension. These steps resulted in the agreement for the July 4th Joint Declaration in 1972. All these efforts by the Park regime were the unmistakable signs of its co-opting the principles of peace proposed by Kim Dae-jung and his unification formula. Judging by the central nature of Park's philosophy and style of leadership, and the fundamental nature of his government (to be revealed later in his Yushin Constitutional System), his change of policy was an unspoken yet eloquent verification of the historical truth that Kim Dae-jung's unification formula accorded perfectly with the winds of historical change and their inevitable trends.

II. The Evolution of the "Three-Stage Unification" Formula

Kim Dae-jung's "Three-Stage Unification" Formula has honed its definition both in depth and structure over the past thirty years, cognizant of the panoramic changes in Korean politics and its climate. The processes of its transformation can be divided into three phases as described below. The first phase is the seventies—the period in which the original ideas were conceived for the primary purpose of peacefully managing the reality of national division, yet envisioning the "Positive Pacifism" in the ultimate attainment of unification.

The second phase, the eighties, was a period of further development of the Formula, in which an institutionalized approach was conceived for the Formula's realism and feasibility. The third period that continues to date, is one of "actual accomplishment of unification" in which the necessary formula refinement is on-going in terms of specificity and concreteness

to reconfirm its aspiration for unification—based on the concept
of a gradualized and peaceful process, as well as the "safety" of
the concept to work as the needed incentive for the two existing
systems to desire an accommodation with each other to seek a
modus operandi in achieving the final unification. We shall now
look at the processes of its change in the context of the contem-
porary internal and external factors and in the context of the two
Koreas' inter-relations.

The Formula—based on the concept of "peaceful coexistence"→"peaceful exchange"→and "peaceful unification"—was
first presented to the public around the time of the presidential
election in South Korea in 1971.[2] The seeds of Kim Dae-jung's
interest, however, in the national unification issue were sown in
the early 1960s. Let us briefly review the growth of his ideas.

The basis of Kim Dae-jung's consciousness on the issue of
national unification which forms the foundation of his "Three-
Stage Unification" Formula can be summarized into the following three fundamental precepts: "unification is the sacred task
for all Koreans"; "diplomacy ought to be based on the principles
of national self-determination and practical self-interest"; and
the "democratization of Korea is not only the shortcut to unification, but actually is its central core."

Of the three basic conceptual foundations, one that Kim Dae-
jung has consistently stressed is the proposition that Korea's unification is a task for all Koreans. In October 1964, in his interpellation of the government in the plenary session of the National
Assembly, he stated that in the matters of utmost national importance, such as unification and diplomacy, the country will have

---

[2]Kim Dae-jung, *Anthology of Kim Dae-jung's Writings [Hukwang Kim Dae-
jung Dae-jun-jib]* 15 vols. (Seoul: Jung-sim-suhwon, 1993), Vol. 3, p. 109.

to assume the "Korea First" posture of "pan-national" efforts.[3]

Two years later in July 1966, he continued to criticize the government for its lack of policy on unification, and added that "the time has come for the establishment of a national consultative body composed of all those, in and out of government, who are devoted to liberal democracy."[4] The unification question, stated Kim, clearly a bipartisan issue of national significance, must be approached in the interest of the "State of Korea" as well as the entire "Korean people." Fundamentally, therefore, it is not and cannot be misused by the rulers of the two Koreas as if it is their own "monopoly" to manipulate and rearrange at will to suit their narrow parochial interests. Accordingly, all Koreans, be they in the South or in the North, all political parties and all social organizations, in South or North Korea, ought to assume the role of the supreme overseer, the arbiter, and that of the booster, to make certain that the means used by the rulers in both Koreas for unification are headed in the right direction; or the substance or the characteristics of the unification that they seek are in the genuine interest of all Koreans.[5] Kim's warning and advice to the nation stemmed from unfortunate experience, namely, that the two ruling governments in Korea habitually exploited the national issue for the sole purpose of preserving their respective governments and keeping the power of the state in their own hands. Kim's consistent conviction, therefore, has been that national unification has to be achieved through demo-

---

[3]The cabinet ministry of the "Board of National Unification" was established on the basis of Kim Dae-jung's efforts at the time.

[4]Kim Dae-jung, *The Federation of the Republics [Konghwa-kuk Yunhap-jae]* (Seoul: Hakmin-sa, 1991), p. 36.

[5]Kim Dae-jung, *Anthology of Kim Dae-jung's Writings [Hukwang Kim Dae-jung Dae-jun-jib]* 15 vols. (Seoul: Jung-sim-suhwon, 1993), Vol. 4, p. 38.

cratic processes with the participation of all Koreans.

As mentioned earlier, his policy recommendations on unification and diplomacy for Korea were truly remarkable in the light of the international situation and the conditions of confrontation on the Korean Peninsula at the time. The twin pillars of his argument were that the fundamental policies ought to be pursued in the interest of "Korea's self-determination and self-interest," and that foreign policy and diplomacy ought to be future-oriented in that the inter-Korean exchanges must begin in non-political and non-controversial areas where inter-Korean consensus was possible.

Again in an interpellation of the government in the National Assembly on July 1, 1966, Kim Dae-jung called for the abandonment of the Hallstein Doctrine and recommended South Korea's decision to seek relations with certain Communist states for the purpose of furthering our national interest.[6] Under the then prevailing political circumstances in South Korea, Kim Dae-jung's statement on that occasion was in direct conflict with the permissible parameter set by the Park government for discussion of the issue of national unity. To no one's surprise, his statement was interpreted as a deliberate intent and reckless recommendation for the exchange with the North Korean "Communist Group"—an object set for destruction by the South, and with the Soviet Union and "Communist China"—the twin masters who incite, provoke, and assist the "puppets" in North Korea. To be sure, it was a deliberate distortion of the real intent and purpose of Kim Dae-jung's policy recommendation for South Korea. Kim Dae-jung's policy line that surfaced in the sixties was based strictly on

---

[6]Kim Dae-jung, *The Federation of the Republics [Konghwa-kuk Yunhap-jae]* (Seoul: Hakmin-sa, 1991), pp. 39-40.

the realities of international relations of the period. Underneath his argument was a surprisingly accurate understanding of the problems that the North Korean system is burdened with. Based on that understanding, he believed sincerely that the maximization of our national interest demanded diversification of our diplomatic relations through dialogue and exchanges with the Communist Bloc in general; and that the maximization of our national interest called for a policy oriented toward the realistic achievement of the unification of Korea. For all this, his advice and recommendation was for South Korea's daring yet realistic approach to seek ways for dialogue and exchange with the Northern regime.

In the same spirit and with the same consistency, Kim also argued against the withdrawal of American forces from Korea and for the "Guarantee of Peace in Korea" by the four great powers. These pragmatic policy proposals based on the correct understanding of Real Politik, however, were twisted and distorted when conveyed to the public, by the past governments of the military dictators. One typical example of the dishonest government black propaganda against Kim Dae-jung has been that by calling for "an early withdrawal of American forces from Korea," he had factually collaborated with the North Korean policy line and thus threatened the security of the Korean Peninsula; and abetted and incited the opposition movement against the basis system and structure of South Korea. Totally lacking legitimacy, the governments of the military dictators at the time were in desperate need of American assistance and support for their very survival in power. Kim Dae-jung's position, in fact, was that the United States ought not provide that support for the dictatorship. The real intent and purpose of Kim's argument was to emphasize that the United States, whose fundamental policy foundation has been traditionally and historically one of supporting democracy and human rights, ought not support the dictatorial governments. As for some who called for the withdrawal of American forces from Korea, he consistently raised the potential dangers of such an argument, and stressed the great significance of the role of the American military presence in the maintenance of strategic equilibrium in Northeast Asia. The only caveat was that the United States policy ought not to err by siding with the illegitimate government of the dictators. Before our eyes, however, the dark shadows of the chain of suspicion and misunderstanding, maliciously cast by the ruling circles, that have always been aimed at his ideas are gradually being lifted.

The other important basis of Kim Dae-jung's unification formula is his firm conviction that peaceful unification will become possible only after democratization is realized as the first step. Only through genuine democracy, he has argued tirelessly since the sixties, can South Korea be effectively and safely protected from insidious penetration by Communist influence and Communist elements; and that democracy alone can provide a realistic chance for unification.

However, the systematic framework of Kim Dae-jung's unification formula has taken shape since the 1970s. The first time the concrete details were presented was in 1971, when he ran as an opposition candidate in the presidential race. In that campaign, he presented three basic policies as the new framework of his unification policy if and when he won the presidency: the reduction of tension; the exchanges between the two Koreas; and the Four Power deterrence to war and guarantee of peace in the Korean Peninsula. More concrete and specific plans for "Three-Stage Unification" Formula soon followed these three policy outlines. Within the larger blueprint, encompassing the three stages of peaceful coexistence, exchange, and unification, the First Stage of Peaceful Exchange was to provide, based on mutual recognition of each other's entity, an institutionalized structure and mechanism for: 1) renunciation of war as the instrument of policy; 2) negotiation of a peace agreement; 3) the establishment of the structure for peaceful coexistence based on the expansion of the mechanism for mutual inspection/oversight; 4) simultaneous membership in the United Nations; and 5) the creation of an institutionalized system for the Four Major Power—the United States, Soviet Union, China, and Japan—guarantee of non-aggression and peace agreement between the two Koreas. The Peaceful Exchange in the Second Stage set the ultimate goal of achieving the restoration of national homogeneity between the two sides through the alleviation and dissolution of mutual hate and distrust, and the diminution of political, economic, social, and other divergences/differences between the two Koreas. To achieve these ends, Kim Dae-jung proposed a comprehensive plan of governmental and non-governmental exchanges in all areas, including Red Cross talks and exchanges in the areas of mass media, culture, the arts, scholarship, sports, religion, and the economy; and particularly the exchanges in television and radio broadcasts by ensuring the mutual opening of the doors in this regard to their respective populations. The Third Stage was to attain the complete unification based on the pan-national consensus, to be reached through the extensive preparation via the previous two mutually integrated stages.

After the election and his defeat, Kim Dae-jung toured five nations—the U.S., Japan, Britain, France, and Germany—and upon his return, he presented the "Three-Stage Unification" Formula as a travel report to a group of people. In that report to the people of Korea, Kim presented his grand vision of how Kore-ans should approach the issue of national unification in a world of evolving East-West thaw, founded on the dual bases of the status quo and peaceful coexistence, and made the case for his proposal[7]: the First Stage of war deterrence; the Second Stage of Inter-Korean exchanges; and the Third and final Stage of com-plete political unification.

In a campaign to promote his plan and its feasibility, in July 1972, he held a major press conference at the Seoul Foreign Cor-respondents Club; and on this occasion, he raised the issue of the two Koreas' simultaneous membership in the United Nations. At a time when North Korea was routinely and naturally called the "North Korean Puppets" and when the Southern policy was its obliteration, his proposal caused a shockwave like a major earth-quake. Despite the general reaction, however, even this proposal was based on his keen observation of the global tidings of recon-ciliation between the two power blocs, and can only be called progressive and prophetic. In his mindset, Korea's grand histori-cal march toward unification can only begin from the premise of realistic mutual recognition as the unavoidable partner for dia-logue. It was, indeed, a classical proposal of pragmatism in that it was to induce the North towards a path of reasonable partici-pation in the world community by helping it to open the door to the world outside.

In October 1972, President Park Chung-hee suspended the constitution and ushered in the notorious "Yushin System." A national emergency was declared and the National Assembly was dissolved. Declaring his opposition, Kim Dae-jung con-

---

[7]Kim Dae-jung, *The Federation of the Republics [Konghwa-kuk Yunhap-jae]* (Seoul: Hakmin-sa, 1991), pp. 119-122.

demned the move as Park's "anti-democratic and anti-unification plot and conspiracy." As a result, Kim Dae-jung was subjected to continuing political repression—an assassination attempt, kidnapping, torture, imprisonment, political exile, and house arrest. Despite the relentless persecution, Kim continued to disseminate the message of his proposal and its rationale in the United States and elsewhere around the world, constantly building on the ideas and improving them. In a way, for Kim Dae-jung, the incarceration, house arrest, and political exile overseas in the seventies and the eighties were the nutrients that helped root the ideas of the "Three-Stage Unification" Formula firmly in reality and make it grow.

Entering the 1980s, Kim Dae-jung's unification formula began to assume systematically the institutional approach to the whole question of national unification. Although his formula still hoped to achieve the implementation of the three basic principles of peaceful coexistence, exchange, and unification as the implementation guidelines, it began to entertain a new concept of the "Federation in order to open the possibilities for national unification—unification that is the ultimate aspiration of all Koreans."[8] Considering the unique set of conditions in the Korean Peninsula, the new concept was based on the understanding that a Federation is needed as a transitional stage before the complete unification is possible.

The unification formula (the "Federation of the Republics") that Kim Dae-jung presented in the mid-1980s, dealt mainly with the first stage of unification. In this stage, a "symbolic federal structure" would be established, composed of the represen-

---

[8]Kim Dae-jung, *The Federation of the Republics [Konghwa-kuk Yunhap-jae]* (Seoul: Hakmin-sa, 1991), pp. 160-162.

tatives of the two sides. Each, however, would maintain their respective independent governments along with their opposing ideologies and systems, to which the two Korean governments would delegate a certain amount of power to discuss and implement matters of peaceful coexistence and peaceful exchange between the two Koreas. Although the designation of "Federation" was used because Kim Dae-jung's concept of the "Federation of the Republics" was considered somewhat similar to the British Commonwealth in some aspects, it was meant to be primarily a period of peaceful coexistence and exchange under a "symbolic federal structure" which can only be defined as a loose confederation. Thus, he believed that the final transition can and will be made to a Federal structure as political power is gradually transferred to the central government from the two independent governments of the divided Koreas. The final work towards the complete unification under the third stage will have to be left in the hands of the next generation, who will have to make the ultimate choice through consultation and adjustment.[9]

In contrast, therefore, to the North Korean proposal that called for a direct transition to a federal structure straight from the present division and confrontation, Kim's "Three-Stage" formula argues for a transitional phase of the Confederation of the two Koreas—as the necessary, and in fact, the inevitable prerequisite to national unification.[10] With the lapse of a reasonable interval of time in which North Korea moves towards a market economy and democracy, the possibility will emerge for the transition to a Federal system. In this context, Kim Dae-jung's proposal is wholly different from that of North Korea.

---

[9]*Ibid.*, pp. 184-185.
[10]*Ibid.*, p. 175.

Nevertheless, Kim Dae-jung's unification proposal was deliberately distorted by the ruling military dictatorship so that it would seem identical to North Korea's. It was the continuation of the Southern government's campaign to paint him "red"; as a result of the insistent efforts of the military rulers, he was singled out for groundless accusations and persecution. For this reason, Kim Dae-jung made an effort to highlight the clear differences between his unification formula and the North Korean proposal. In the context of this effort, he clarified his views on national security as well as on national unification through the principles of the "Three Nos": no-violence, no-Communism, and "no" anti-Americanism. Non-violence, he insisted, is the most important principle to be observed in the struggle for democratization. He believed consistently that the effort for democracy must follow the examples of the "people power" revolution in the Philippines and the June 1987 struggle for democracy in Korea (against the Chun Doo-hwan dictatorship). Second, the principle of "non-Communism" has to be the basis of Korea's unification: namely, that unification through the communization of Korea ought to be rejected outright. However, his opposition to North Korean Communism must not be confused with an indefinite delay in unification. His argument has been that, although democracy should be the ultimate goal for Korea, efforts must still be made to provide opportunities for North Korea so that it can voluntarily accept the principles of democracy and, through it, achieve peaceful unification of the nation. To enable such a process of evolution, there has to be peaceful coexistence between the two Koreas as well as dialogue and negotiation.

Third, he believes that non-"Anti-Americanism" must be the basis of Korea's independence and self-reliance. Although he supports the principle of autonomous national efforts for unification, he warns that it must not be allowed to cause the rise of unconditional anti-Americanism. If the United States supports the dictatorship, opposes democracy, and pursues policies, detrimental to Korea's unification, we must resolutely oppose the policies. However, as long as the United States is helpful to us in preserving peace in Korea and achieving our national unification, we must fully cooperate with the United States. This has been the core and gist of his principle of "non-Anti-Americanism." This philosophy and his views on the United States have been fully reflected in the policies that he proposed to realize the unification through the "Three-Stage" formula.

While Kim Dae-jung was engaged in efforts to clarify his policies and the differences from the North Korean plan, the July 7th Declaration was issued in 1988. Although, in principle, he was in agreement with President Roh Tae-woo's July 7th Declaration, he still regretted that it contained no reference at all concerning a peace structure between the two Koreas. To fill that important gap, he accelerated his efforts to systematize the concepts and ideas behind his formula. Nevertheless, his unification formula at the time still lacked sufficient explanation on several important points. Despite the fact that it mentions the need for and the role of the Confederation as an indispensable step towards unification, it did not yet fully clarify and explain either the inter-relations between Confederation and Federation or process of transition from Confederation to Federation to full unification. That job was undertaken in the 1990s.

The plan for the "Confederation of the Two Korean Republics," announced in April 1991, finally addressed these key issues, and as such it was on its way toward the completion of refinement. What is noteworthy here is that the previous expression of the "loose Federal stage" was changed to the " Stage of

Confederation" during this period of refinement. Another revision concerned the principles of peaceful coexistence, exchange, and unification—previously considered to be three stages of unification in themselves; they are now judged to be three basic principles in the guidelines for unification during the first stage of Confederation. This change reflected the change in basic perception of the likely issues between the two sides; specifically, that peaceful exchange does not necessarily require the precondition of peaceful existence in place, as previously thought. To put it still differently, a realization dawned that there could be two different kinds of exchanges: "peaceful exchange *within* peaceful coexistence" and "peaceful coexistence *from* peaceful exchange." These perceptional changes accelerated the systematization of the realistic formula.

The newly revised "Three-Stage" Formula concludes first that there must be a peace agreement and non-aggression treaty between the two Koreas to realize peaceful coexistence. It also calls for arms control measures, firm verification procedures and an international guarantee of the Korean peace structure. Second, the realization of peaceful exchange depends on active inter-Korean exchange based on the agreement for peaceful coexistence between the two sides. Third, peaceful unification ought to be truly peaceful—it should depend neither on the superiority of power by either side, nor should it depend on the sudden absorption of one side by the other.

Under the plans envisioned by the "Confederation of the Two Korean Republics," the two Koreas will be headed toward unification guided by the three basic principles and through the processes of three stages. Kim Dae-jung explains the processes as follows: the two independent governments will first coalesce under a state-to-state Confederation, followed by a Federation in which the two governments will be transformed into regional authorities, which will then head towards the final stage of complete unification with either a centralized system or a Federal system like the United States and Germany.

After refinement and important revision, Kim Dae-jung's unification formula assumed a new name as well. Considering the symbolism and importance of the South-North Confederation in the first stage, the "Confederation of the Two Korean Republics" was an appropriate designation at the time before refinement/revision. Kim Dae-jung, however, felt that his unification formula needed a new comprehensive title to stress the following: the operative principles for each stage of the unification process; the appropriate level of the necessary institutionalization for each stage, the procedural matters involved in the implementation of various measures in each stage of the process, and the specific tasks to be accomplished for the process. And since the "Confederation of the Two Korean Republics" represented merely the first step in the "Three-Stages" of the unification process, the entire formula was officially redesignated as "Kim Dae-jung's 'Three-Stage Unification' Formula." Chart 6-1 below summarizes the process of systematization of Kim Dae-jung's "Three-Stage Unification" Formula.

III. The Efforts to Implement the "Three-Stage Unification" Formula

An ideology or a plan, however superior, would be like "throwing a pearl to a swine," if it is not feasible or if there are no policy efforts to guide it toward reality. To realize the "Three-Stage Unification" Formula, Kim Dae-jung has continued to offer

*[Chart 6-1] The Developmental Process of Kim Dae-jung's
"Three-Stage Unification" Formula.*

Period	Period of Initial Conception ('70s)	Period of Development ('80s)	Period of Maturity ('90s)
Designation	"3-Stage Unification Plan"	The "Federation of the Two Korean Republics" Unification Plan (aka: The "Confederation of the Two Korean Republics" Unification Plan.	Kim Dae-jung's "Three-Stage Unification" Formula
3 Principles	Self-reliance, Peace, and Democracy	Self-reliance, Peace, and Democracy	Self-reliance, Peace, and Democracy
3 Stages	① Peaceful Coexistence ② Peaceful Exchange ③ Peaceful Unification	① Peaceful Coexistence & Exchange under Symbolic Federal Structure ② Federation ③ Complete Unification	① The South-North Confederation ② Federation ③ Complete unification
First Stage	Peaceful Coexistence: Treaty of Renunciation of War; Peace Agreement; and 4-Power Guarantee of Korean Peace	Phase of Peaceful Coexistence & Exchange under the Symbolic "Federal" Structure (the Confederation Stage): The two independent Korean governments (with different ideology and system) continue to be in charge of their respective foreign relations, internal and military affairs; the "symbolic" federal government maintains and administers peaceful coexistence & exchange.	The Stage of South-North Confederation: The institutionalization of the system for mutual cooperation by the two Koreas on the basis of their existing sovereign independence; the establishment of the Confederal Summit Meeting, the Confederal Council, the Confederal Ministerial Council; the tasks of the Confederal bodies are to implement the 3 basic guidelines (Peaceful Coexistence, Exchange, and Unification)

Second Stage	Peaceful Exchange: Exchange/Cooperation in all areas.	The Phase of Federation: The Federal Gov't in charge of foreign relations, defense, major internal affairs; the two Koreas will retain their own gov'ts as "regional" authorities.	The Stage of Federation: The Federal Gov't in charge of foreign relations, defense, and important internal affairs; the establishment of Federal President & Federal Parliament; Two Koreas still retain autonomous regional gov'ts
Third Stage	Peaceful Unification: Opposition to unification through military means and unification without freedom	The Phase of Complete Unification: The realization of national unification on the basis of ongoing active peaceful coexistence & exchange,	The Phase of Complete Unification: Complete centralization or federal system (a là U.S or Germany); the unified state's ideology and system — democracy, market economy, social welfare, moral/ethical advanced state, pacifism.
Historical Significance	The very first gradualistic unification plan in history	Progressive development of unification plan	The completion of the systematic & specific unification plan.

realistic alternatives, and positively responded to the test of history and reality. From these ceaseless efforts were born the consistent display of rationalism and foresight, and creative flexibility which have attracted attention and respect both from domestic scholars and experts as well from their foreign counterparts. Consequently, his unification plan has become a "living organism" and will continue to be a process of "adjustment and resistance."

Let us reappraise once more Kim Dae-jung's efforts to walk the path toward unification with the people of Korea. First, he has persistently and consistently worked for the democratization of Korea against all odds—as the absolutely necessary precondition for unification. His belief has rested on the fundamental assumption that an approach toward peaceful unification must necessarily begin with the cool headed appreciation of the problems and difficulties that now exist between the two divided Koreas. After that, any realistic solution to the problems must come from the efforts and wisdom of the entire nation; and the means of approaching the task will have to be diverse, based on the free expression of ideas. To accommodate such a need, "one hundred voices from one hundred schools" must be freely heard and debated in order finally to reach a consensual formula for unification. For this reason, Kim Dae-jung has argued for the policy of "democratization first" in spite of his personal suffering.

As a concrete measure of seeking the answers, he established the "Kim Dae-jung Peace Foundation for the Asia-Pacific Region (KPF)" in January 1994. In December of the same year, he organized and sponsored an international conference of democratic leaders in Seoul to assist and accelerate democratization in the Asia-Pacific region; established a "Forum of Democratic Leaders in the Asia-Pacific (FDL-AP)" and created an international NGO, headquartered in Seoul, Korea with regional branch and liaison offices in several key Asian cities. The publication of this book in mid-1995 is part of Kim Dae-jung's continuing effort for "unification through democracy."

Besides these efforts, Kim Dae-jung made further efforts in other areas as well in accordance with his conviction that democracy must precede unification. In this context, he argued that the "Basic Agreement" between the two Koreas should be reviewed by the National Assembly for its "advice and consent"; that the military ought to be made neutral in internal politics and the military intelligence agencies' surveillance of the civilian population must be stopped completely; and that the infamous National Security Law and the National Security Planning Agency Law must be improved through revision.

He also tried to renovate the legal and systemic structures to effectively and efficiently manage the tasks necessary for ultimately achieving national unity. As mentioned earlier, to raise and improve the level of specialization and efficiency in the government's handling of the unification tasks, he made an initial proposal (which was accepted by the government) to unify all the scattered and disorganized government functions related to the unification issue under a single ministry [the newly established Board of National Unification, a post of a Deputy Prime Minister today]. He demanded that the newly established ministry, with centralized functions, adapt itself skillfully and in a timely fashion to the rapidly changing international situation and maintain consistency in our basic policies and approaches to the unification issue. He cautioned, however, that if the centralized unification ministry is to function properly, the National Security Planning Agency ought to be stopped from monopolizing all intelligence matters and decision-making towards North Korea. The NSP's role must, he argued, be confined to a supporting role for the ministry.

But his special contribution has been to take the first step to realize inter-Korean coexistence: such as the meticulous and good faith implementation of the "Joint Declaration for Denuclearization," arms control and mutual inspection, the peaceful use of the De-militarized Zone, and others. In addition, he made a proposal for a national security structure within Northeast Asia in consideration of the new conditions created by the end of the Cold War. The proposal included the recommendation for a relevant buildup of national defense capabilities to cope with the security conditions in the region; and for the continued American military presence until a reliable peace structure is in place for Korea and the region. For him, the central mechanism for national security and peace in the Korean Peninsula will have to be the continued existence of the collective security structure between the United States and South Korea, to be reinforced by an additional layer of security guarantees from a multilateral security setup involving both Koreas as well as the four major powers—the United States, China, Japan, and Russia.

Lastly, he has tried to effect viable progress towards peaceful exchange between the two Koreas. In 1992, during the presidential campaign, he promised that he would give top priority to achieving humanitarian exchange visits and reunion for the separated families; and that he would achieve tangible results within one year of his presidential term in office. As a specific step, he would push for the reunion and exchange of mail after establishing the whereabouts of the surviving family members, and set up a permanent meeting place either along the DMZ or inside the Panmunjom area.

Many of the policy alternatives that the "Three-Stage" formula presents have been recognized as rational and creative proposals. One example wherein Kim Dae-jung's policy ideas proved their worth was in 1993 in solving the thorny issues during the crisis caused by the North Korean nuclear weapons project. That his proposals for a "package deal" and for former President Jimmy Carter's visit to North Korea played a decisive role in making a breakthrough is well known.

The terminology, "package deal," that is now more generally in use in "international studies" began to have new meaning when Kim gave it a fresh significance during his stay in Britain in April 1993. The core of his "package deal" was to settle the North Korean nuclear issue by one sweeping agreement in which North Korea would give up the nuclear project in return for diplomatic and economic concessions/assistance.

At the time, in some quarters of South Korean government, there were judgments that North Korea still harbored intentions to overthrow the Southern system through the strategy of Communist Revolution and that the North was far from being a proper counterpart for dialogue, compromise, and negotiation. Kim Dae-jung, however, understood the implications of the end of the Cold War on North Korea. Citing the examples of several important North Korean laws and specific projects (such as the Rajin and Sunbong "Free Trade" Zones) for partial opening of the country in the early 1990s, Kim Dae-jung concluded that North Korea would have to face the reality of at least a partial opening of the country for its survival.

His prognoses and conclusion at the time were accepted by many in Korea and overseas as "persuasive." Finally, an agreement was extracted in Geneva in October 1994 between the two sides, based on a package deal that took into account both the staked position and the interest of both sides. The U.S.-North Korea agreement in Geneva not only fully demonstrated the rational utility of a successful negotiation based on the concept of a "package deal," but provided one more opportunity to attract world-wide attention to Kim Dae-jung's North Korean policy concepts and unification plans. This does not mean, however, that the package deal approach was smooth sailing from the start. In fact, in May 1994, the United States and North Korea were in agreement to open a three-tier negotiations in the aftermath of the

IAEA inspection of North Korea's nuclear facilities. There was cautious optimism about the prospect of these projected talks at the time. But ignoring demands by the IAEA and the United States on selective extraction and safe-keeping of the fuel rods, North Korea proceeded to make extraction by itself. In response, the United States and South Korea were seriously considering economic and military sanctions against the North, while North Korea countered by withdrawing from the IAEA, and threatened to consider any sanction as "a declaration of war."

On the other hand, the planning for economic sanctions against North Korea soon hit a snag and serious doubts were raised as to its effectiveness as China was expressly opposed to it and Russia proposed an "eight-power" meeting in an attempt to increase its influence on the Northern nuclear issue. Just at this juncture, Kim Dae-jung while in the United States, suggested that a solution would be impossible without a direct meeting with Kim Il Sung and that the person to do the talking would be former President Jimmy Carter.[11] Kim Dae-jung's proposal was relevant on several counts. First, North Korea made it clear that it intended to negotiate only with the United States and nobody else by withdrawing from the IAEA. Second, the United States was not in a position to officially propose negotiations with North Korea as it was considering sanctions. On the other hand, North Korea could not ignore Jimmy Carter as a possible trouble-shooter. In a way, he was the most suitable person for North Korea. As a former president, Carter was a senior statesman,

---

[11]Refer to Kim Dae-jung's luncheon speech before the National Press Club in Washington, D. C. on May 12, 1994. For the text of the speech and other related speeches by Kim, see Kim Dae-jung, *Korea and Asia: A Collection of Essays, Speeches, and Discussions* (Seoul: The Kim Dae-jung Peace Foundation [KPF], 1994), pp. 11-31.

and had a specially suitable political weight in a Democratic administration. Besides, as president of the United States, Carter once called for the withdrawal of American forces from South Korea. For North Korea, he was the most ideal person for dialogue and negotiation, and was best suited to draw the North Koreans away from a course of potentially dangerous confrontation. In fact, Carter went to North Korea and had a series of talks with Kim Il Sung before his death in July, and was instrumental in turning the confrontational situation to one of dialogue and negotiation.

Here, we have to note Kim Dae-jung's long standing conviction that politics must be based on dialogue and compromise for mutual benefits; his clear understanding of North Korea's international isolation and its domestic difficulties as well as his superior perception of North Korea's unique "political culture" as the bases of his suggestions for a package deal and Jimmy Carter as the person to carry the message. On this, Li Rui-hwan, Chairman of the Consultative Conference, and the fourth-ranking leader in China, later commented to Kim Dae-jung during his trip to China, that a great cause for peace in Korea was served by the wise role played by Kim in making the Carter trip possible. Much the same appreciation was expressed by President Carter himself and the officials of the U.S. State Department for Kim Dae-jung's contribution.

Indeed, Kim Dae-jung's timely role in making the "package deal" and Carter's North Korean visit a reality, was one additional evidence of the rationality and feasibility of his ideas on the best means to deal with North Korea. We are convinced that these processes have convinced the people of Korea that "South Korea's policies toward the North will have to be changed fundamentally to account for the end of the Cold War." Kim Dae-jung's "Three-Stage Unification" Formula will continue to adjust and adapt to the evolving future to deserve its role as the most logical and feasible plan of unification for Korea in the years to come until we as a nation reach that goal.

Selected Bibliography

Ahn Doo-soon, *Korean Unification & Economic Integration: The Problems That Need Attention in Light of the German Experience* (Seoul: 1992).

The Bank of Korea, *A Comparison of Major Economic Indicators of the Two Koreas in 1993* (Seoul: June 1994).

Bela Balassa, *The Theory of Economic Integration* (Homewood, Illinois: Richard D. Irwin, Inc., 1961).

Bureau of Exchange/Cooperation, Board of National Unification,Republic of Korea, *Status of Inter-Korean Exchange/Cooperation* [Monthly], No. 44, 1995.

Bureau of Exchange/Cooperation, Board of National Unification, Republic of Korea, *South-North Korean Exchanges and Cooperation Today* [Monthly], March-April, 1995.

Bureau of International Economics, Ministry of Foreign Affairs, *The Final Report of the High Level Officials on Environmental Cooperation* (Seoul, 1993).

Committee for the Promotion of Foreign Economic Cooperation, DPRK, *The Golden Triangle: The Investment Guide for the Rajin-Sunbong Free Trade Zone* (Pyongyang: 1993).

Cha Young-koo, "[We will] Enter an Era of Common Defense between the Two Koreas from Year 2000," *The Unification Era That Will Open in Year 2000* (Seoul: The Presidential Commission on the 21st Century, 1993).

Chang Meng-yul, "Problems of North Korean Economy and Its Internal Structure: Internal Approaches," in Hwang Eui-gak, *et al.*, *The Stagnation of North Korea's Socialist Economy and Responses* (Seoul: Kyungnam University Press, 1995).

Chang Young-sik, *The Energy Economy in North Korea* (Seoul: Korea Development Institute [KDI], 1993).

Cho Chung-kon, "The Settlement of Disputes in Inter-Korean Exchanges and Trade, and in Investment through the Mediation by International Trading Companies," in *Anthology of Articles Dealing with North Korea and Unification Issues II: The Inter-Korean Exchanges and Cooperation* (Seoul: National Board of Unification, 1993).

Cho Min, "Unification Culture and Korean National Community," *The Korean Journal of Unification Studies*, Vol. 2, No. 2., 1993. (Seoul: The Research Institute for National Unification, 1993).

Chun Hong-taek, "North Korea's Investment Environment and Strategies for Investment in the North," *The Korea Development Review*, Vol. 15, No. 2, November 1993 (Seoul: KDI, 1993).

Chun Soo-tae & Choi Chul-ho, *Comparative Study of the Languages in South and North Korea: For the Unification of National Language in the Era of Division* (Seoul: Nokjin, 1989).

Chun Sung-hoon, *On Verification of Arms Control: Based on Theories and Historical Cases* (Seoul: Research Institute for National Unification, 1992).

Chung Hyung-soo, "The Realities of North Korea's Broadcasting," in *North Korea's Newspapers and Broadcasting* (Seoul: Board of National Unification, Republic of Korea, 1979).

Chung Kyung-bae, *et al.*, *The Comparative Study of the Social Security System in South and North Korea* (Seoul: Korea Institute for Health and Social Affairs, 1992).

Doh Hong-ryul, "Proposal for Information and Human Exchanges between the Two Koreas," in *The Opening of the Era of Reconciliation and Cooperation and Inter-Korean Relations* (Seoul: Board of National Unification, Republic of Korea, 1992).

Educational Books Publishing Co., *The Korean History: For the Third and Fourth Grades in High Middle School* (Pyongyang, 1983).

The Environmental Protection Agency, Republic of Korea, *White Paper on Environment* (Seoul, 1993).

Maurice Ernst, "Postwar Economic Growth in Eastern Europe (A Comparison with Western Europe)," *New Directions in the Soviet Economy*, Part IV (Washington, D. C.: Joint Economic Committee, Congress of the United States, 1966).

Richard Evans, *Deng Xiaoping and the Making of Modern China* (New York: Viking, 1994).

Robert Gilpin, *The Political Economy of International Relations* (Princeton, N.J.: Princeton University Press, 1987).

Han Kyun-tae, "On North Korea's Broadcast Policy and System," *Study of Broadcasting [Bang-song Yunkoo]* (Seoul: Broadcast Committee, 1989).

Hahm Taek-young, "A Study of Arms Competition between the Two Koreas and the Military Balance," in Hahm Taek-young, *et al.*, *The Arms Competition and Arms Control between the Two Koreas* (Seoul: Kyungnam University Press, 1993).

Ralph Hawtrey, *Economic Aspects of Sovereignty* (London: Longmans, 1952).

IISS, *Military Balance*, 1994.

Kang Jung-koo, "Policies for the Establishment of the Inter-Korean Social-Cultural Community," in In *Search of Rapid Restoration of Common National Identity* (Seoul: Board of National Unification, Republic of Korea, 1993).

Kim Dae-jung, *Anthology of Kim Dae-jung's Writings [Hukwang Kim Dae-jung Dae-jun-jib]* 15 vols. (Seoul: Jung-sim-suhwon, 1993).

Kim Dae-jung, *The Federation of the Republics [Konghwa-kuk Yun-*

hap-jae] (Seoul: Hakmin-sa, 1991).

Kim Dae-jung, *Korea and Asia: A Collection of Essays, Speeches,* and Discussions (Seoul: The Kim Dae-jung Peace Foundation [KPF], 1994).

Kim Dae-jung, *My Way and My Ideas: The Great Transition of World History and Strategy for National Unification [Na-eui Gil Na-eui Sasang: Saegae-sa eui Dae-junhwan-gwa Minjok Tongil-eui Bang-ryak]* (Seoul: Hangilsa, 1994).

Kim Kook-jin, "An Approach to a Multilateral Security Regime in Northeast Asia," *Journal of Area Studies,* 6, 1994 (The Korean Consultative Research Council for Area Studies/*Hankuk Jeeyuk Yunku Hyup-eui-hoe*).

Kim Mun-hwan, "On Increasing the Level of Cultural Homogeneity between South and North Korea," in *The Seminar on the Means to Form the Cultural Community between South and North Korea* (Data Book) (Seoul: Association for the Promotion of Cultural Exchange between South and North Korea, 1993).

Kim Sang-koo, "On the Means for the Sports Exchanges between the Two Koreas," *The Anthology of Research Articles for the Sungkyunkwan University,* Vol. 35, No. 2 (Seoul: Sungkyunkwan University, 1986).

Kim Tae-sung & Sung Kyung-ryung, *On State Social Welfare* (Seoul: Nanam, 1993).

Kim Woo-ryong, "In Search of Modalities for the Exchange of Inter-Korean Broadcasts," in *Journal of Unification Studies* (Seoul: Board of National Unification, 1993).

The Korean Broadcasting Institute, *On the Technological Tasks for the Inter-Korean Broadcasting Exchange* (Seoul, 1992).

The Korean Broadcasting Institute, *The Korean Broadcasting System* (KBS) (Seoul: 1992).

Korea Advanced Energy Research Institute, *The Energy Problems in North Korea Today and Inter-Korean Cooperation* (Seoul: 1994).

The Korea Development Institute (KDI), *The Basic Ideas for Economic Relations between the Two Koreas* (Seoul: 1991).

The Korea Development Institute (KDI), *Economic Evaluation of the Three Years of German Unification and Its Applicability in Inter-Korean Economic Relations* (Seoul: 1993).

Korea Institute for International Economic Policy, *The Study of Korean-Chinese Environmental Cooperation* (Seoul. 1993).

Korean Broadcasting Institute, *Investigation into Various Technical Problems for the Inter-Korean Exchange in Broadcasting* (Seoul: 1992).

The Korean Broadcasting Institute, *On the Technological Tasks for the Inter-Korean Broadcasting Exchange* (Seoul, 1992).

KOTRA, *Facts about Investment in North Korea* (Seoul: KOTRA, 1993).

KOTRA, *North Korea's Leading Economic Indicators 1993* (Seoul, 1993).

Michael Krakowski, "System Transformation and System Integration in Eastern Germany and Eastern Europe: Some Lessons," a preliminary version, presented at the International Seminar on *"Two Years Since the German Unification: Implications for the Unification of Korea,"* sponsored by the Korea Institute for International Economic Policy and Friedrich Ebert Stifung in Seoul, Korea, 1992.

Lee Bong-seoug, "National Income and Industrial Growth during the Developmental Period in North Korea," in Hwang Eui-gak, *et al.*, *The Political Economy of North Korea's Socialist Economy Construction* (Seoul: Kyungnam University Press, 1993).

Lee Chang-hee, "The Problems in the Promotion of Scholarly Exchanges between University Professors of South and North Korea," in *The Reality and Prospect in the Scholarly Exchanges of the Professors and the Students between South and North Korea* (Seoul: Committee for the Promotion of Scholarly Exchanges of University Professors between South and North Korea, 1992).

Lee Chong-seoug, "The Substance and Limitations of 'Socialism Our Style'," in Hwang Eui-gak, *et al., The Stagnation of North Korea's Socialist Economy and Responses* (Seoul: Kyungnam University Press, 1995).

Lee Hong-koo, *The March Towards Unification through the Establishment of National Community* (Seoul: Board of National Unification, 1989).

Lee Sang-man, *On "Unification Economy": North Korean Economy and South-North Korean Economic Integration* (Seoul: Hyungsul, 1994).

Lee Sang-woo, "The Unification Scenario: Economic Integration in the Year 2000, Political Integration in 2010, and the Unified Republic in 2020," *The Era of Unification in the 2000s* (Seoul: The Tong-A Ilbo, 1993).

Lee Yong-pil, "The Theoretical Bases for Functional Integration: Approaches and Relevance," in *On the Integration of the Two Koreas* (Seoul: Ingan-sarang, 1992).

Arend Lijphart, *Democracies: Patterns of Majoritarian & Consensus Government in Twenty One Countries* (New Haven: Yale University Press, 1984).

Lim Dong-won, "Arms Control on the Korean Peninsula is the Historic Demand of Our Times," *Hankuk Nondan* (A monthly journal in Seoul), July, 1990.

Lim Dong-won, *The Basic Concepts on the Management of the Inte-*

grational Process between the Two Koreas (Seoul: Board of National Unification, 1989).

Lim Dong-won, *The Communist Revolutionary War and Counterinsurgency* (Seoul: Tamgudang, 1967).

Andrew Marton, Terry McGee and Donald G. Paterson, "Northeast Asian Economic Cooperation and The Tumen River Area Development Project," *Pacific Affairs*, Vol. 68, No. 1, Spring 1995.

Ministry of Defense, Republic of Korea, *National Defense White Paper*, 1993-1994 (Seoul: Ministry of Defense, 1993-1994).

Ministry of Education, *History in High School*, 2 vols. (Seoul: Korea Textbooks Co., 1993).

Ministry of Finance and Economy, *Farm, Forestry, and Fisheries Statistics* (Seoul: 1995).

Ministry of Foreign Affairs, *The Report on the High Level Meeting on the Environmental Cooperation in Northeast Asia* (Seoul: Ministry of Foreign Affairs, 1993).

Ministry of Foreign Affairs, Republic of Korea, *Thirty Years of Korea's Diplomacy, 1948-1979* (Seoul: Ministry of Foreign Affairs, 1979).

Nam Man-kwon, "Plans for Inspection and Verification of Arms Control Agreements between South and North Korea," *Defense Journal(Kukbang-nonjib)*, 14, Summer, 1991.

Nam Young-sook, "The Inter-Korean Environmental Cooperation and the Study of Plans to Integrate Environmental Policies" in *Proceedings of Baedal Green Federation Symposium* (Seoul, 1995).

Oh Jae-hak, "North Korea's Road and Railroad Systems Today and the Proposal for the Linkup of the two Koreas' Land Transportation System," *North Korean Studies [Bukhan Yunku]*, Summer, 1994 [Seoul: Daeryuk Yunkuso].

Park Hyung-sook, "Problems and Prospect of Broadcasting Exchanges between the Two Koreas," *The Press Exchanges between South and North Korea* (Seoul: The Korean Press Institute, 1992).

Park Young-ho and Park Jong-chul, *On the Method of Establishing a South-North Korean Political Community* (Nambuk-han Jungchi Gongdongchae Hyungsung Bang-an Yungu) (Seoul: The Research Institute for National Unification, 1993).

Gareth Porter and Janet Welsh Brown, *Global Environmental Politics* (Boulder, Colorado: Westview Press, 1991).

The Presidential Commission on the 21st Century, *Korea in the 21st Century* (Seoul: Seoul Press, 1994).

Stephen Rainbow, *Green Politics* (Auckland, Oxford, New York: Oxford University Press, 1993).

The Research Institute for North Korea, *Bukhan Chong-ram [North Korean Handbook]* (Seoul: Research Institute for North Korea, 1983).

Roh Jae-bong, "Vision for Asia-Pacific Economic Cooperation and the Direction of Its Development," in Lee Jae-sung, ed., *New Direction in Asia-Pacific Economic Cooperation* (Seoul: Korea Institute for International Economic Policy & Korea Committee for Pacific Economic Cooperation, 1993).

Science Encyclopedia Publishing Company, *History of the Chosun War [Chosun Junsa]* (Pyongyang: 1981-1982).

Sohn Ki-woong, "On Mutual Cooperation between the Two Koreas over Environmental Issues," *Collection of Research Articles on North Korea & Unification, II, 1993* (Seoul: Board of National Unification, 1994).

Suh Jae-il, *Proposal for the Promotion of Cooperation in Light Industries between the Two Koreas* (Seoul: Korea Institute for Industrial Economics & Trade [KIET], 1994).

Lester Thurow, *Head to Head: The Coming Economic Battle Among Japan, Europe, and America* (New York: William Morrow and Co., 1992).

Yang Ho-min, *The Reappraisal of North Korean Society* (Seoul: Hanwool, 1987).

Yoon Mi-ryang, *North Korea's Policy on Women* (Seoul: Han-ul, 1991).

Yun Ha-chung, *North Korea's Economic Policies and Implementation* (Seoul: KDI, 1994).

Yun Mi-ryang, *North Korea's Policy on Women* (Seoul: Hanwool, 1991).

Wortlaut des Protokolls, in "Europäische Gemeinschaft" Nr. 2/71, S.10.

APPENDIX 1

AGREEMENTS WITH NORTH KOREA

1) Korean Armistice Agreement between the Commander-in-Chief, United Nations Command, on the one hand, and the Supreme Commander of the Korean People's Army and the Commander of the Chinese People's Volunteers, on the other hand, Concerning a Military Armistice in Korea, together with Annex and Supplementary Agreement. July 27, 1953 [Excerpt]

2) The July 4th Joint Declaration between South and North Korea. July 4, 1972

3) Agreement on Reconciliation, Nonaggression and Exchanges and Cooperation between the South and the North, Signed by South and North Korean Prime Ministers at the Fifth Round of the Inter-Korean High-Level Talks. December 13, 1991

4) Protocol for Reconciliation, Signed and Entered into Force on September 17, 1992

5) Protocol for Nonaggression, Signed and Entered into Force on September 17, 1992

6) Protocol for Exchanges and Cooperation, Signed and Entered into Force on September 17, 1992

7) Joint Declaration of the Denuclearization of the Korean Peninsula: To Enter into Force as of February 19, 1992

1. Korean Armistice Agreement between the Commander-in-Chief, United Nations Command, on the one hand, and the Supreme Commander of the Korean People's Army and the Commander of the Chinese People's Volunteers, on the other hand, Concerning a Military Armistice in Korea, together with Annex and Supplementary Agreement. July 27, 1953 [Excerpt]

Preamble

The undersigned, the Commander-in-Chief, United Nations Command, on the one hand, and the Supreme Commander of the Korean People's Army and the Commander of the Chinese People's Volunteers, on the other hand, in the interest of stopping the Korean conflict, with its great toll of suffering and bloodshed on both sides, and with the objective of establishing an armistice which will insure a complete cessation of hostilities and of all acts of armed force in Korea until a final peaceful settlement is achieved, do individually, collectively, and mutually agree to accept and to be bound and governed by the conditions and terms of armistice set forth in the following Articles and Paragraphs, which said conditions and terms are intended to be purely military in character and to pertain solely to the belligerents in Korea.

Article I
Military Demarcation Line and Demilitarized Zone

1. A Military Demarcation Line shall be fixed and both sides shall withdraw two (2) kilometers from this line so as to establish a Demilitarized Zone between the opposing forces. A Demilitarized Zone shall be established as a buffer zone to prevent the occurrence of incidents which might lead to a resumption of hostilities.

2. The Military Demarcation Line is located as indicated on the attached map (Map 1).

3. The Demilitarized Zone is defined by a northern and a southern boundary as indicated on the attached map (Map 1).

6. Neither side shall execute any hostile act within, from, or against the Demilitarized Zone.

7. No person, military or civilian, shall be permitted to cross the Military Demarcation Line unless specifically authorized to do so by the Military Armistice Commission.

10. Civil administration and relief in that part of the Demilitarized Zone which is south of the Military Demarcation Line shall be the responsibility of the Commander-in-Chief, United Nations Command; and civil administration and relief in that part of the Demilitarized Zone which is north of the Military Demarcation Line shall be the joint responsibility of the Supreme Commander of the Korean People's Army and the Commander of the Chinese People's Volunteers. The number of persons, military or civilian, from each side who are permitted to enter the Demilitarized Zone for the conduct of civil administration and relief shall be as determined by the respective Commanders, but in no case shall the total number authorized by either side exceed one thousand (1,000) persons at any one time. The number of

civil police and the arms to be carried by them shall be as pre-scribed by the Military Armistice Commission. Other personnel shall not carry arms unless specifically authorized to do so by the Military Armistice Commission.

Article II
Concrete Arrangements for Cease-Fire And Armistice

A. General

12. The Commanders of the opposing sides shall order and enforce a complete cessation of all hostilities in Korea by all armed forces under their control, including all units and person-nel of the ground, naval, and air forces, effective twelve (12) hours after this Armistice Agreement is signed. (See Paragraph 63 hereof for effective date and hour of the remaining provisions of this Armistice Agreement.)

B. Military Armistice Commission

1. Composition

19. A Military Armistice Commission is hereby established.

20. The Military Armistice Commission shall be composed of ten (10) senior officers, five (5) of whom shall be appointed by the Commander-in-Chief, United Nations Command, and five (5) of whom shall be appointed jointly by the Supreme Com-mander of the Korean People's Army and the Commander of the Chinese People's Volunteers. Of the ten members, three (3) from each side shall be of general or flag rank. The two (2)

remaining members on each side may be major generals, brigadier generals, colonels, or their equivalents.

2. Functions and Authority

24. The general mission of the Military Armistice Commission shall be to supervise the implementation of this Armistice Agreement and to settle through negotiations any violations of this Armistice Agreement.

25. The Military Armistice Commission shall:

a. Locate its headquarters in the vicinity of PANMUNJOM (37° 57'29"N, 126° 40'00"E). The Military Armistice Commission may re-locate its headquarters at another point within the Demilitarized Zone by agreement of the senior members of both sides on the Commission.

b. Operate as a joint organization without a chairman.

c. Adopt such rules of procedure as it may, from time to time, deem necessary.

d. Supervise the carrying out of the provisions of this Armistice Agreement pertaining to the Demilitarized Zone and to the Han River Estuary.

e. Direct the operations of the Joint Observer Teams.

f. Settle through negotiations any violations of this Armistice Agreement.

g. Transmit immediately to the Commanders of the opposing sides any reports of investigations of violations of this Armistice Agreement and all other reports and records of proceedings received from the Neutral Nations Supervisory Commission.

h. Give general supervision and direction to the activities of the Committee for Repatriation of Prisoners of War and the

Committee for Assisting the Return of Displaced Civilians, hereinafter established.

i. Act as an intermediary in transmitting communications between the Commanders of the opposing sides; provided, however, that the foregoing shall not be construed to preclude the Commanders of both sides from communicating with each other by any other means which they may desire to employ.

j. Provide credentials and distinctive insignia for its staff and its Joint Observer Teams, and a distinctive marking for all vehicles, aircraft, and vessels, used in the performance of its mission.

3. General

31. The Military Armistice Commission shall meet daily. Recesses of not to exceed seven (7) days may be agreed upon by the senior members of both sides; provided, that such recesses may be terminated on twenty-four (24) hour notice by the senior member of either side.

C. Neutral Nations Supervisory Commission

1. Composition

36. A Neutral Nations Supervisory Commission is hereby established.

37. A Neutral Nations Supervisory Commission shall be composed of four (4) senior officers, two (2) of whom shall be appointed by neutral nations nominated by the Commander-in-Chief, United Nations Command, namely SWEDEN and SWITZERLAND, and two (2) of whom shall be appointed by neutral nations nominated jointly by the Supreme Commander

of the Korean People's Army and the Commander of the Chinese People's Volunteers, namely, POLAND and CZECHOSLOVAKIA. The term "neutral nations" as herein used is defined as those nations whose combatant forces have not participated in the hostilities in Korea. Members appointed to the Commission may be from the armed forces of the appointing nations. Each member shall designate an alternate member to attend those meetings which for any reason the principal member is unable to attend. Such alternate members shall be of the same nationality as their principals. The Neutral Nations Supervisory Commission may take action whenever the number of members present from the neutral nations nominated by one side is equal to the number of members present from the neutral nations nominated by the other side.

2. Functions And Authority

41. The mission of the Neutral Nations Supervisory Commission shall be to carry out the functions of supervision, observation, inspection, and investigation, as stipulated in Sub-paragraphs 13c and 13d and Paragraph 28 hereof, and to report the results of such supervision, observation, inspection, and investigation to the Military Armistice Commission.

42. The Neutral Nations Supervisory Commission shall:

a. Locate its headquarters in proximity to the headquarters of the Military Armistice Commission.

b. Adopt such rules of procedure as it may, from time to time, deem necessary.

c. Conduct, through its members and its Neutral Nations Inspection Teams, the supervision and inspection provided for in Sub-paragraphs 13c and 13d of this Armistice Agreement at the ports of entry enumerated in Paragraph 43 hereof, and the special observations and inspections provided for in Paragraph 28 hereof at those places where violations of this Armistice Agreement have been reported to have occurred. The inspection of combat aircraft, armored vehicles, weapons, and ammunition by the Neutral Nations Inspection Teams shall be such as to enable them to properly insure that reinforcing combat aircraft, armored vehicles, weapons, and ammunition are not being introduced into Korea; but this shall not be construed as authorizing inspections or examinations of any secret designs or characteristics of any combat aircraft, armored vehicle, weapon, or ammunition.

d. Direct and supervise the operations of the Neutral Nations Inspection Teams.

e. Station five (5) Neutral Nations Inspections Teams at the ports of entry enumerated in Paragraph 43 hereof located in the territory under the military control of the Commander-in-Chief, United Nations Command; and five (5) Neutral Nations Inspection Teams at the ports of entry enumerated in Paragraph 43 hereof located in the territory under the military control of the Supreme Commander of the Korean People's Army and the Commander of the Chinese People's Volunteers; and establish initially ten (10) mobile Neutral Nations Inspection Teams in reserve, stationed in the general vicinity of the headquarters of the Neutral Nations Supervisory Commission, which number may be reduced by agreement of the senior members of both sides on the Military Armistice Commission. Not more than half of the mobile Neutral Nations Inspection Teams shall be dispatched at any one time in accordance with requests of the senior member of either side on the Military Armistice Commission.

f. Subject to the provisions of the preceding Sub-paragraph, conduct without delay investigations of reported violations of this Armistice Agreement, including such investigations of reported violations of this Armistice Agreement as may be requested by the Military Armistice Commission or by the senior member of either side on the Commission.

g. Provide credentials and distinctive insignia for its staff and its Neutral Nations Inspection Teams, and a distinctive marking for all vehicles, aircraft, and vessels, used in the performance of its mission.

3. General

44. The Neutral Nations Supervisory Commission shall meet daily. Recesses of not to exceed seven (7) days may be agreed upon by the members of the Neutral Nations Supervisory Commission; provided, that such recesses may be terminated on twenty-four (24) hour notice by any member.

Article IV
Recommendation To The Governments
Concerned on Both Sides

60. In order to insure the peaceful settlement of the Korean question, the military Commanders of both sides hereby recommend to the governments of the countries concerned on both sides that, within three (3) months after the Armistice Agreement is signed and becomes effective, a political conference of a higher level of both sides be held by representatives appointed respectively to settle through negotiation the questions of the withdrawal of all foreign forces from Korea, the peaceful settlement of the Korean question, etc.

Article V
Miscellaneous

⁕61. Amendments and additions to this Armistice Agreement must be mutually agreed to by the Commanders of the opposing sides.

62. The Articles and Paragraphs of this Armistice Agreement shall remain in effect until expressly superseded either by mutually acceptable amendments and additions or by provision in an appropriate agreement for a peaceful settlement at a political level between both sides.

63. All of the provisions of this Armistice Agreement, other than Paragraph 12, shall become effective at 2200 hours on 27 July 1953.

Done at Panmunjom, Korea, at 1000 hours on the 27th day of July, 1953, in English, Korean, and Chinese, all texts being equally authentic.

KIM IL SUNG	PENG TEH-HUAI	MARK W. CLARK
Marshall, Democratic People's Republic of Korea Supreme Commander, Korean People's Army	Commander, Chinese People's Volunteers	General, United States Army Commander-in-Chief United Nations Command

PRESENT

NAM IL	WILLIAM K. HARRISON, JR.
General, Korean People's Army Senior Delegate, Delegation of the Korean People's Army and the Chinese People's Command Delegation	Lieutenant General, United States Army Senior Delegate, United Nations Command Delegation

2. The July 4th Joint Declaration between South and North Korea.
July 4, 1972

South-North Joint Communique

Recently there were talks held both in Pyongyang and Seoul to discuss problems, of improving South-North relations and unifying the divided Fatherland.

Director Hu Rak Lee of the Central Intelligence Agency of Seoul visited Pyongyang from 2 to 5 May 1972 to hold talks with Director Young Joo Kim of the Organization and Guidance Department of Pyongyang. Second Vice Premier Sung Chul Park, acting on behalf of Director Young Joo Kim, also visited Seoul from 29 May to 1 June 1972 to hold further talks with Director Hu Rak Lee.

With the common desire to achieve peaceful unification of the Fatherland as early as possible, the two sides in these talks had frank and openhearted exchanges of views, and made great progress in promoting mutual understanding.

In the course of the talks, the two sides, in an effort to remove the misunderstandings and mistrust and mitigate increased tensions that have arisen between the South and the North as a result of long separation, and further to expedite unification of the Fatherland, have reached full agreement on the following points.

1. The two sides have agreed to the following principles for unification of the Fatherland:

First, unification shall be achieved through independent Korean efforts without being subject to external imposition or interference.

Second, unification shall be achieved through peaceful means, and not through the use of force against each other.

Third, as a homogeneous people, a great national unity shall first be sought, transcending differences in idea, ideologies, and systems.

2. In order to ease tensions and foster an atmosphere of mutual trust between the South and the North, the two sides have agreed not to slander or defame each other, not to undertake armed provocations whether on a large or small scale, and to take positive measures to prevent inadvertent military incidents.

3. The two sides, in order to restore severed national ties, promote mutual understanding and to expedite independent peaceful unification, have agreed to carry out various exchanges in many fields.

4. The two sides have agreed to cooperate positively with each other to seek early success of the South-North Red Cross talks, which are underway with the fervent expectations of the entire people.

5. The two sides, in order to prevent the outbreak of unexpected military incidents, and to deal directly, promptly and accurately with problems arising between the South and the North, have agreed to install a direct telephone line between Seoul and Pyongyang.

6. The two sides, in order to implement the aforementioned agreed items, solve various problems existing between the South and the North, and to settle the unification problem on the basis of the agreed principles for unification of the Fatherland, have agreed to establish and operate a South-North Coordinating Committee co-chaired by Director Hu Rak Lee and Director Young Joo Kim.

7. The two sides, firmly convinced that the aforementioned

agreed items correspond with the common aspirations of the entire people, who are anxious to see an early unification of the Fatherland, hereby solemnly pledge before the entire Korean people that they will faithfully carry out these agreed items.

July 4, 1972
UPHOLDING THE DESIRES OF THEIR RESPECTIVE
SUPERIORS
HU RAK LEE   YOUNG JOO KIM

3. Agreement on Reconciliation, Nonaggression and Exchanges and Cooperation between the South and the North, Signed by South and North Korean Prime Ministers at the Fifth Round of the Inter-Korean High-Level Talks. December 13, 1991

WHEREAS in keeping with the yearning of the entire people for the peaceful unification of the divided land, the South and the North reaffirm the unification principles enunciated in the July 4 (1972) South-North Joint Communique:

WHEREAS both parties are determined to resolve political and military confrontation and achieve national reconciliation:

WHEREAS both desire to promote multifaceted exchanges and cooperation to advance common national interests and prosperity:

WHEREAS both recognize that their relations constitute a special provisional relationship geared to unification: and

WHEREAS both pledge to exert joint efforts to achieve peaceful unification.

THEREFORE, the parties hereto agree as follows:

South-North Reconciliation

Article 1: The South and the North shall respect each other's political and social system.

Article 2: Both parties shall not interfere in each other's internal affairs.

Article 3: Both parties shall not slander and vilify each other.

Article 4: Both parties shall not attempt in any manner to sabotage and subvert the other.

Article 5: Both parties shall endeavor together to transform the present armistice regime into a firm state of peace between the South and the North and shall abide by the present Military Armistice Agreement (July 27, 1953) until such time as such a state of peace has taken hold.

Article 6: Both parties shall cease confrontation on the international stage and shall cooperate and endeavor together to promote national interest and esteem.

Article 7: To ensure close consultations and liaison between both parties, a South-North liaison office shall be established at Panmunjom within three months of the effective date of this agreement.

Article 8: A South-North Political Subcommittee shall be established within the framework of the Inter-Korean High-Level Talks within one month of the effective date of this agreement with a view to discussing concrete measures to ensure the implementation and observance of the accords on South-North reconciliation.

South-North Nonaggression

Article 9: Both parties shall not use armed force against each other and shall not make armed aggression against each other.

Article 10: Differences of opinion and disputes arising between the two parties shall be peacefully resolved through dialogue and negotiations.

Article 11: The South-North Demarcation Line and areas for nonaggression shall be identical with the Military Demarcation Line specified in the Military Armistice Agreement of July 27, 1953 and the areas that have been under the jurisdiction of each party respectively thereunder until the present.

Article 12: To abide by and guarantee nonaggression, the two parties shall create a South-North Joint Military Committee within three months of the effective date of this agreement. The said Committee shall discuss and carry out steps to build military confidence and realize arms reductions, including the mutual notification and control of major movements of military units and major military exercises, the peaceful utilization of the Demilitarized Zone, exchanges of military personnel and information, phased reductions in armaments including the elimination of weapons of mass destruction and surprise attack capabilities, and verifications thereof.

Article 13: A telephone hot line shall be installed between the military authorities of both sides to prevent accidental armed clashes and avoid their escalation.

Article 14: A South-North Military Subcommittee shall be established within the framework of the Inter-Korean High-Level Talks within one month of the effective date of this agreement in order to discuss concrete measures to ensure the implementation and observance of the accords on nonaggression and to resolve military confrontation.

South-North Exchanges and Cooperation

Article 15: To promote an integrated and balanced development of the national economy and the welfare of the entire people, both parties shall conduct economic exchanges and cooperation, including the joint development of resources, trade in goods as a kind of domestic commerce and joint investment in industrial projects.

Article 16: Both parties shall carry out exchanges and cooperation in diverse fields, including science, technology, education, literature, the arts, health, sports, the environment and publishing and journalism, including newspapers, radio, television and publications in general.

Article 17: Both parties shall guarantee residents of their respective areas free inter-Korean travel and contacts.

Article 18: Both parties shall permit free correspondence, reunions and visits between family members and other relatives dispersed south and north, shall promote the reconstitution of divided families on their own and shall take measures to resolve other humanitarian issues.

Article 19: Both sides shall reconnect railroads and roads that have been cut off and shall open South-North land, sea and air transport routes.

Article 20: Both parties shall establish and link facilities needed for South-North postal and telecommunications services and shall guarantee the confidentiality of inter-Korean mail and telecommunications.

Article 21: Both parties shall cooperate on the international stage in the economic, cultural and various other fields and carry out joint business undertakings abroad.

Article 22: To implement accords on exchanges and cooperation in the economic, cultural and various other fields, both parties shall establish joint committees for specific sectors, including a South-North Economic Exchanges and Cooperation Committee, within three months of the effective date of this agreement.

Article 23: A South-North Exchanges and Cooperation Subcommittee shall be established within the framework of the Inter-Korean High-Level Talks within one month of the effective date of this agreement with a view to discussing concrete measures to ensure the implementation and observance of the accords on South-North exchanges and cooperation.

Amendments and Effectuation

Article 24: This agreement may be amended or supplemented by concurrence between both parties.

Article 25: This agreement shall enter into force as of the day both parties exchange instruments of ratification following the completion of their respective procedures for bringing it into effect.

Date: December 13, 1991

Chung Won-shik
Prime Minister
Republic of Korea

Yon Hyong-muk
Premier
Administration Council
Democratic People's
Republic of Korea

4. Protocol for Reconciliation, Signed and Entered into Force on September 17, 1992

The South and the North,

As a result of concrete negotiations to ensure compliance with and implementation of Chapter I, Reconciliation, of the Agreement on Reconciliation, Nonaggression, and Exchanges and Cooperation Between the South and the North,

Have agreed as follows:

Chapter I
Recognition of Each Other's Systems

Article 1: The South and the North shall recognize and respect each other's political, economic, social and cultural systems.

Article 2: The South and the North shall guarantee the freedom to disseminate information about the truth of the other's political, economic, social and cultural systems and institutions.

Article 3: The South and the North shall recognize and respect the authority and competence of the other's authorities.

Article 4: The South and the North shall have a working-level legal group discuss and resolve issues of revising or scrapping legal and institutional devices that infringe on the Agreement on Reconciliation, Nonaggression, and Exchanges and Cooperation Between the South and the North.

Chapter II
Noninterference in Each Other's Internal Affairs

Article 5: The South and the North shall not interfere in the legal system and policies of the other side.

Article 6: The South and the North shall not interfere in the external relations of the other side.

Article 7: The South and the North may request the other side to redress any matter that infringes on the Agreement on Reconciliation, Nonaggression, and Exchanges and Cooperation.

Chapter III
Cessation of Vilification and Slander

Article 8: The South and the North shall not slander or vilify the other side through the news media, leaflets or other means.

Article 9: The South and the North shall not revile specific persons of the other side.

Article 10: The South and the North shall not vilify and slander the authorities of the other side.

Article 11: The South and the North shall not distort facts about the other side nor fabricate and disseminate false facts.

Article 12: The South and the North shall not regard as slander or vilification objective and factual media coverage of the other side.

Article 13: The South and the North shall not vilify or slander the other side within the Demilitarized Zone through broadcasts, billboards or any other means.

Article 14: The South and the North shall not vilify or slander the other side at mass meetings or events.

Chapter IV
Prohibition Against Sabotage and Subversion

Article 15: The South and the North shall not attempt any acts of sabotage or subversion against the other in any form, direct or indirect, violent or nonviolent, including acts of terror, abduction, recruitment, murder or injury.

Article 16: The South and the North shall not resort to propaganda or agitation aimed at sabotaging or subverting the other side.

Article l7: The South and the North shall not organize, support or protect any terrorist organization in its own area, the area of the other side, or overseas, intended to sabotage or subvert the political or legal system of the other side.

Chapter V
Transformation of State of Armistice into State of Peace

Article 18: The South and the North, in order to transform the present state of armistice into a solid state of peace between the South and the North, shall sincerely comply with and implement the Agreement on Reconciliation, Nonaggression, and Exchanges and Cooperation and the Joint Declaration of the Denuclearization of the Korean Peninsula.

Article 19: The South and the North shall adopt appropriate measures in order to transform the present state of armistice into a solid state of peace between the South and the North.

Article 20: The South and the North shall sincerely abide by the Military Armistice Agreement until a solid state of peace has been established between the South and the North.

Chapter VI
Cooperation in the International Arena

Article 21: The South and the North shall not vilify and slander each other in the international arena, including at international meetings, and shall closely cooperate with each other in order to maintain the dignity of the Korean people.

Article 22: The South and the North shall consult with each other on matters effecting national interests and take the necessary joint measures.

Article 23: The South and the North, in order to promote the common interests of the Korean people, shall maintain close contacts between their diplomatic missions overseas in areas where both sides have diplomatic missions.

Article 24: The South and the North shall champion and protect the ethnic rights of overseas Koreans and shall endeavor to promote reconciliation and unity among them.

Chapter VII
Implementation Mechanisms

Article 25: The South and the North, to implement Chapter I, South-North Reconciliation, of the Agreement on Reconciliation, Nonaggression and Exchanges and Cooperation Between the South and the North, shall organize and operate the South-North Joint Reconciliation Commission. An agreement to establish the South-North Joint Reconciliation Commission shall be separately adopted.

Article 26: The South-North Joint Reconciliation Commission shall have a working-level legal group and a working-level group for cessation of slander and vilification. It may form additional working-level groups with concurrence of both sides. Accords concerning organization and operation of the working-level groups shall be adopted by the South-North Joint Reconciliation Commission.

Chapter VIII
Amendments and Effectuation

Article 27: This Protocol may be amended or supplemented by agreement between the two sides.

Article 28: This Protocol shall enter into force the day it is signed and exchanged by the two sides.

Supplementary Note

The following provisions proposed by the North but not included in his Protocol shall be further discussed in the South-North Political Committee:

1) The North and the South shall endeavor to affiliate with international organizations under a single name for a single seat;

2) The North and the South shall endeavor to participate in political events including international meetings as a single delegation representing the entire Korean people;

3) The North and the South shall not side with nor cooperate with attempts by a third country in the international arena to undermine the interest of the other side; and

4) The North and the South shall have the working-level legal group discuss and resolve the issue of revising or abolishing treaties or agrements signed by either side with other countries which run counter to the unity and interests of the Korean people.

DATE: September 17, 1992

Chung Won-shik   Yon Hyong-muk
Prime Minister   Premier

Republic of Korea   The Administration Council
and   Democratic People's
Chief Delegate to the   Republic of Korea
South-North High-Level Talks and
                                     Chief Delegate to the South-
                                     North High-Level Talks

5. Protocol for Nonaggression, Signed and Entered into Force
   on September 17, 1992

The South and the North,

As a result of concrete negotiations to resolve military confrontation as well as to comply with and implement Chapter II, Nonaggression, of the Agreement on Reconciliation, Nonaggression, and Exchanges and Cooperation Between the South and the North.

Have agreed as follows:

Chapter I
Nonuse of Military Power

Article 1: The South and the North shall prohibit the use of military power, including shooting, bombarding, bombing and other forms of attack and destruction, against the people, property, vehicles and civil and military ships and airplanes on the other side of its jurisdiction including the Demilitarized Zone. Neither side shall resort to armed provocation that inflicts damage to the other side.

Article 2: The South and the North shall not infiltrate into or attack by military force the administrative region of the other side or even temporarily occupy part or whole of the area of the other side. Under no circumstances, shall the South and the North infiltrate a regular or irregular force into the administrative region of the other side with any means or method whatsoever.

Article 3: The South and the North shall not engage in hostile acts against citizens from the other side, who are visiting in accordance with an agreement between the two sides, or their belongings or transportation vehicles nor block their way.

In addition, the issues of the nonreinforcement of military power along the Demilitarized Zone, suspension of scouting activities against the other side, and nonblocking of territorial waters and air space of the other side—all proposed by the North—and the issue of guaranteeing the security of Seoul and Pyongyang—proposed by Seoul—shall continue to be discussed in the South-North Joint Military Commission.

Chapter II
Peaceful Settlement of Disputes and Prevention of Accidental Armed Clashes

Article 4: The South and the North, upon detection of any sign of deliberate armed aggression from the other side, shall immediately notify the other side and demand clarification and shall adopt necessary measures so as to prevent it from escalating into an armed clash.

The South and the North, upon the discovery of any unintentional armed clash or aggression due to misunderstanding, misperception, mistake or unavoidable accident, shall immediately notify the other side in accordance with the signals agreed to by both sides, and shall adopt precautionary measures to prevent such incidents.

Article 5: When an armed group, an individual, a vehicle, a civil or military ship or airplane has violated the administrative region of the other side due to natural calamity, navigational error or other unavoidable cause, the trespassing side shall immediately notify the other side of the incident along with the fact that it has no aggressive intent and shall abide by instructions of the other side. The other side shall immediately confirm the incident, guarantee the safety of the persons and equipment concerned and take measures to repatriate them.

Repatriation shall be completed within a month in principle but may be further delayed.

Article 6: In the event of an outbreak of a dispute such as accidental aggression or armed clash between the South and the North, the military authorities of both sides shall immediately have the hostile acts of the armed group of its own side stopped, and shall immediately notify the military authorities of the other side through the military hotline or other available means of communications.

Article 7: The South and the North shall discuss and resolve all military disputes and confrontation through a mechanism agreed to by the military authorities of both sides.

Article 8: The South and the North, whenever either side has violated this Protocol on the compliance with and implementation of the nonaggression chapter of the Basic Agreement, shall conduct a joint investigation to determine the cause of and responsibility for the violation and shall adopt measures to prevent the recurrence of such an incident.

Chapter III
Demarcation Line and Areas of Nonaggression

Article 9: The South-North demarcation line and areas for nonaggression shall be identical with the Military Demarcation Line specified in the Military Armistice Agreement and the areas that have been under the jurisdiction of each sides until the present time.

Article 10: The South-North sea nonaggression demarcation line shall continue to be discussed. Until the sea nonaggression demarcation line has been finalized, the sea nonaggression zones shall be identical with those that have been under the jurisdiction of each side until the present time.

Article 11: The air nonaggression demarcation line and zone shall be the skies over the land and sea demarcation lines.

Chapter IV
Establishment and Operation of Military Hotlines

Article 12: The South and the North, in order to prevent the outbreak or an escalation of any armed clash, shall establish and operate direct military hotlines between the Minister of Defense in the South and the Minister of the People's Armed Forces in the North.

Article 13: The direct military hotlines shall use means of communication agreed to by both sides to send the texts of messages over telex, facsimile or telephone. If necessary the military authorities of both sides may directly converse with each other over the telephone.

Article 14: Technical and practical matters concerning the establishment and operation of the hotlines shall be discussed and resolved by a working-level communications group, composed of five members from each side, as soon as possible following the coming into force of the Protocol.

Chapter V
Mechanisms for Consultation and Implementation

Article 16: The South-North Joint Military Commission shall carry out its duties and functions as provided in Article 12 of the Basic Agreement and Article 2 of the Agreement to Establish a South-North Joint Military Commission.

Article 17: The South-North Joint Military Commission shall discuss and adopt concrete measures on issues both sides recognize need to be resolved to effectively comply with and implement the nonaggression chapter of the Basic Agrement and remove the military confrontation between the South and the North.

Chapter VI
Amendments and Effectuation

Article 18: This Protocol may be amended or supplemented by agreement between the two sides.

Article 19: This Protocol shall enter into force on the day it is signed and exchanged by the two sides.

DATE: September 17, 1992

Chung Won-shik   Yon Hyong-muk
Prime Minister   Premier
Republic of Korea   The Administration Council
and   Democratic People's

Chief Delegate to the   Republic of Korea
South-North High-Level Talks and
Chief Delegate to the
South-North High-Level Talks

6. Protocol for Exchanges and Cooperation, Signed and Entered into Force on September 17, 1992

The South and the North,

As the result of discussions on concrete measures to ensure the compliance with the implementation of Chapter III, South-North Exchanges and Cooperation, of the Agreement on Reconciliation, Nonaggression and Exchanges and Cooperation between the South and the North,

Have agreed as follows:

Chapter I
Economic Exchanges and Cooperation

Article 1: The South and the North shall engage in economic exchanges and cooperation, including joint development of resources, exchanges of goods as domestic commerce, and joint investment in order to promote unified and balanced development of the national economy and the welfare of the entire people.

1. The South and the North shall carry out exchanges of goods and projects of economic cooperation for the joint development of such resources as coal, minerals and seafood and in such other fields as manufacturing, agriculture, construction, banking and finance, and tourism.

2. The South and the North shall determine the objectives and forms of such projects of economic cooperation as the joint development of resources and joint ventures and investment and the types and quantities of goods to be exchanged through consultations in the Joint Commission for Economic Exchanges and Cooperation.

3. Such practical matters as the scale of such projects of economic cooperation as the joint development of resources and joint ventures and investment and the quantity and terms of trade of each product to be traded shall be determined through discussions between the parties from the two sides directly involved in exchanges and cooperation.

4. Parties directly involved in South-North economic cooperation and exchanges of goods shall be trading houses, companies or business firms which have been registered as juridical persons or public economic agencies, providing, however, that depending on the situation, individuals may also be involved.

5. The South and the North shall have exchanges of goods and projects of economic cooperation carried out under contracts signed by parties directly involved after the contracts have gone through their respective required procedures.

6. The prices of goods to be exchanged shall be determined through consultations between the parties directly involved in consideration of international market prices.

7. South-North exchanges of goods shall be carried out on the principle of reciprocity and complementarity.

8. In principle, payments for goods exchanged between the South and the North shall be settled through an open account, providing, however, that when necessary other methods of settlement may be used by agreement between both sides.

9. The South and the North shall determine by mutual con-

currence matters necessary to the settlement of payments and capital movement, including the designation of banks to handle open accounts and the selection of currencies for settlement.

10. The South and the North shall not impose tariff on goods exchanged and shall discuss and take measures to develop South-North economic relations into domestic links.

11. In order to smoothly carry out economic exchanges and cooperation, the South and the North shall exchange various data and information, including industrial standards, and will inform the other side of relevant laws and regulations that the parties directly involve must comply with.

12. The South and the North shall determine, through mutual consultation, the procedures for guaranteeing investment, avoiding double taxation and arbitrating disputes and other matters necessary to smoothly carry out economic exchanges and cooperation.

13. The South and the North shall guarantee free economic activities and essential services to personnel from the other side who participate in economic exchanges and cooperation in their own areas.

Article 3: The South and the North shall reconnect railroads and roads that have been severed and shall open sea and air routes.

1. Initially, the South and the North shall open sea routes between the ports of Inchon, Pusan and Pohang (in the South) and the ports of Nampo, Wonsan and Chongjin (in the North).

2. As the scale of South-North exchanges and cooperation expands and as military confrontation is resolved, the South and the North shall open additional sea routes, connect the Seoul-Shinuiju Railroad, the Munsan-Kaesong Highway and other land routes and shall open an air route between the Kimpo Air-

port and the Sunan Airport.

3. When necessary to allow exchanges of people and goods even before regular transportation routes are established, the South and the North may open temporary routes.

4. The South and the North shall exchange information and conduct technological cooperation necessary to ensure the smooth opening and administration of land, sea and air routes.

5. Goods to be exchanged between the South and the North shall be transported directly along the land, sea and air routes that have been opened by mutual concurrence.

6. The South and the North shall extend emergency assistance to the means of transportation from the other side that have fallen into distress in their respective areas.

7. The South and the North shall respect the relevant international agreements governing the establishment and administration of transportation routes.

8. The South and the North shall determine, through discussions in the Joint Commission for Economic Exchanges and Cooperation such other practical matters involved in the opening and administration of transportation routes as the entry and exit procedures for the means of transport and their crews that operate between the South and the North, the modes of operating means of transportation and the selection of points of passage.

Article 4: The South and the North shall install and connect facilities necessary to exchange mail and telecommunications and shall guarantee their confidentiality.

1. The South and the North shall exchange and connect mail and telecommunications services through Panmunjom at an early date and shall exchange information and conduct technological cooperation necessary to exchange mail and telecommunications.

2. In exchanging mail and telecommunications, the South and the North shall guarantee priority to official and humanitarian activities and shall progressively expand the scope of such services.

3. The South and the North shall guarantee the confidentiality of mail and telecommunications exchanged and shall not use them for a political or military purposes under any circumstances.

4. The South and the North shall respect the relevant international agreements governing exchanges of mail and telecommunications.

5. Such other practical matters as the kinds and fees of mail and telecommunications exchanged between the South and the North and the methods of collecting and delivering mail shall be determined through consultations in the Joint Commission for Economic Exchanges and Cooperation.

Article 5: The South and the North shall cooperate with each other in various sectors of the international economy and shall promote their joint presence abroad.

1. The South and the North shall cooperate with each other in various international events and international organizations in the economic field.

2. The South and the North shall discuss and carry out measures to promote their joint presence abroad in the economic field.

Article 6: The South and the North shall support and guarantee
exchanges and cooperation in the economic field.

Article 7: The South and the North shall decide the issue of creating agencies needed to carry out exchanges and cooperation in the economic field and other relevant practical matters through consultations in the Joint Commission for Economic Exchanges and Cooperation.

Article 8: The South-North Joint Commission for Economic Exchanges and Cooperation shall implement Chapter I, Economic Exchanges and Cooperation, of this Protocol and shall discuss and carry out details involved therein.

Chapter II
Social and Cultural Exchanges and Cooperation

Article 9: The South and the North shall carry out exchanges and cooperation in such various fields as education, literature, the arts, health, athletics, and publishing and journalism, including newspapers, other publications, radio and television.

1. The South and the North shall exchange information and data about such various fields as education, literature, the arts, health, athletics, publishing and journalism, including those about achievements, experience and research, and publications, media reports, and catalogues thereof.

2. The South and the North shall carry out multifaceted cooperation, especially technological cooperation, in such various fields as education, literature, the arts, health, athletics, publishing and journalism.

3. The South and the North shall promote contacts and exchanges between public agencies, other organizations and individuals in such various fields as education, literature, health, athletics, publishing and journalism through cross-country group tours and the invitation and dispatch of delegations and observers.

4. The South and the North shall carry out joint research and surveys, joint publication projects and joint events in such various fields as education, literature, the arts, health, athletics, publishing and journalism and shall also exchange exhibitions of

works of art, cultural relics, and books and other publications.

5. The South and the North shall take measures worked out by mutual concurrence to protect various copyrights of the other side.

Article 10: The South and the North shall allow free visits and contacts between their citizens.

1. The South and the North shall take joint measures to enable all their citizens to freely travel to the other area as they wish.

2. Citizens wishing to travel between the two areas may use any of the land, sea and air routes established between the South and the North as they see fit and may also use international air routes depending on the situation.

3. The South and the North shall allow free activities of citizens visiting their areas and shall guarantee their personal safety and safe return home.

4. The South and the North shall take measures to ensure that citizens visiting the other area will travel to and from and contact residents there without breaching law and order in the area visited.

5. Citizens traveling between the South and the North shall bear the necessary certificates with them and may carry goods with them within the scope agreed to by both sides.

6. The South and the North shall provide services necessary to enable visitors from the other side to travel between the two areas and accomplish their purposes of visit.

7. The South and the North shall provide emergency assistance to visitors from the other side when they fall into distress.

8. The South and the North shall establish, through consultations in the Joint Commission for Social and Cultural Exchanges and Cooperation, procedures and other practical matters needed

to allow free visits and contacts between their citizens.

Article 11: The South and the North shall cooperate on the international stage in the social and cultural fields and promote a joint international presence.

1. The South and the North shall cooperate with each other in international events and international organizations in the social and cultural fields.

2. The South and the North shall discuss and take measures to promote their joint presence abroad in the social and cultural fields.

Article 12: The South and the North shall support and guarantee exchanges and cooperation in the social and cultural fields.

Article 13: The South and the North shall settle, through consultations in the Joint Commission for Social and Cultural Exchanges and Cooperation, the issue of creating agencies needed to carry out exchanges and cooperation in the social and cultural fields and other relevant practical issues.

Article 14: The South-North Joint Commission for Social and Cultural Exchanges and Cooperation shall implement Chapter II, Social and Cultural Exchanges and Cooperation, of this Protocol and discuss and carry out relevant details involved therein.

Chapter III
The Solution of Humanitarian Issues

Article 15: The South and the North shall allow free correspondence, free reunions and free visits between immediate members of dispersed families and other dispersed relatives and their free travel to and from the other area and the reconstitution of dispersed families of their own free volition and shall take measures to solve other humanitarian issues.

1. The scope of dispersed families and relatives shall be defined through discussions between the Red Crosses of the two sides.

2. The South and the North shall allow immediate members of dispersed families and other dispersed relatives to travel freely to and from the other area and freely visit each other in accordance with travel procedures worked out by agreement between the two sides.

3. The South and the North shall have the Red Crosses of the two sides discuss and resolve the issue of establishing reunion centers for dispersed immediate member of families and other relatives.

4. The South and the North shall discuss and take measures to allow the reconstitution of dispersed families, including immediate and more distant relatives, of their own free volition.

5. With a humanitarian spirit and a sense of compatriotic kinship, the South and the North shall help each other in case of a natural or other disaster in the other area and shall assist in the disposition of the personal effects of deceased immediate members of dispersed families and other deceased dispersed relatives and the transfer of their remains.

Article 16: The South and the North shall actively cooperate with each other to have the Red Crosses of both sides resume at an early date their talks that were already in progress.

Article 17: The South and the North shall respect agreements reached by the Red Crosses of both sides to alleviate the misfortune and suffering of dispersed immediate members of families and other dispersed relatives and shall support and guarantee the smooth implementation of such accords.

Article 18: The Red Crosses of the two sides shall implement Chapter III, The Solution of Humanitarian Issues, of this Protocol and shall discuss and carry out details involved therein.

Chapter IV
Amendments and Effectuation

Article 19: This Protocol may be amended or supplemented by agreement between the two sides.

Article 20: This Protocol shall enter into force the day it is signed and exchanged by the two sides.

DATE: September 17, 1992

Chung Won-shik	Yon Hyong-muk
Prime Minister	Premier
Republic of Korea	The Administration Council
and	Democratic People's
Chief Delegate to the	Republic of Korea
South-North High-Level Talks	and
	Chief Delegate to the
	South-North High-Level Talks

7. Joint Declaration of the Denuclearization of the Korean Peninsula: To Enter into Force as of February 19, 1992

The South and North,

Desiring to eliminate the danger of nuclear war through denuclearization of the Korean Peninsula, and thus to create an environment and conditions favorable for peace and peaceful unification of our country and contribute to peace and security in Asia and the world,

Declare as follows:

1. The South and the North shall not test, manufacture, produce, receive, possess, store, deploy or use nuclear weapons.

2. The South and the North shall use nuclear energy solely for peaceful purposes.

3. The South and the North shall not possess nuclear reprocessing and uranium enrichment facilities.

4. The South and the North, in order to verify the denuclearization of the Korean Peninsula, shall conduct inspection of the objects selected by the other side and agreed upon between the two sides, in accordance with procedures and methods to be determined by the South-North Joint Nuclear Control Commission.

5. The South and the North, in order to implement this joint declaration, shall establish and operate a South-North Joint Nuclear Control Commission within one (1) month of the effectuation of this joint declaration.

6. This Joint Declaration shall enter into force as of the day the two sides exchange appropriate instruments following the completion of their respective procedures for bringing it into effect.

Signed on January 20, 1992

Chung Won-shik
Prime Minister of the
Republic of Korea
Chief delegate of the
South delegation of the
South-North High-Level Talks

Yon Hyong-muk
Premier of the
Administration Council of the
Democratic People's
Republic of Korea
Head of the
North Delegation of the
South-North High-Level Talks

APPENDIX 2

DOCUMENTS ON SOUTH-NORTH RELATIONS AND UNIFICATION ISSUES

1) President Roh Tae-woo's Special Address Concerning National Unification Delivered Before the National Assembly: Presenting a Formula for Korean National Unification, Seoul, September 11, 1989

2) Statement Issued by President Kim Young Sam on the Occasion of the 49th Anniversary of National Liberation Day, Manifesting His Government's Basic Position on National Unification and North Korean Policies: "Unification Formula for the Korean National Community," Independence Hall in Mokchon, Chonan-gun, South Chungchong Province, August 15, 1994

3) The "July 7th Special Declaration" for Korea's Independence, Unification, and Prosperity [by President Roh Tae-woo on july 7, 1988]

4) North Korea's 10-Point Unification Program Adopted by the Fifth Session of the Ninth Supreme People's Assembly of North Korea, Pyongyang, April 7, 1993.

5) R.O.K.-U.S. Mutual Defense Treaty, October 1, 1953

1. President Roh Tae-woo's Special Address Concerning
   National Unification Delivered Before the National Assem-
   bly: Presenting a Formula for Korean National Unification,
   Seoul, September 11, 1989

... On October 4 last year, I promised in this hall to present, in due course, a feasible and reasonable formula for peacefully unifying our homeland in response to the will of our people and in keeping with newly changing circumstances. The administration has since worked out a new unification formula to fulfill the popular yearning. It is based on an extensive pooling of the views and wisdom of citizens from all walks of life, including experts, and on the outcome of hearings conducted by the National Assembly.

In line with the solemn duty that the Constitution imposes on the President, I am going to outline the Korean National Community Unification Formula. It calls for a merger of South and North Korea, under the principles of independence, peace and democracy, in a unified democratic republic, which is to be built upon a Korean Commonwealth to be formed in an interim stage.

Our unified homeland must be a single national community in which every citizen is his own master, that is to say, a democratic nation that guarantees the human rights of every individual and his right to seek happiness. The entire Korean people have long craved a democratic republican system which will assure every citizen the right of participation as well as equal opportunity and under which diverse creeds and opinions can be freely voiced and represented. This is the only choice for a unified Korea if it is to achieve grand national unity.

Accordingly, a unified homeland must not tolerate special privileges, dominant positions or the usurping and wielding of dictatorial powers by any specific individual, group or class. A unified homeland should be the kind of nation that promotes welfare for all and guarantees permanent national security, while maintaining good neighborly relations with all nations and contributing to world peace and global well-being.

The Korean people are one. Therefore, a unified Korea must be a single nation. This is what the Korean people long for. No system for bringing the two parts of Korea together will accomplish genuine unification so long as it is aimed at perpetuating two states with differing ideologies and political system. Indisputably, unification must be achieved independently in keeping with a spirit of national self-determination and under the principles of peace, non-use of military force, and grand national unity through democratic procedures.

Unification should be achieved as quickly as feasible. However, the reality is that it will be impossible to achieve unification overnight without ending the long-standing deep distrust, confrontation and antagonism that have been built up between the South and the North over the past 40-odd years since the partitioning of the land into two halves committed to different ideologies and political systems.

For millenniums until that partitioning, we had lived in a single national community which evolved on the Peninsula, cemented by common ethnic origin and common language, culture and traditions. This national heritage still binds our people together, even though we are forced to live in a divided land. It is the reason why the Korean people must become one again. It is the ultimate guarantee that we will succeed.

Our territorial division has deepened into a national schism due initially to bloody rightist-leftist clashes in the wake of liberation and subsequently to the savage fratricidal war sparked by

North Korea's invasion of the South on June 25, 1950. Having thus lived for nearly half a century in a land divided into two hostile polities, Koreans in the South and the North have come to follow different lifestyles and different values. As long as our national community remains so deeply divided and differentiated, it will be impossible to re-form a single country. Properly restoring and developing our national community is the key to realizing unification at the earliest possible date.

It is thus imperative for the South and the North to set an interim stage toward unification in which both will recognize each other and seek co-existence and co-prosperity, irrespective of the existence of different political systems and will endeavor to speed the homogenization and integration of the national community. This, of course, will require expanding openness, exchanges and cooperation between the South and the North to build mutual trust that will be the basis for integrating them into a single nation-state. If a single social, cultural and economic community is thus progressively developed, while issues pending between the South and the North are resolved one after another, conditions for political integration will ripen.

To institutionalize such moves to speed unification, I propose to create, under a charter agreed to by both parties, a kind of commonwealth to link the South and the North together. In such a commonwealth, the South and the North would be formed into a common sphere of national life to promote common prosperity and restore national homogeneity, thereby accelerating the development of a national community.

I propose that the Korean Commonwealth have a Council of Presidents, or chief executives from both parts of Korea, as the highest decision-making organ. There would be a Council of Ministers, composed of delegates from both governments and a

Council of Representatives, to be composed of members of the legislatures in both the South and the North.

To logistically support the activities of the Council of Ministers and the Council of Representatives, to help implement agreed matters and to handle other administrative affairs, the South and the North would set up a joint secretariat and exchange resident liaison missions to each other's capital, named Seoul and P'yongyang. I propose that the joint secretariat and other institutions and facilities of the Korean Commonwealth be established in a Peace Zone to be created within the Demilitarized Zone. The Peace Zone should gradually be developed into a City of Unification and Peace.

The Council of Ministers would be co-chaired by the Prime Ministers of the South and the North and would comprise around 10 cabinet-level officials from each side. Under the council, a number of standing committees could be created to deal with humanitarian, political, diplomatic, economic, military, social, cultural and other affairs. The Council of Ministers would discuss and adjust all pending South-North issues and national problems and would ensure the implementation of its decisions. Among other things, it could work on the following agenda, with assistance from its standing committees in relevant areas:

In the humanitarian field, the Council of Ministers should solve the issue of reuniting dispersed families, whose members are estimated to total 10 million.

In the political and diplomatic fields, the Council of Ministers should take measures to ease political confrontation between the South and the North, prevent counterproductive inter-Korean rivalry on the world scene that only wastes national energies, promote the interests of overseas Koreans and otherwise advance national interests jointly.

In the economic, social and cultural fields, that Council should accelerate the opening of South and North Korean societies, promote multi-faceted inter-Korean exchanges, trade and cooperation and jointly foster national culture. The formation of a common economic zone to achieve mutual prosperity would facilitate the development of both the South and the North, thereby enhancing the quality of life for all.

In the military field, measures should be taken to build confidence and control arms with the goal of ending the costly arms race and confrontation between the two parts of Korea. Replacing the current armistice agreement with a peace agrement could also be on the Council's agenda.

The Council of Representatives should be composed of around 100 legislators, with equal numbers representing the two parts of Korea. It should draft the constitution of a unified Korea, develop methods and procedures to bring about unification and advise the Council of Ministers at its request.

In drafting the constitution of a unified nation, the Council of Representatives should discuss and agree on the political ideals, name and form of government for a unified Korea, its basic domestic and foreign policies and the methods, timing and procedures for a general election to constitute its legislature. Both the South and the North would present their own proposals for the constitution of a unified Korea to the Council of Representatives so they can be combined into a single draft.

The agreed draft of the constitution of a unified Korea should be finalized and promulgated through democratic methods and procedures. General elections would then be held under the promulgated constitution to form both a unified legislature and a unified government.

I suggest that the legislature of the unified homeland be a

bicameral parliament, composed of an upper house based on regional representation and a lower house based on population.

In the manner I have just described, it should be possible to establish a unified democratic republic, thus accomplishing the momentous task of unification.

I am convinced that the Korean National Community Unification Formula represents a most rational and realistic route to unification in compliance with the ideals and wishes of our people. Ever since the birth of the sixth Republic, I have repeatedly emphasized that the most effective way to make a decisive move toward South-North reconciliation and unification is through a summit meeting between Seoul and P'yongyang. I hope that a South-North summit will take place as quickly as possible to successfully launch joint efforts to work out an agreed charter for opening an era of full-fledged inter-Korean cooperation and unification. Such a charter could contain a comprehensive package of agreement covering a basic formula for attaining peace and unification, mutual non-aggression arrangements and the founding of a Korean commonwealth as an interim stage toward unification.

I look forward to the preparation and promulgation of such a charter of the Korean national community at the earliest possible date. And I hope that a breakthrough to peace and unification between South and North Korea will be found by August 15 next year—the 45th anniversary of the partitioning of Korea. In that way, we should be able to accomplish the mission that history has imposed on our generation of Koreans to open a new era of national unification....

2. Statement Issued by President Kim Young Sam on the Occasion of the 49th Anniversary of National Liberation Day, Manifesting His Government's Basic Position on National Unification and North Korean Policies: "Unification Formula for the Korean National Community," Independence Hall in Mokchon, Chonan-gun, South Chungchong Province, August 15, 1994

... As the President of the Republic of Korea, I have not forgotten for even a single moment my responsibility for the security, survival, unification and prosperity of our 70 million people. It was with this acute sense of responsibility that this past July I pursued a South-North summit meeting.

Now that both the currents of world history and the trend of South-North relations are entering a new phase, I hereby wish to redefine the basic position of our Government on unification.

Over the past century, the Korean people have tirelessly striven to secure independence, freedom and democracy. National liberation will have been truly completed only when we have built a unified Korea marked by blooming democracy and brimming prosperity.

World history has already proclaimed the victory of freedom and democracy. We are now living in the age of ever-spreading democracy. With the advent of this civilian government, democracy is spreading its roots into our soil ever deeper and firmer. We will defend our hard-won freedom and democracy at any cost. I want to make it clear once again that any challenges to our free and democratic system will not be tolerated.

The basic philosophy behind our quest for unification is also centered on the values of freedom and democracy. Without freedom, there can be no democracy. Without democracy, there can be no genuine freedom and peace. With firm faith in democracy and on the strength of the independent abilities of our nation, we must strive harder to overcome the lingering remnants of the Cold War and end the territorial division in order to achieve the long-cherished goal of peaceful unification without fail.

The unification process should be focused not on how to distribute power but on how to enable our people to live together. Unification should be grounded on the values of freedom, democracy and well-being for all, rather than on any ideology focused narrowly on a specific class or group. Efforts toward unification should be concerned not so much with developing a hypothetical structure of a unified state as with building a national community within which all Koreans can live together.

Unification would be achieved on our own according to the wishes of our people and by virtue of our inherent national capabilities. Unification must be achieved peacefully without fail. It must not be achieved through war or one side overthrowing the other. Unification must be achieved democratically on the strength of the freedom and rights of all Koreans.

It will not be possible to unify the South and the North overnight, because the two parts of Korea have ben locked into mutual hostility and distrust for as along as they have consistently pursued distinctly different ideologies and markedly different political and social systems. Unification should be a gradual and phased process of building a single national community.

The Government has already made public a three-state unification formula for building a single national community. It calls first for reconciliation and cooperation between the South and the North, next for forming a Korean commonwealth and lastly for completing a single unified nation-state.

First of all, the presently hostile and confrontational South-

North relations must be replaced with an amicable and cooperative relationship. Yemen failed to prevent a civil war even after it
was politically unified. This is because it was unified hastily and
superficially without having gone through a process of real reconciliation and cooperation.

South and North Korea must first promote coexistence and
coprosperity and then join together in a Korean commonwealth
to ensure lasting peace. During the commonwealth stage, the two
areas of Korea should form and develop a single socio-economic
community to lay the groundwork for political integration.

In short, the Government's Three-Stage Unification Formula
for Building a Korean National Community is designed to ultimately build a single nation-state after going through interim
stages of integration. The path to unification must also be the
path to democracy and prosperity. A unified homeland which
will belong to all 70 million Koreans must be built on a national
community and must guarantee every individual citizen freedom, welfare and human dignity ....

3. The "July 7th Special Declaration" for Korea's Independence, Unification, and Prosperity [by President Roh Tae-
   woo on July 7, 1988]

A Single National Community; Special Declaration in the
Interest of National Self-Respect, Unification and Prosperity

My sixty million compatriots,
Today, I am going to enunciate the policy of the Sixth Republic to achieve the peaceful unification of our homeland, a long-
standing goal dear to the hearts of the entire Korean people.

We have been suffering the pain of territorial division for almost half a century. This national division has inflicted numerous ordeals and hardships upon the Korean people, thus hindering national development. Dismantling the barrier separating the South and the North and building a road to a unified and prosperous homeland is a duty that history has imposed on every Korean alive today.

The South and the North, divided by different ideologies and political systems, have gone through a fratricidal war. The divided halves of the single Korean nation have distrusted, denounced and antagonized each other since the day of territorial partition, and this painful state has yet to be remedied. Though the division was not brought about by our own volition, it is our responsibility to achieve national unification through our independent capabilities.

We must all work together to open a bright era of South-North reconciliation and cooperation. The time has come for all of us to endeavor in concert to promote the well-being and prosperity of the Korean people as a whole.

Today, the world is entering an age of reconciliation and cooperation transcending ideologies and political systems. A brave new tide of openness and exchange is engulfing people of different historical and cultural backgrounds. I believe we have now come to a historic moment when we should be able to find a breakthrough toward lasting peace and unification on the Korean Peninsula which is still threatened with the danger of war amidst persisting tension and confrontation.

My fellow compatriots,

The fundamental reason why the tragic division has still to be overcome is that both the South and the North have been regarding each other as an adversary, rather than realizing that both halves of Korea belong to the same national community, so that inter-Korean enmity has continued to intensify. Having lived in a single ethnic community, the Korean people have shaped an illustrious history and cultural traditions, triumphing over almost ceaseless trials and challenges with pooled national strength and wisdom.

Accordingly, developing relations between the South and the North as members of a single national community to achieve common prosperity is a shortcut to realizing a prosperous and unified homeland. This is also the path to national self-esteem and integration.

Now the South and the North must tear down the barrier that divides them and implement exchanges in all fields. Positive step after positive step must be taken to restore mutual trust and strengthen our bonds as members of one nation.

With the realization that we both belong to a single community, we must also put a stop to confrontation on the international scene. I hope that North Korea will contribute to the community of nations as a responsible member and that this will accelerate the opening and development of North Korean society. South and North Korea should recognize each other's place in the international community and cooperate with each other in the best interests of the entire Korean people.

My sixty million fellow compatriots,

Today, I promise to make efforts to open a new era of national self-esteem, unification and prosperity by building a social, cultural, economic and political community in which all members of Korean society can participate on the principles of independence, peace, democracy and welfare. To that end, I declare to the nation and to the world that the following policies will be pursued:

We will actively promote exchanges of visits between the people of South and North Korea, including politicians, businessmen, journalists, religious leaders, cultural leaders, artists, academics, sportsmen and students, and will make necessary arrangements to ensure that Koreans residing overseas can freely visit both parts of Korea.

Even before the successful conclusion of the North-South Red Cross talks, we will promote and actively support, from a humanitarian viewpoint, all measures which can assist separated families in their efforts to find out whether their family members in the other part of the Peninsula are still alive and to trace their whereabouts, and will also promote exchanges of correspondence and visits between them.

We will open doors for trade between South and North Korea, which will be regarded as internal trade within the national community.

We hope to achieve a balanced development of the national economy with a view to enhancing the quality of life for all Korean people—in both the South and the North—and will not oppose nations friendly with us trading with North Korea, provided that this trade does not involve military goods.

We hope to bring to an end counter-productive diplomacy characterized by competition and confrontation between the South and the North, and to co-operate in ensuring that North Korea makes a positive contribution to the international community. We also hope that representatives of South and North Korea will contact each other freely in international forums and will co-operate to pursue the common interests of the whole Korean nation.

To create an atmosphere conducive to durable peace on the Korean Peninsula, we are willing to co-operate with North Korea in its efforts to improve relations with countries friendly to us, including the United States and Japan; and in tandem with this, we will continue to seek improved relations with the Soviet Union, China and other socialist countries.

I trust that North Korea will respond positively to the measures outlined above. If the North shows a positive attitude, I should like to make it clear that even more progressive measures will be taken one after another. I hope that this declaration today will serve to open a new chapter in the development of inter-Korean relations and will lead to unification. I believe that if the entire 60 million Korean people pool their wisdom and strength, the South and the North will be integrated into a single social, cultural and economic community before this century is out. On that basis, I am confident that we will accomplish the great task of uniting in a single national entity in the not so very distant future.

4. North Korea's 10-Point Unification Program Adopted by the Fifth Session of the Ninth Supreme People's Assembly of North Korea, Pyongyang, April 7, 1993.

To put an end to the nearly half a century of division and confrontation and reunify the country is the unanimous demand and desire of the whole nation. For the independent and peaceful reunification of the country it is necessary to achieve the great unity of the whole nation. All those who are concerned about the destiny of the nation, whether they be in the north, or in the south, or overseas, and whether they be communists or nationalists, rich or poor, atheists or believers, must unite as one nation, transcending all their differences, and together pave the way for national reunification.

Those with strength devoting their strength, those with knowledge giving their knowledge and those with money donating their money, all should make a tangible contribution to the reunification of the country and the development and prosperity of a reunified land, so putting an end to national division and displaying the dignity and honor of the reunited 70 million fellow countrymen to the world.

1. A unified state, independent, peaceful and neutral, should be founded through the great unity of the whole nation.

The north and the south should found a pan-national unified state to represent all parties, all groupings and all the members of the nation from all walks of life, while leaving the existing two systems and two governments intact. The pan-national unified state should be a confederal state in which the two regional governments of the north and the south are represented equally, and an independent, peaceful and nonaligned neutral state which does not lean to any great power.

2. Unity should be based on patriotism and the spirit of national independence.

All the members of the nation should link their individual destiny with that of the nation, love their nation passionately and unite with the single desire to defend the independence of the nation. They should display dignity and pride in being members of our nation and reject sycophancy and national nihilism that erode the nation's consciousness of independence.

3. Unity should be achieved on the principle of promoting do-existence, co-prosperity and common interests and subordinating everything to the cause of national reunification.

The north and the south should recognize and respect the existence of different beliefs, ideas and systems, and achieve joint progress and prosperity, with neither side encroaching on the other. They should promote the interests of the whole nation before regional and class interests and direct every effort to the accomplishment of the cause of national reunification.

4. All political disputes that foment division and confrontation between fellow countrymen should be ended and unity should be achieved.

The north and the south should refrain from seeking or fomenting confrontation, end all political disputes between them and stop abusing and slandering each other. As fellow countrymen they should not be hostile to each other and, through the united efforts of the nation, they should counter foreign aggression and interference.

5. The fear of invasion from both south and north, and the ideas of prevailing over communism and communization should be dispelled, and north and south should believe in each other and unite.

The north and the south should not threaten and invade each other. Neither side should try to force its system on the other or to absorb the other.

6. The north and south should value democracy and join hands on the road to national reunification, without rejecting each other because of differences in ideals and principles.

They should guarantee the freedom of debate on and of activities for reunification and should not suppress, take reprisals against, persecute or punish political opponents. They should not arrest anyone because of their pro-north or pro-south tendencies and should release and reinstate all political prisoners so that they may contribute to the cause of national reunification.

7. The north and south protect the material and spiritual wealth of individuals and organizations and encourage their use for the promotion of great national unity.

Both before reunification and after it they should recognize state ownership, cooperative ownership and private ownership and protect the capital and property of individuals and organizations, as well as all interests concerned with foreign capital. They should recognize the social reputation and qualifications of individuals in all domains including science, education, literature, the arts, public debate, the press, health care and sports, and continue to guarantee the benefits granted to people who have performed meritorious services.

8. Understanding, trust and unity should be built up across the nation through contact, exchange visits and dialogue.

All the obstacles to contact and exchange visits should be removed and the door should be opened for everyone without discrimination to undertake exchange visits.

All the parties, groupings and people of all social standings should be given equal opportunities to conduct dialogue, and bilateral and multilateral dialogue should be developed.

9. The whole nation, north, south and overseas, should strengthen its solidarity for the sake of national reunification.

Things beneficial to national reunification should be supported and encouraged in an unbiased manner and things harmful to it should be rejected in the north, in the south and overseas, and all should assist and cooperate with one another, going beyond their own narrow enclosure. All political parties, organizations and the people from all walks of life in the north, in the south and overseas should be allied organizationally in the patriotic work to achieve national reunification.

10. Those who have contributed to the great unity of the

nation and to the cause of national reunification should be hon-
ored.

Special favors should be granted to those who have performed exploits for the sake of the great unity of the nation and
the reunification of the country, to patriotic martyrs and to their
descendants. If those who had turned their back on the nation in
the past return to the patriotic road, repentant of their past, they
should be dealt with leniently and assessed fairly, according to
the contribution they have made to the cause of national reunification.

5. R.O.K.-U.S. Mutual Defense Treaty, October 1, 1953

The Parties to this Treaty,

Reaffirming their desire to live in peace with all peoples and
all governments and desiring to strengthen the fabric of peace in
the Pacific area;

Desiring to declare publicly and formally their common
determination to defend themselves against external armed
attack so that no potential aggressor could be under the illusion
that either of them stands alone in the Pacific area;

Desiring further to strengthen their efforts for collective
defense for the preservation of peace and security pending the
development of a more comprehensive and effective system of
regional security in the Pacific area;

Have agreed as follows:

Article I

The Parties undertake to settle any international disputes in
which they may be involved by peaceful means in such a man-

ner that international peace and security and justice are not endangered and to refrain in their international relations from the threat or use of force in any manner inconsistent with the purposes of the United Nations, or obligations assumed by any Party toward the United Nations.

Article II

The Parties will consult together whenever, in the opinion of either of them, the political independence or security of either of the Parties is threatened by external armed attack. Separately and jointly, by self-help and mutual aid the Parties will maintain and develop appropriate means to deter armed attack and will take measures in consultation and agreement to implement this Treaty and to further its purposes.

Article III

Each Party recognizes that an armed attack in the Pacific area on either of the Parties in territories now under their respective administrative control, or hereafter recognized by one of the Parties as lawfully brought under the administrative control of the other, would be dangerous to its own peace and safety and declares that it would act to meet the common danger in accordance with its constitutional processes.

Article IV

This treaty shall be ratified by the United States of America and Republic of Korea in accordance with their respective constitutional processes and will come into force when instruments of ratification thereof have been exchanged by them at Washington.

Article V

This Treaty shall remain in force indefinitely. Either party may terminate it one year after notice has been given to the other Party.

In witness Whereof the undersigned Plenipotentiaries have signed this Treaty.

Done in duplicate at Washington, in the English and Korean languages, this first day of October 1953.

For the Republic of Korea:

Y.T. Pyun

For the United States of America:

John Foster Dulles